The Defeat of the Luftwaffe

The Defeat of the Luftwaffe

The Eastern Front 1941–45
A Strategy for Disaster

JONATHAN TRIGG

AMBERLEY

Other books by this author:

Hitler's Legions series
Hitler's Gauls: The History of the French Waffen-SS
Hitler's Flemish Lions: The History of the Flemish Waffen-SS
Hitler's Jihadis: The History of the Muslim Waffen-SS
Hitler's Vikings: The History of the Scandinavian Waffen-SS

Hastings 1066
Death on the Don: The Destruction of Germany's Allies on the
   Eastern Front 1941–44

First published 2016

Amberley Publishing
The Hill, Stroud
Gloucestershire, GL5 4EP

www.amberley-books.com

British Library Cataloguing in Publication Data.
A catalogue record for this book is available from the British Library.

ISBN 978 1 4456 5186 6 (hardback)
ISBN 978 1 4456 5187 3 (ebook)

Map design by Thomas Bohm, User design.
Typesetting and Origination by Amberley Publishing.
Printed in the UK.

Contents

Preface

I have been a student of the Second World War, and the cataclysmic fighting on the Eastern Front in particular, for more years than I care to remember, but the prism through which I have viewed the latter has primarily been the land battles, the great sweeping movements of tanks, artillery and endless columns of marching infantry. Throughout my studies I have rarely, if ever, made more than a cursory nod to the war waged in the skies above the battling armies, and when I have my mind has conjured up a series of wildly different images. The first is the Stuka. Its distinctive gull wings emblazoned with the black German cross, its sirens – the infamous 'Trumpets of Jericho' – blaring madly and, beneath it, soldiers and civilians cowering in terror. The Stuka was a symbol, a symbol of Nazi blitzkrieg and the years of crushing German victories, and as with all good symbols it metamorphosed into a kind of short-hand for the superiority of German arms at the time. At a time when most other armed forces seemingly still relied on masses of infantry and cavalry dash, the Stuka and the German panzer screamed 'modern' and epitomised the future of warfare – never mind that the reality was a German Army still overwhelmingly reliant on the horse and boot leather – it was the Luftwaffe, the all-conquering Luftwaffe, that was prevalent.

Along with the Stuka were the images of smiling fighter aces – the knights of the skies – and their individual scores of downed enemy aircraft. Flying with the RAF were Douglas Bader, twenty-two; 'Paddy' Finucane (Irish), thirty-two; 'Sailor' Malan (South African), twenty-seven; and Bob Stanford Tuck, twenty-nine. In the other Allied air forces there were: Dick Bong, forty (USAAF); Stanislaw Skalski, twenty-two and a half (Polish Air Force); and Ivan Kozhedub, sixty-four (Soviet Air Force). Yet their scores pale in comparison next to their Luftwaffe opponents, the famed '*Experten*': Heinrich Erler, 206 kills; Theodor Weissenberger, 208; Heinz Bär, 220; Hermann Graf, 212; Otto Kittel, 267; Günther Rall, 275; Gerhard Barkhorn, 301; and of course Erich Hartmann, with an incredible 352.

The men who achieved these incredible statistics were all clearly top pilots and extremely brave men, but the men of the Luftwaffe were fighting for a cause that has rightly been condemned as one of the vilest in human history. As the US Civil War general, and later President, Ulysses S. Grant said about the fall of the slave-owning Confederacy: 'I felt like anything rather than rejoicing at the downfall of a foe who had fought so long and valiantly, and had suffered so much for a cause, though that cause was, I believe, one of the worst for which a people ever fought, and one for which there was the least excuse.'

The Nazis and the Luftwaffe were intertwined from the very beginning. It was the Nazis who created the Luftwaffe, and there was a saying in German military circles of the time that Germany had 'an Imperial Navy, a Prussian Army, and a National Socialist Air Force'. The Nazis fell in love with air power. It was everything they wanted for themselves, new, powerful and destined to rule, and indeed Hitler and his propaganda chief, Goebbels, pioneered a winning combination of air power and politics. Goebbels would have Hitler criss-cross the country in his own plane before every election, seeming to be everywhere, and appearing from the heavens as a messiah to his adoring crowds, and once elections were no longer necessary in totalitarian Germany, air power became a way for the Nazis to project their might on to their neighbours. Visiting diplomats and politicians were treated to carefully choreographed fly-pasts by armadas of warplanes, and the message was clear: 'We can reach you wherever you are.'

So, lauded and nurtured by the Nazis, the Luftwaffe came to embody Hitler's Germany. Instrumental in the conquest of the west and the Balkans, it was in the east with the launch of Operation Barbarossa – the invasion of the Soviet Union – that the Luftwaffe was to reach its zenith. As the army rolled inexorably eastwards, the Luftwaffe flew above it providing a vast protective canopy. Final victory was within reach, and yet ... And yet the certainty of that victory proved a mirage, leaving only a monumental war of attrition that ground the Luftwaffe into bloody shreds. As the Duke of Wellington might have commented had he seen another German attempt at European domination come to naught: 'They came on in the same old way, and we saw them off in the same old way.'

The reasons for the defeat of the Luftwaffe in the east were complex, and what I have tried to achieve in this account is not a day-by-day description of the air war, rather a demonstration of just how inter-related the fighting was for the Luftwaffe across so many spheres – how, in effect, the strategic bombing of Germany by the Anglo-Americans, German industrial failure, the dispersion of effort to secondary sectors, the lack of effective leadership at the highest levels of command, and so on, all had a cumulative effect that in the end crushed the Nazis' air force in a huge vice. As far as is possible I have also tried to capture that miraculous journey in the words of the men and women who were there.

Beyond these macro-economic, political and military factors, there is one simple, undeniable truth to the victory of the Soviets over the Luftwaffe, and that is that ultimately, the Luftwaffe in the east, despite its undoubted brilliance, was destroyed by an opponent who, when staring defeat and extinction in the face, stood up and said 'No'. The Soviets made mistakes on a hitherto unimaginable scale, particularly during the first year or so of the war, but their ruthlessness, their courageous stubbornness, and their utter belief in final victory saw them through to a conclusion of the war no-one back in the autumn of 1941 would ever have dreamed of. The volte face was then complete. The same air force that on 22 June 1941 won the greatest ever victory over a rival power lay in ruins less than four years later as that same enemy flew unopposed over the centre of Berlin.

In terms of the text itself, the Soviet Union is now defunct of course, and its successor states and peoples have almost all grasped the freedom they were for so long denied. However, at the time, the country in question was still very much the Soviet Union, and I have used that title for the country, its peoples and its armed forces. This is rather than using the short-hand 'Russian', which was very much the German catch-all title of the time that, in my view, fails to adequately describe the multi-ethnic dimension of the conflict: this was not Russians versus Germans – if it was then where would the VVS ace and winner of the Order of the Red Banner, Sultan Amet-Khan sit, a fighter pilot born to a Muslim Dagestani father and a Crimean Tatar mother. These seismic changes have also seen the rebirth of languages such as Ukrainian, and the reversion of many towns and cities to their pre-Soviet names – even for some their pre-Tsarist ones – so Kharkov is now Kharkiv, and Lvov is Lviv. However, this doesn't hold true universally: Stalingrad is still a Russian city but is not known by its pre-Revolutionary name of Tsaritsyn, but as Volgograd. With names I have gone with the spelling as described to me by the source, or indeed the individual themselves. I have used the German umlaut where appropriate, but have used the anglicised version of Goering as it is very commonly known. Apart from that I have tried to stay true to the names as they were at the time simply for ease, my apologies if any national sensibilities are offended. For ranks, both Soviet and German, I have used the English translation so a Luftwaffe *Hauptmann* is a captain, and a VVS *podpolkovnik* is a lieutenant colonel, except where a rank is quoted: these I have left alone. A table of ranks and their equivalent is included as an appendix. I have tried to be as accurate as possible, particularly when expressing the words and thoughts of the veterans and witnesses themselves, and so if there are any mistakes or errors they are mine and mine alone and I apologise.

Acknowledgements

As ever when writing military history, the end result is only as good as the research that goes into it, and the support the author receives from a network of people, most of them experts in their own right. All the sources I have used fit into the 'expert' category and I would like to thank them all, although I will content myself with mentioning three if I may: firstly, I would like to pay tribute to Christer Bergstrom and his various collaborators for their superb books and research into the 1941 and 1942 campaigns in particular, and I would also like to thanks Sönke Neitzel and Harald Welzer for their ground-breaking work in *Soldaten,* where they brought, for the first time, to a wider audience a treasure trove of secretly recorded conversations between German POWs from all service branches while in British captivity. The British government had fitted microphones in cells and rooms, used 'turned' POWs as agents provocateurs and generally excelled themselves in getting prisoners to open up and talk about their experiences of the war without resorting to torture or physical assaults of any kind. The results are both shocking and fascinating. From a historical perspective they shed an enormous amount of light on the eternal conundrum of the German experience of the war; were the vast majority of decent, ordinary Germans betrayed by a minority of individuals – the SS, Gestapo etc – who committed genocide and horrific atrocities in their name, or were the majority in some way complicit, either by action or through passive compliance – in effect trying to answer the question – 'did they know what was happening?' Neitzel and Welzer's studies would suggest that while participation in, and even knowledge of, brutality and murder was not universal, it was pretty widespread. Rape, bombing of civilians, the murder of Jews – these were not hidden away in some far dark corner, but an accepted part of the war in the east – why? I am no psychologist. My friend Ben Amponsah – who is a psychologist and a very good one at that, and who devotes much of his time to pro bono work to help asylum seekers who have been victims of torture, murder and genocide – would provide a far better answer than I ever could, but in all my studies I keep on coming back to the words of Freidrich Wilhelm Heinz. Heinz was a First World War veteran who became a Nazi Brownshirt. He proceeded to lose faith in Nazism and eventually became a member of the anti-Hitler resistance. He ended the war in hiding. His view on war and peace is probably the most concise I have read: 'Everyone told us the war was over. That was a laugh; we ourselves were the war.'

The rest of the list of those I wish to thank is long and exhaustive, so I will limit myself to a representative handful: to Jimmy McLeod for coming out of his comfort zone and helping track down Luftwaffe veterans, to Shaun Barrington for his ever-helpful editorship, and to Tim Shaw for his by-now standard photographic genius.

I dedicate this book to my beautiful wife Rachel, and my rapidly growing children, Maddy and Jack, and most especially to my father – Robert – who remains the only member of my immediate family who not only reads everything I write but insists on going into almost every book shop he sees to make the same enquiry of the counter staff: 'Do you have anything by Jonathan Trigg? He's very good you know.' Thank you.

PART ONE

'War takes to the skies!'

CHAPTER 1

Military Air Power Begins

Wilbur and Orville Wright only made their first powered flight in December 1903, and yet just over a decade later their incredible invention was one of the cutting edges in military technology as the Great Powers of the world slugged it out on battlefields across the globe. At first, aerial warfare was almost laughable in its amateurism; pilots and observers armed with pistols and rifles fired at each other in the sky, or dropped hand grenades out of their open cockpits onto enemy troops below. The allure of the plane was singular, though, in a war that came to be quickly dominated by the concept of 'industrialised mass slaughter'. Air power managed to recreate something of the 'lost glamour' of battle that has enraptured young men in particular since time immemorial – whether modern society likes that idea or not.

> To be alone, to have your life in your hands, to use your own skill, single-handed, against the enemy, it was like the lists in the Middle Ages, the only sphere where there was still honour and chivalry. You did not sit in a muddy trench while someone who had no personal enmity against you loosed off a gun five miles away and blew you to smithereens. That was not fighting; it was murder, senseless, brutal, ignoble.

These were the sentiments of Cecil Lewis, a pilot from Great Britain's Royal Flying Corps (RFC) who joined up as a seventeen-year-old direct from Oundle public school and later wrote a best-selling autobiography of his wartime service. His words perfectly capture a commonly held view of fighting in the air as being something apart, something quintessentially more honourable, and less like slaughter – a view that simply does not stand up to any sort of challenge. Over 116,000 aircraft were lost during the First World War to all causes (27,737 German, 52,640 French and 35,973 British, not including Russia, the USA and Austria-Hungary), and with parachutes a rarity, and the ever-present danger of fire, the human cost was enormous. The great French ace Raoul Lufbery, revered for his flying prowess and gentlemanly conduct in the air, came to a gruesome end at the hands of a German Albatros pilot. His extremely flammable, resin-covered, wooden plane was set alight by his enemy's machine-gun fire, and his comrades were forced to watch, helpless, as Lufbery climbed out of his cockpit in mid-air and clung on, straddling the fuselage, until the flames became too much for him to bear and he jumped to his death. His crushed and eviscerated body was found impaled on a fence post.

The deaths of so many other pilots may have been less well documented, but they were nevertheless just as horrific as they were riddled with machine gun bullets or shrapnel, crushed on impact or burnt alive strapped into their aircraft. What of these men then? Were they in a sense a 'breed apart' from other combatants? The answer is no; pilots were, and are, roughly the same mixture of personalities as in every other branch of the armed services.

A distinguished US Army infantry officer from the Second World War wrote of his experiences: 'A few guys carry your attack, and the rest sort of participate and arrive on the objective afterwards.'

His US Army colleague Colonel William DePuy said much the same: 'The average man, like nine out of ten say, does not have an instinct for the battlefield, doesn't relish it, and will not act independently except under direct orders.'[1]

The same was absolutely true for pilots. For the majority, the primary goal is survival, and not to wreak death and destruction on the enemy. The bulk of every squadron in every air force in both world wars was made up of men who not only didn't want to be killed, but had no overwhelming desire to kill other pilots either. They took to the air, did their duty, and fired their guns if they had to. It was only ever a small handful of flyers that actively sought out combat with the enemy and claimed the kills. Post-action investigation proved this beyond doubt. For example, in the RFC's crack 56 Squadron, just two of the more than forty pilots who served were responsible for ninety-four of the unit's entire wartime total of 427 German aircraft shot down.[2] That was not to say that any of the other pilots were cowards – far from it: it would be preposterous to claim that any of those ridiculously young men were anything other than heroic; rather it is about understanding the nature of pilots, and particularly fighter pilots, as it would be them who would very much come to dominate the air war between Nazi Germany and the Soviet Union in the Second World War.

Back at the dawn of aerial warfare, it was the British, as so often in history, who were the early pioneers of this new area of study in trying to understand the psychological make-up of pilots; they broke relatively new ground when they applied their burgeoning knowledge to the selection process for prospective candidates for the newly created Royal Flying Corps. A psychological research adviser was employed to brief medical examiners on identifying three distinct personality types from among the mass of volunteers coming forward to join the glamorous new service – these were paranoids, psychopaths and impulsives, the latter being men given to acting in a reckless, thoughtless manner only suited to satisfying their own immediate needs – and then weeding them out. However, further research by the same adviser on existing pilots within the RFC found that almost all who had achieved ace status (classified by the British as having shot down five or more enemy aircraft) were drawn from one of those self-same categories. The conclusion was clear – being an ace pilot usually meant being a killer of men. Captain William R. O'Brien, a successful pilot in the United States Army Air Force's (USAAF) 357th Fighter Group credited with six kills in the Second World War while flying his P-51 Mustang – *Billy's Bitch* – instinctively understood this when he talked openly and honestly about the best way to shoot down opponents: 'It's just like being in a knife fight in a dirt-floor bar. If you want to fix a fella, the best way to do it is to get behind him and stick him in the back. It's the same in an air fight. If you want to kill the guy, the best thing to do is get around behind him where he can't see you ... and shoot him.'[3]

America's most successful ace in the First World War embodied this approach completely. Eddie Rickenbacker was a second generation immigrant of Swiss-German descent, and an ex-racing driver and mechanic. He chalked up twenty-five kills over France in a very short time by adopting an attacking profile designed to give his opponents no chance whatsoever. He would fly alone, searching out enemy aircraft, and then get in position above and behind them to give himself the advantages of speed in the dive and the element of surprise; he also liked to attack out of the sun so he wasn't even seen by his intended target. The first they would know about it would be Rickenbacker's bullets riddling them and their aircraft. Young Eddie was successful not just because he adopted a better attack tactic but also because he appreciated another golden rule of air fighting – kill novices and avoid experienced flyers.

All fighter planes were, and still are to an extent, inherently unstable in their design to both deliver the ultra-responsiveness needed in combat and achieve great speed in flight, and while in the hands of an experienced pilot this makes them lethal weapons of war, in the hands of a novice they are usually more dangerous to the individual at the controls. The statistics bear this out. In both world wars pilots who had flown fewer than twenty combat missions accounted for fully 80 per cent of casualties, and the vast majority of every ace's kills were new pilots. The priority for a new pilot therefore was to survive and little more, until they had built up experience; then and only then could you become an effective aerial killer.

As it was, aerial warfare briefly grabbed the headlines in the First World War, before Imperial Germany and her Central Power allies were comprehensively defeated and much of the world sank back into an exhausted peace. It seemed then as if the future of air power was uncertain, despite the loud proclamations of a handful of aerial evangelists like the American First World War commander, Brigadier General Billy Mitchell: 'The day has passed when armies on the ground or navies on the sea can be the arbiter of a nation's destiny in war. The main power of defence and the power of initiative against an enemy has passed to the air.'

CHAPTER 2

Goering and *His* Luftwaffe

In post-Imperial Germany, the air force was disbanded and the now humbled country banned from all forms of military aviation under the terms of the Treaty of Versailles. Hundreds of fighter planes were piled haphazardly on top of each other in breakers yards and farmers' fields, their wings and struts rotting, their engines rusting away. Relatively few men were affected; after all, only 3 per cent of Germany's military manpower were involved in the air force, against a full 58 per cent who were officers or soldiers in the infantry.[4] Those men who did survive the Allied aerial onslaught and the wreckage of defeat were scattered to the four winds. Some, like Ernst Udet, went abroad and drifted while others, like Erhard Milch, continued their careers and found work in Germany's growing civil aviation industry. Many would go on later to prominence in the Luftwaffe. None more so than the man who would found the service and be its driving force throughout its early years, the same man who would, for better or worse, utterly dominate the Luftwaffe's entire brief existence, and would ultimately lead it to its utter defeat in the east – Hermann Wilhelm Goering.

To understand Goering was to understand how and why the Soviet Union would eventually grind the vaunted Luftwaffe into dust. The man himself was something of a minor celebrity in Weimar Germany. A war hero and recipient of the coveted 'Blue Max', the last commander of Von Richthofen's legendary Flying Circus, *Jagdgeschwader 1*, he even possessed the delicious whiff of scandal from his aristocratic Swedish wife, Carin von Kantzow, who had divorced her estranged army-officer husband to marry the dashing German ex-flyer. Five years Hermann's senior, the glamorous Carin was a scion of Denmark's well-known von Rosen family and a distant relative of the Anglo-Irish

Beamish brewing clan, and Goering was infatuated with her. Settling in Munich, the Goerings became involved in politics and Hermann himself joined the infant Nazi Party after hearing its new leader, Adolf Hitler, speak at a small rally. Goering rose extremely quickly through the party's ranks, helping organise the brown-shirted bully boys of the Sturmabteilung – the SA, the Nazis' own storm troopers, before Hitler became Chancellor in 1933. Two years previously, Carin had died from a heart condition, and a heartbroken Goering had thrown himself into political work, although the addictions to morphine and paracodeine he had picked up from his treatment for the wounds he suffered at Hitler's side during the failed 1923 Beer Hall Putsch continued to plague him. Hitler, however, considered Goering one of his most organised acolytes: 'He is the only one of the SA heads that ran it properly. I gave him a dishevelled rabble. In a very short time he had organised a division of 11,000 men.' This was a remarkable comment to make in view of Goering's utter desertion from hard work just a few short years later. But if this wasn't enough praise, Hitler went on to say, 'In time of crisis he is brutal and ice-cold. I've always noticed that when it comes to the breaking point he is a man of iron, without scruple.' Goering revelled in his nickname, *'der Eiserne'* (the Iron Man), and Hitler wasn't the only one who regarded Goering highly. The man destined to become probably his most successful subordinate in the Luftwaffe, 'Smiling' Albert Kesselring, a man who would cast a very long shadow in the Luftwaffe's war in the east, said of the ex-fighter pilot's pre-war efforts, 'He was always at his best under pressure, when the rest of us were completely exhausted, he was still able to go on.'

This manic drive helped Goering amass a plethora of important posts and offices as the Nazis consolidated their grip on power in Germany. Goering was at one and the same time the Plenipotentiary for the Four Year Plan, Chairman of the Council of Ministers for the Defence of the Reich, Minister President of Prussia, President of the Reichstag and even head of Germany's hunting association. Yet the one title he craved above all others was commander-in-chief of a new German air force. The creation and nurturing of that same air force was a labyrinthine process of deception and infighting, and one that was intimately tied up with Hitler's determination to throw off the shackles imposed on Germany by the hated Treaty of Versailles. Hitler was determined to establish his country once again as a major military power in Europe, and the Luftwaffe would be a key part of that vision. Goering's love of flying had never left him, and his major role in Hitler's plan was to create and build the air force that would be the

envy of the world. So, with Hitler's blessing, he began his undercover
task the moment the Nazis took power.

Deals were done with the country's aviation firms – already mostly
in hock to the government after years of covert subsidies – to focus on
military designs, and an agreement was even reached with the Soviet
Union that allowed the training in secret of German pilots deep in the
country's interior at the air base at Lipetsk.

By 1935 Hitler felt strong enough to publicly disavow Versailles's
military restrictions, and announce to the world the existence of the
Luftwaffe. In full view of the Allied Powers, the Nazi Chancellor and now
Führer then began a military build-up of quite dramatic proportions. The
transformation it wrought was very concisely detailed in a lecture in 1939
given by General Georg Thomas, head of the German Foreign Office's
War Economy and Armaments Office. Thomas, whose receding chin
and accompanying hairline made him look like a village schoolmaster in
uniform, outlined to his appreciative audience how Germany's Weimar-era
Reichswehr army of seven infantry and three cavalry divisions had
ballooned in 4 short years into the new Heer of no less than fifty-one
divisions all told, including three of motorised infantry and five of panzers.
This growth was mirrored at sea, where Germany's earlier bath-tub navy
was now a Kriegsmarine of two battleships, two armoured cruisers,
seventeen destroyers and forty-seven deadly U-boats. In the air, Germany
had gone from nothing to a new Luftwaffe that boasted a ration strength
of a quarter of a million, with almost 300 batteries of anti-aircraft guns
and no fewer than twenty-one frontline squadrons of modern aircraft.
These were the component parts of the Nazi Wehrmacht – the national
Armed Forces – who would be commanded by the Oberkommando der
Wehrmacht (OKW), the High Command of the Armed Forces, with
each service having its own leadership and command structure. For the
Luftwaffe that meant the Oberkommando der Luftwaffe (OKL), based in
the Air Ministry on Berlin's Wilhelmstrasse, with its own chief of staff,
and above him Reichsmarshall Goering himself.

Building an air force from the ground up will inevitably lead to
some compromises and decisions that with the benefit of hindsight can
either be viewed as flawed, or strokes of near-genius. The Luftwaffe
encapsulated this truism beautifully. With no existing stocks of aircraft
filling the country's hangars, the Luftwaffe was able to opt for a host
of new aircraft designs at the leading edge of aviation technology.
Some would fail, but others would become the backbone of the most
advanced aerial armada of the time: aircraft such as the Messerschmitt
Bf 109 single-engine fighter (the most mass-produced fighter of all
time), the Heinkel He-111 and Junkers Ju-88 twin-engine bombers,

and the iconic Junkers Ju-87 Stuka dive-bomber. These aircraft were faster, more manoeuvrable and better armed than almost anything any other air force in the world possessed. The missing link in the armoury was a strategic bomber – dubbed in the Luftwaffe 'the Ural bomber', so no prizes for guessing who it was envisaged to be deployed against. Goering's first chief of staff, the amiable and extremely intelligent ex-Army officer Walther Wever, was a big advocate of the Ural bomber programme, but when he died in a flying accident in 1936 so did Berlin's enthusiasm for a fleet of heavy behemoths and any sense of a strategic and not purely tactical role for the foetal Luftwaffe – as Von Richthofen put it extremely succinctly, the new air force would be 'the army's whore'. Another ex-Army officer, Albert Kesselring, was Wever's replacement, and under pressure from Goering to fill the skies with the swastika, he opted instead for a mass of medium, all-purpose, twin-engine tactical bombers. He was strongly supported in his decision by another man who would be instrumental in the Luftwaffe's future in the East – Erhard Milch. After his wartime service as a pilot, Milch had gone on to work his way up the ranks of the civil aviation industry before effortlessly sliding into the senior echelons of the Nazi administration despite doubts over his 'Aryan' blood (his father Anton was alleged to be Jewish). Protected by Goering ('I will decide who is Jewish in the Luftwaffe'), Milch believed that German industry only had the raw materials and capacity to produce about 1,000 four-engine heavy bombers, but many times that number of twin-engine ones. At their urging, Goering ordered a halt to all work on the strategic bomber programme in the spring of 1937, just at the moment the Luftwaffe's own Technical Office had passed the Ju-89 and Do-19 heavy bomber models ready for testing.

That same Technical Office – a sprawling octopus of conflicting departments, sections, programmes and egos – was headed up by probably Goering's most disastrous appointment, Ernst Udet. After the Red Baron, Udet was Germany's most famous First World War fighter ace – and unlike the great man himself, Udet was still alive to be feted. His sixty-two victories, charisma and playboy charm made him the darling of the press and society alike, and Goering believed he had scored a huge coup when he got Udet to agree to become his Chief of Supply and Procurement. '*Udlinger*', as he was affectionately known, was a spectacular failure in the job. He was utterly devoid of every skill and attribute needed to make the role a success, and under his supposed leadership the entire future equipment programme of the Luftwaffe became a train wreck. After seeing trials of dive-bombers during his time stunt flying in the USA after the war, he was an unbridled enthusiast for precision bombing, insisting that just about every aircraft destined for the Luftwaffe have a dive-bombing capability. This was fine for the Stuka of course, but when applied to the Ju-88 the modifications needed more than doubled its weight and neutralised its main selling point as a lightweight, ultra-fast bomber. In the end, one of the only innovations he introduced which proved its worth was the Stuka's famous, ear-splitting klaxon that he christened the 'Trumpets of Jericho'.

Not that Goering was any better. The once dashing and muscular fighter pilot had now become corpulent and extremely egotistical, although he was one of the only senior Nazis who didn't take offense at hearing jokes about himself, 'no matter how rude', as he exclaimed, taking them as a sign of public popularity. Germans joked about his pretensions, saying that he would wear an admiral's uniform to take a bath, and, of course, his weight, joking that 'he sits down on his stomach'. One joke went that he had sent a wire message to Hitler after his visit to meet the pope in the Vatican: 'Mission accomplished. Pope unfrocked. Tiara and pontifical vestments are a perfect fit.'

He proved himself the worst of leaders, though. By turns lazy, hyperactive, uninterested, paranoid, indecisive, blustering and prone to cronyism, he set up a sort of kitchen cabinet derisively called the 'Little General Staff' by those in the know, through which he undermined and bypassed the proper chain of command; its members included ex-comrades from the First World War like Bruno Loerzer, political bedfellows such as State Secretary Paul 'Pilli' Koerner (Goering's deputy for both the Four Year Plan and Prussia's presidency), the Bavarian General of Flyers Karl Bodenschatz (Goering's liaison at Hitler's headquarters), his adjutants Colonel Bernd von Brauchitsch (son of the head of the Wehrmacht, Field Marshal Walther von Brauchitsch) and Lieutenant Colonel Werner Teske and even his own physician, Dr Ramon von Ordarza. Goering picked none of them for their competence in matters military.

As to the Luftwaffe's organisational structure, at the frontline of the new service was its most basic unit, the Staffel (in Anglo-American terms, the 'squadron'), usually consisting of nine aircraft, though it could be more, commanded by a captain or senior lieutenant, with around ten or more pilots and eighty or so ground crew – the so-called 'black men', named on account of both the colour of their uniforms and their propensity to be covered in oil. Typically, three Staffeln and a headquarters flight (a Stab) would form a Gruppe. The Gruppe would be led by a senior captain or major, have over 300 'black men' and thirty to forty pilots on its roster. The operational formation next up the ladder was the Geschwader – equivalent to the RAF

Wing; a Geschwader would usually have three Gruppen, but it could be up to five. A senior major, lieutenant colonel or full colonel would command the ninety-plus aircraft, with the Geschwader having a prefix denoting it as a fighter unit, 'Jagd'; bomber, 'Kampf'; dive-bomber, 'Sturzkampf'; ground attack, 'Schlacht'; and so on. Each Geschwader had a number, and some of the fighter Geschwader also had 'honour titles' such as Jagdgeschwader 2 Richthofen. The Geschwader could then be grouped into divisions – Flieger Division; corps – Fliegerkorps; and giant air fleets – Luftflotte, as required by the situation. The fighter arm as a whole was known as the 'Jagdwaffe'.

The pilots themselves were predominantly very young men in their early to mid-twenties, with a few *alte Adler* (Old Eagles) as they were known from the First World War – the latter men like the celebrated Theo Osterkamp. The youngsters had learnt to fly in Germany's plethora of state-sponsored gliding clubs, classed as sports associations to get round the Versailles restrictions. Flying was seen as a huge adventure by these youngsters who dreamt of little else apart from progressing from a glider to a military aircraft: 'As soon as I was old enough I took up gliding, and with a C Class Glider Pilot's License I joined the Luftwaffe ...'[5] And all of them had been reared on the legend of the greatest German flying ace of them all – Baron Manfred Freiherr von Richthofen – the Red Baron. So powerful has been his legacy that as late as the 1970s the US studies of air combat over Vietnam over the preceding twenty or so years were codenamed 'Red Baron'.

It was in vain, however, that the new service looked for written inspiration from the man himself. He had left a diary, that was true; but his widow refused to allow it to be published as her late husband had not used its pages to expound his views on tactics or operations, but rather to insult and pour scorn on a whole host of other German flyers and senior officers. Obsessed with winning victories and the glory that came with them, one of the few statements he did leave, however, just about summed up his views on air warfare: 'Fighter pilots should have an allotted area to cruise around in as it suits them, but when they see an opponent they must attack and shoot him down. Anything else is absurd. Nothing else matters but the aerial victory.' This basically became the dogma of the German fighter arm – the Jagdwaffe – and with it the cult of the ace, the *Experte*. The desire to become one, and then to achieve ever higher scores, would become a dominant characteristic of the Luftwaffe in its battle with the Soviet Union.

It was left to other men, primarily two young fighter pilots, Werner Mölders and Günther Lützow, fighting in the sun-drenched skies above Spain in the late 1930s, to come up with the defining flying tactics of their era. The two of them devised the 'finger four' formation, where each Staffel was divided into three *Schwärme* (singular: *Schwarm*, 'swarm'), or flights, consisting of four to six aircraft. A fighter Schwarm was then sub-divided into two *Rotten*, or 'pairs' of aircraft. The Rotte was the basic fighting unit, consisting of a leader and a wingman – a '*Katschmarek*'. A bomber Schwarm was likewise divided into a *Kette* ('chain') of three aircraft flying in a 'V' formation.

The Spanish Civil War – and the Nazis' commitment of the Condor Legion to it to fight on the side of Franco's Nationalists – enabled the infant Luftwaffe to test out everything from new aircraft models to flying formations to terror bombing tactics such as those practiced on the helpless Basque inhabitants of Guernica. It gave them invaluable operational experience and produced a core of fighter pilots and bomber crews who would go on to lead the Luftwaffe's battle against the Soviets two years later.

CHAPTER 3

Stalin's Purges and the VVS

The First World War had seen the end of Tsarist Russia, the three-hundred-year-old Romanov dynasty washed away in rivers of blood and revolutionary fervour. Vladimir Ilyich Lenin, the architect of the Revolution, had died; his most likely successor, Leon Trotsky, had been murdered in exile with an ice axe through his head on the orders of the man who took on the mantle of leadership of the Communist Party and the Soviet Union – Joseph Stalin. A Georgian by birth, Joseph Vissarionovich Djugashvili had murdered millions of his own people in a forced collectivisation of agriculture and subsequent state-sponsored famines and had then pushed through mass industrialisation to try and drag the Soviet economy into the twentieth century. Dangerously paranoid, in the late 1930s he feared the growing power of the Soviet military, especially the potential ambition of the 'Red Napoleon' – Soviet Marshal Mikhail Tukhachevsky. Stalin's answer was a 'red terror' that became infamously known as the Great Purges. Tukhachevsky was the first to die. His torture-induced confession document, spattered by his own blood, sealed his fate at a show-trial where he was heard to mutter, 'I feel I'm dreaming,' before being led away a condemned man. Just hours later, Stalin's chief NKVD (the Soviet secret police) executioner, Vasily Blokhin,[6] put a bullet into the back of Tukhachevsky's head while watched by his gloating boss, Nikolai Yezhov. With tragic irony, a mere three years later Yezhov himself would die screaming for mercy at the tail end of the Purges he himself had so enthusiastically carried out. As for Blokhin, he would die by his own hand in 1955, alone and insane, his last few years washed away by the vodka bottle.

After Tukhachevsky's death the Purge swiftly gathered momentum, swallowing hundreds of thousands in its greedy maw. It started at the very top. The Party was decimated. Every living member of Lenin's original Cabinet was executed, along with most of the Party leadership. In the armed forces it was even worse. Three out of five Marshals of the Soviet Union were shot, along with fifteen of sixteen Army commanders, fifty of fifty-seven Corps commanders, 154 of 186 divisional commanders, and 401 of 456 colonels. The scythe swept through lower officer ranks too, often culling men for no other reason than that their name appeared on the wrong list at the wrong time. After a while the whole pogrom became institutionalised and quotas were set and required to be filled, regardless of any notion of guilt. By the end some 700,000 people had been slaughtered, among them 30,000 military personnel, almost all of them officers. Stalin further underscored his control of the military by reasserting the role of political commissars – the loathed '*politruk*' – at divisional level and below to oversee the political loyalty of the Armed Forces to the regime, and maintain the 'dual-command' structure. As the historian Lloyd Clark said: 'Stalin not only cut the heart out of the armed forces, he also gave them brain damage.'

This was most definitely true in the Soviet air force, the VVS – *Voyenno-Vozdushnye Sily*, literally 'Military Air Forces' – which was in total and utter disarray from the terror. The VVS's commander before the German invasion, the thirty-year-old Spanish Civil War veteran Lieutenant General Pavel Rychagov, was its third in three years, his two predecessors having been arrested, interrogated and thrown into prison on trumped-up charges. Both of them, the bald and bulldog-like Aleksandr Loktionov and the Jewish veteran of Spain and Khalkhin Gol Yakov Smuchkevich, would survive for a while before Yezhov's successor as head of Stalin's secret police – his fellow Georgian, Lavrenti Beria – decided the time was right to have them executed. They were moved to the main prison in Kuybyshev (Stalin's 'alternate' capital should Moscow have fallen to the Nazis) and shot. Joining them under the executioner's hammer was their successor, Rychagov; Rychagov's wife; the head of Soviet Long Range Aviation, Lieutenant General Ivan Proskurov; and a dozen or more other air force officers, including the noted female pilot, Major Mariya Nesterenko.

The next man in the VVS hot seat was the bullet-headed Lieutenant General Pavel Zhigarev, an officer with very little experience at a senior rank and naturally fearful of what awaited him. The men under his direct command were much the same; 91 per cent of his major formation commanders had been in post for less than six months at that point, the majority of their predecessors having been imprisoned or executed. As for the by-now dead Rychagov, he had specifically been arrested for criticising the obsolete nature of most VVS aircraft – 'flying coffins' as he termed them – and he had a point. The Soviets had surged forward in the late 1920s with aircraft design; however, a decade later most of their standard aircraft types were dated and obsolete. A re-equipment programme had been put in place, and newer models like the MiG-3 fighter, the Pe-2 bomber and the Il-2 Shturmovik, with its 66-mm-thick, bullet-resistant cockpit glass and steel armour round the engine, cockpit and fuel tanks, were coming on stream as the frontline units reorganised into squadrons of twenty to thirty planes, and regiments of sixty aircraft, three to five of which were then grouped into an Air Division – but it all took time, and was only 20 per cent complete by the time of Barbarossa. As one pilot, Lieutenant Alexsandr Pavlichenko, recalled, 'The fighter pilots were frustrated. They waited and hoped, "Perhaps tomorrow we will receive modern aircraft?"'[7]

The VVS's airborne tactics were also outdated. A core of pilots had flown and fought in Spain and had seen at first hand the success of the German Rotte, Kette and Schwarm formations; however they returned to a Soviet Union in the throes of the Purges, where anyone who had spent time outside the country fell under immediate suspicion of treachery. Discussing their experiences and how they could be applied back home was actively discouraged, and as far as the high command was concerned, air doctrine was set in stone, and watchful eyes kept a look-out for anyone who would deviate from accepted procedure.

As for Soviet industry, it was struggling somewhat in terms of aircraft manufacture as the country transited from being an agricultural nation to one with a huge base of heavy industry. In these circumstances the highly technical aviation sector was always going to lag behind due to its reliance on advanced engineering and non-ferrous metallurgy. Key industrial subsets such as engine design, instrument technology, electronics and radio were slower to develop, as was the practical ability to produce components such as carburettors and roll bearings. Soviet frontline aircraft suffered as a result. For example, on the eve of Barbarossa the Western Border Military Districts of Leningrad, Baltic, Odessa, Western Special and Kiev Special fielded 4,226 fighters, of which 42 per cent were I-16s (nicknamed *Ishaks* in Russian, 'Donkeys' in English), of which as few as 150 were fitted with RSI-3 Orel radios. In combat they would come up against Bf 109s which were faster, better armed and were all equipped with proven FuG-7 two-way radio. Metallurgy was another issue. In Western Europe and the United States, aircraft production mainly used aluminium and magnesium; these strategic materials were not readily available to Moscow, so to try and fill the gaps, the Soviets improvised, turning to the types of material they had in abundance at home – timber, steel and plywood. This meant big compromises in terms of armaments, armour, fuel and ammunition carriage to try and keep the overall weight down while retaining strength in the structure. The Germans, despite their own raw materials shortages, did not have an issue on the same scale, so while an I-16 could only carry 1,600 rounds of machine-gun ammunition, its opponent the Bf 109 would have 2,000, plus 120 20-mm cannon rounds – big, heavy shells that could tear an aircraft apart.

Then, on 23 August 1939, the world woke to the shocking news that the two greatest ideological enemies in the world were now the best of friends – the Molotov–Ribbentrop Non-Aggression Pact had been signed between Berlin and Moscow, in what *Time* magazine christened the 'Communazi Pact', with its participants only half-jokingly labelled 'communazis'. The pact stood on twin pillars. The first was the 'secret protocols', denied to have even existed by the Soviet Union until the late 1980s – these clauses divided Europe up into agreed spheres of influence and condemned the Baltic States, Finland, Romania and Poland to aggression, invasion, subjugation and oppression from one or both signatories. The second was a trade agreement based on an internal German government study that identified Nazi Germany's biggest needs for the future as cereals, petroleum products, manganese ore and raw phosphates. To get them, the Nazis would send Moscow advanced German manufactured goods, especially weaponry. Before long, Soviet rolling stock was steaming west and offloading vast amounts of much needed food for hungry German mouths. In the first year of the agreement alone the Soviet Union shipped to Germany one million tons of cereals, half a million tons of wheat and a million tons of Manchurian soybeans. Along with the foodstuffs came the raw materials German industry was crying out for: 900,000 tons of petroleum products, 500,000 tons of phosphates, 100,000 tons of cotton, 50,000 tons of crucial manganese ore, and 900 kg (almost a ton!) of platinum.[8]

In return the Soviets were salivating in anticipation at getting their hands on cutting-edge German military technology: the as-yet unfinished naval cruiser *Blücher*, the technical plans for the pocket battleship *Bismarck*, heavy naval guns, thirty brand-new aircraft models including the Bf 109, 110 and the Ju 88, electric equipment, locomotives, turbines, generators, diesel engines, machine tools and samples of modern German artillery, panzers, explosives and chemical-warfare equipment. Berlin even ordered IG-Farbenindustrie to hand over to the Soviets their newly developed process for manufacturing toluene. This chemical process was the jewel in the German industrial conglomerate's crown and had cost huge sums to develop. With it you could produce aviation fuel with much higher octane levels that would deliver greater flight speed and significantly improved performance all-round.[9] The Kremlin was also going to be paid cold, hard cash and lots of it – millions of Reichmarks in fact.

As it turned out, they would only get a fraction of what they promised – cash or otherwise.

PART TWO

The War Begins

CHAPTER 4

1939–41: Poland, Finland and Blitzkrieg in the West

Before a single train carriage of goods had headed west, or the first 100 Reichmark note had changed hands, there was the small matter of the two dictatorships invading and carving up Poland. For Case White, as it was codenamed, the Luftwaffe concentrated over 2,000 aircraft, with a clear plan to destroy their opponents on the ground and achieve aerial supremacy as fast as possible before switching to support the ground troops, in what would become their standard operating procedure. The Polish Air Force (*Lotnictwo Wojskowe*), with only around 600 mainly obsolete aircraft, was outnumbered and outclassed in just about every department apart from the quality of their pilots, who were top drawer. The Poles believed in the pre-eminence of the bomber, and its main strike force was the so-called 'Bomber Brigade'. It also had a 'Pursuit Brigade' and various squadrons attached to support ground armies. Polish fighters were a generation older than their German counterparts: the PZL P.11 fighter – produced in the early 1930s – had a top speed of only 227 mph, and was slower than almost all of the Luftwaffe's bombers. When the attack came, a lot of aircraft were hit on their own airfields, but by no means all, and the Luftwaffe were forced to fight the Poles in the air before the campaign closed, in what was a triumph for the new German air force.

Even though the Soviets had also invaded Poland, and now occupied the east of the country, their pilots had no real chance to test their mettle against their Polish opponents, as the survivors of the Luftwaffe's onslaught escaped abroad to continue the fight: 'We didn't have any battle encounters with the Poles, and were soon relocated to Kaunas in Lithuania.'[10]

Their chance finally came with the Soviet invasion of tiny Finland. Emulating the terror attacks of their German partners, the Soviets began their offensive by bombing Helsinki one hour after announcing the invasion. Overhead, wings of SB2 medium bombers from the Red Banner Baltic Fleet bases in Estonia swept in, dropping 500 lb bombs on the city as well as thousands of leaflets exhorting the populace to rise up and overthrow their bourgeois rulers and welcome their Soviet brothers – clearly the apparent irony of exhorting the populace to revolt while at the same time bombing them had not occurred to the Soviet planners!

The attack was timed to coincide with an emergency meeting of the Finnish Cabinet called to discuss the Soviet assault, and was a conspicuous failure. Over 200 civilians were killed by the bombers and their escorting fighters, who even dived down to strafe the streets of the Finnish capital, but the attack did not produce either a wholesale collapse in Finnish morale or an uprising against the government. Added to this, the Soviet legation itself was hit and badly damaged, several of its staff being wounded by their own air force. The Finns resisted the Soviets as bitterly as the Poles resisted the Germans, and turned the whole campaign into a debacle for Moscow as their ill-equipped and poorly led troops froze in the Finnish landscape, their white-clad enemy stalking them in the silent forests. In the air, the outnumbered Finns also showed their quality, as they hunted the Soviets in the blue near-Arctic sky.

For the Soviets overall it was a rude awakening, and even if Moscow denied the errors of the campaign the men at the front were only too aware of the mistakes that had been made by the men at the top:

> We were based on Lake Kolajarvi, west of Kandalaksha, and our main tasks were reconnaissance and bombing raids ... we were lucky not to come across any Finnish planes, as it was suicide to engage them in our R-5s. We only had a PV-1 machine-gun at the front – basically a Maxim fitted for airplanes, and two Degtyarev machine-guns in rear. It was not a good war. Our leadership sucked. What could those infantry boys do in their ankle boots, leg wrappings, thin overcoats and *budyonovka* hats? In fact two divisions froze to death.[11]

The VVS pilots, miles away from the ground battles, were not immune to the horrors described by the fighter pilot Ivan S. Gaidenko: 'One day we went to the steam bath as they brought in a truckload of frozen dead. The corpses were contorted and twisted, so they were put in the steam bath, warmed up and then straightened out. It was an awful sight.'[12] Gaidenko was under no illusions as to just how poor a showing the Soviet air force had made during the fighting: 'We were lucky the Finns had no anti-aircraft artillery in our sector. They fired their small arms at us without effect. Our squadron's only casualty came on the return flight to Gatschina ... the Political Officer's propeller caught a pile of wooden bomb crates, breaking the tips.'[13]

Even among the ranks of the political commissars there was grave disquiet at the poor performance of Soviet arms against the Finns: 'We have just confronted Finland. You know that our fighters couldn't even down one of their old Bristol Blenheims?'[14]

After Poland the Nazis turned west, invading and occupying Denmark and Norway in quick succession before slicing over the River Meuse at Sedan and subjecting the French and British to blitzkrieg. As was now the pattern, close air support from the Luftwaffe was vital. Hans von Luck's unit, part of Erwin Rommel's 7th Panzer Division, got to La Bassée Canal and used light boats to get across the waterway but couldn't establish a proper bridgehead. 'Only when the Stukas came into action was the crossing finally successful.' Von Luck was also appreciative of the job the air force had done in Rouen in Normandy: 'The Luftwaffe had done quite a job. From afar we could already see huge clouds of black smoke hanging in the sky, we could see the burning oil tanks and harbour.'[15]

With the fall of France, Great Britain and her empire stood alone. Over-confident, the Nazis began a half-baked campaign to subdue Great Britain and were soundly beaten. The Battle of Britain was a disaster for the Luftwaffe, with 3,700 aircraft written off and another 2,300 damaged. Along with the aircraft, the Germans lost 3,700 experienced aircrew killed and another 3,000 missing, most of the latter ending up in British POW camps. Neither German industry nor the training schools could make good losses on this scale, and when Operation Sea Lion (the Wehrmacht's plan to invade Britain) was shelved, the Luftwaffe was left with fewer planes and fewer crew than at any time since the start of the war. It was badly in need of a rest and a refit – it was to get neither.

PART THREE

'Barbarossa: The Largest Invasion in History'

CHAPTER 5

The Luftwaffe v. the VVS

By the winter of 1940, Nazi Germany stood at the very height of her power. In German eyes all the wrongs of Versailles, real or imagined, had been righted and the First World War Austro-German infantry corporal-cum-Nazi dictator had jigged in delight over the total defeat of the hated French giant. Great Britain and her empire still held out, but had neither the ground forces nor the strategic air arm to threaten German hegemony in Europe. Hitler now had a choice to make: he could choose to pour his considerable military might into the fighting in the Mediterranean and North Africa, capture Egypt and cut the Suez Canal, Britain's lifeline to her Indian empire, securing the oil-rich Middle East into the bargain. This course of action would make a reality of Mussolini's idle boast of the Mediterranean being '*il mare nostrum*', and Hitler could then turn his formidable political talents to reaching a diplomatic solution with the British that would leave their empire intact in return for acceptance of German dominance in mainland Europe – this was basically the 'Halifax approach'. It would also echo Hitler's own dictum, 'The art of leadership consists of consolidating the attention of the people against a single adversary and taking care that nothing will split up this attention ... The leader of genius must have the ability to make different opponents appear as if they belonged to one category.'[16]

Alternatively, the Nazi dictator could give vent to his rabid hatred of Bolshevism, overturn the Non-Aggression Pact that had served him so well for the last year, and turn to face the largest military power on earth. Hitler, the inveterate gambler, decided to reach for the dice once more and committed his racist state to a two-front war – something he had always given his word he would never do.

Wednesday 18 December 1940 dawned cold and overcast. Hitler, due to give a speech at the Berlin Sportspalast to young officer cadets, strode down the steps of the Chancellery, acknowledging the salutes of the black-clad SS-Leibstandarte sentries before climbing into the black Mercedes that would take him the short distance across the capital to the arena. Sitting in the back on the deep leather seat, he reflected on the speech he was about to give, going over phrases in his mind. As usual, the speech was designed for the attention of a wider audience than the one who would be sitting in front of him. Hitler had riddled the text full of righteous indignation about the world's treatment of the German racial *Volk* and the prejudices it supposedly laboured under – he would tell his listeners that the German people 'is one of the most disadvantaged peoples of the world', stoking the resentment he was always keen to nurture. He would then go on to argue that the Germans needed *Lebensraum*, 'living space', to allow them to fulfil their destiny as the master race. The speech was all part of a carefully orchestrated campaign to prepare the German people for the next phase in his supreme plan.

That next phase was embodied in Hitler's Directive No. 21 – *Unternehmen Barbarossa* (Operation Barbarossa) – which he had formally signed at his desk just before heading out to give his speech: 'The Wehrmacht must be prepared to crush Soviet Russia in a quick campaign even before the end of the war against England. For this purpose the Army will have to employ all available units with the reservation that the occupied territories must be safeguarded against surprise attack ...'

As an example of muddled military thinking at the highest level, this document has few equals. For a start it accepted a two-front war as fact, but made no provision to resolve that dilemma, and it even set a non-existent geographical concept as the final goal: 'The ultimate objective of the operation is to establish a defence line against Asiatic Russia from a line running approximately from the Volga River to Archangel.'

The paper was nonsense, and yet it was not a senior General Staff-trained officer that led the opposition to its institution, but Hitler's own deputy and anointed successor – Hermann Goering.

The Reichsmarshall profoundly disagreed with the turn eastwards, preferring the Mediterranean option instead, and he was forthright with Hitler: 'The Luftwaffe is the only branch of the Wehrmacht which hasn't had a breathing space since the war began. I told you when we first went to war that I was going into battle with my training squadrons, and now they're all gone. I'm not at all sure you can beat

Russia in six weeks. There's nothing I'd like better than to have you proven right, but, frankly, I doubt that you will be.'[17]

Perhaps Goering was spurred on by the fact that only ten days previously Hitler had ordered the establishment of an Air Command Mediterranean with the 370-aircraft strong Fliegerkorps X based in Sicily to assist the desperately ineffective Italians in the campaign against the British. This dispersion of the Luftwaffe's limited forces was set out perfectly in the 226-word opening page of the Barbarossa Directive that stated the Luftwaffe's role as follows:

> The Airforce will have to make available for this eastern campaign supporting forces of such strength that the Army will be able to bring land operations to a speedy conclusion and that eastern Germany will be as little damaged as possible by enemy air attack. This build-up of a focal point in the east will be limited only by the need to protect from air attack the whole combat and arsenal area which we control, and to ensure that attacks on England, and especially upon her imports, are not allowed to lapse.

In essence, Hitler was demanding the continuation of the war against Britain and the aerial defence of the entire occupied European continent, while committing the air force to an overwhelming effort against the Soviet Union – how could a weakened Luftwaffe do all three tasks? This dilemma would be a major factor in the Luftwaffe's defeat in the east.

But Goering's forebodings were not shared by his own chief of staff, Hans Jeschonnek, who on hearing the news delightedly exclaimed to Goering's Head of Intelligence, Josef 'Beppo' Schmid, 'At last a proper war!'[18] As it was, it was Hitler himself who put an end to the dissension in his usual bullying manner: 'Goering, why don't you stop trying to persuade me to drop my plans for Russia? I've made up my mind!' And with that the Luftwaffe fatefully turned to the east.[19]

What awaited them in the east was a true leviathan. Soviet communism had almost been destroyed at birth by the counter-revolutionary Whites and their overseas allies, and as a consequence had been left with an indelible fear and suspicion of the outside world. Stalin's answer was to seek sanctuary in massive military power. The foe the Nazis would face had no fewer than 5,370,000 men under arms, over 4 million of them in the Red Army, and this from a population of 190 million with 16 million men of military age. In comparison there were just 85 million Germans. When the Red Army marched into eastern Poland in September 1939, Moscow had an inventory of some 8,105 planes in service and counting – the Germans, by contrast, had just 2,916.[20] By the time the Nazis invaded the Soviet Union that number would have rocketed to almost double the 1939 total, making the VVS the largest air force on the planet. They were backed by a manufacturing base created in the mass industrialisation of the 1920s and 1930s and a political ideology that, just as with the Nazis, held aviation up as a powerful symbol of the new regime: modern, innovative and youthful. In the 1930s the Party created the slogan 'Our country needs 150,000 pilots!' and launched a campaign that glamorised aviation and specifically targeted the recruitment of Party and Komsomol [the Communist Party's youth organisation] members to become the pilots of the future. The sons of Party high-ups flocked to volunteer, youngsters such as Leonid Nikitovich Khrushchev, son of the senior Commissar and future Premier Nikita Khrushchev, and this phenomenon was not just confined to the Soviet Union. In Fascist Italy, Il Duce himself, and two of his sons, Bruno and Vittorio, became qualified pilots, and even in autocratic Hungary the Regent's eldest boy, Istvan Horthy, eagerly enlisted to become a fighter pilot. Vitaly I. Klimenko spoke for most of the Soviet volunteers:

> Why did I become a pilot? That was the fashion of our time! Pilots were heroes; Chkalov, Levanevski…Gromov. We wanted to be like them … I dreamt of getting a pilot's leather coat, a smart uniform and of flying a fighter plane. So, with these dreams and the recommendation of the Komsomol I entered the Rogan Air Force Academy … I graduated from the Academy in September 1940 having studied four types of aircraft and with a total flight time of 40–45 hours.[21]

Germany and the Soviet Union were both instinctively land powers, and saw war primarily through the prism of the army, but they appreciated the potential value of air power and aped each other in their approach to their air forces. On the other side of the border the German equivalents of Vitaly Klimenko could be found in the network of glider clubs set up by the Nazis all over the country under the auspices of the National Socialist Flyers Corps (*Nationalsozialistisches Fliegerkorps*; NSFK) – young men such as Norbert Hannig from Silesia, who would go on to become a Luftwaffe fighter pilot in the east: 'The launch crew disappeared beneath me as I soared over their heads. The bracing wires sang like a finely-tuned violin … I was flying!'[22]

For both countries, the corps of flyers who had begun their training in the Nazi-sponsored gliding clubs or the Soviet Komsomol flying academies would go on to become the hard wood of their wartime services. Those young men benefited from extensive pre-war training and combat experience. For the Soviets this meant up to two and a half years in an air force academy, and then action in the Spanish Civil War against the Germans and Italians, or versus the Japanese in the Far East Khalkhin-Gol campaign, or even up in the far north fighting the outnumbered Finns. For the Germans, training was almost as long and even more comprehensive, with rookie pilots having to acquire multiple gradings and master everything from aerobatics to formation and foul weather flying to finally achieve pilot status. For many, it was then the selfsame experience as their Soviet counter-parts in the skies over Spain – but on the other side with the Nazi Condor Legion, fighting on behalf of Franco's Nationalists against the Soviet-backed Republican government. Following on was the full-blooded air campaigns over France, the Low Countries and finally Great Britain.

The Luftwaffe that then began to move east in early 1941 was an experienced, powerful weapon of war, equipped with some of the most modern aircraft in the world and formed around a cohort of well-trained, experienced pilots. Not that it was invulnerable. For a start, given the tasks it had been set, it was small. The sources disagree on the exact figures, but the Luftwaffe would begin Barbarossa with between 2,232 and 2,598 frontline aircraft in the east – far less than the 3,826 it had to launch the invasion of the west in the previous year, and even considerably fewer than the 3,705 it concentrated for the Battle of Britain.[23] Of this slimmed-down armada, just 619 were single-engine fighters, although this was a full two-thirds of the entire Jagdwaffe at the time, while the 838 bombers were almost exactly half the total deployed to attack France.

Luftwaffe Intelligence estimated this limited force would have to face some twenty-three VVS divisions, equipped with around 7,300 aircraft, with an additional 3,000 in the interior and about 2,000 in the Far East facing the Japanese.[24] In reality there were seventy-nine VVS divisions, with 7,850 planes in the western districts facing the Germans, and more than another 7,000 scattered across the country's vastness.[25] However, some sources put the VVS total strength at closer to an astronomical 20,000. Whatever the truth of the number itself, the reality would be that the Luftwaffe would be vastly outnumbered in every category of aircraft: fighters, bombers, ground attack, reconnaissance, and even seaplanes! Indeed, the German fighters alone would face odds of 5 to 1 against.

As well as being small, the Luftwaffe of 1941 was dispersed, tired and showing some disturbing signs of combat fatigue.

For the launch of Barbarossa the Luftwaffe was structured to mirror the ground forces it would be tied to. So, it would be Colonel General Alfred 'Bomben' Keller's Luftflotte 1 who would support Field Marshal Wilhelm Ritter von Leeb's Army Group North. The personally brave but tactically unimaginative Keller was given eight bomber and three and a third single-engine fighter Gruppen, but no dive-bombers at all for ground attack, and so would be forced to rely on Junkers Ju 88s for that task. The Luftflotte's frontage was only 125 miles, but stretched back more than 500 miles to encompass Leningrad – the Army Group's main objective. Keller was an 'Old Eagle', an *alte Adler* from the First World War, a bomber specialist, an ardent Nazi and a member of Goering's 'Little General Staff'. His sector would always be the poor relation of the Luftwaffe's war in the East.

To Keller's south was the Luftwaffe's main striking force, Albert Kesselring's Luftflotte 2. Hitler and his generals considered the 186-mile-long central section of the front the most important and so gave Fedor von Bock's Army Group Centre the lion's share of the air force: between 1,223 and 1,500 planes (accounts differ)[26] grouped into two fliegerkorps – Fliegerkorps VIII (without doubt the best close support unit in the Luftwaffe) with three bomber, five and a third dive-bomber, two twin-engine fighter, three single-engine fighter and one air transport Gruppen, and Fliegerkorps II with five bomber, three dive-bomber, two twin-engine fighter and one air transport Gruppen.

Kesselring's southern neighbour was Colonel-General Alexander Löhr's Luftflotte 4. For the Germans, the southern axis was of secondary importance to what would happen further north on the main route to Moscow, but Soviet plans were markedly different, with Moscow believing that the rolling tank country of the south would be the main area of operations, hence their major armoured and VVS forces were concentrated there. To combat them along the longest frontage for any Luftflotte at 215 miles, the Austrian 'little emperor' (as Löhr was nicknamed on account of his slightly Oriental looks) was given 630 German planes in two Fliegerkorps: Fliegerkorps IV with four bomber and three single-engine fighter Gruppen, and Fliegerkorps V with a further eight bomber and three single-engine fighter Gruppen. The German OKW had also agreed with the Bucharest government that the Romanian air force would act in support of Gerd von Runstedt's Army Group South, as well as protect its own homeland from Soviet attack.

In overall terms what this translated into was built-in inferiority from the very outset of the invasion. The stark fact was that the Luftwaffe would not outnumber the VVS anywhere along the thousand miles of front. The only way it could achieve local supremacy would be to continually shift Gruppen and Fliegerkorps from sector to sector as the situation demanded – with all the consequent wear and tear this would inevitably mean.

That same stress was becoming evident among the existing Luftwaffe air crews even before the advent of Barbarossa. As Goering pointed out to Hitler before Directive 21 was signed, the air force was the only service not to have had a significant break since the beginning of the war to rest, recover and rebuild its strength. The army had been able to bask in the glory of the victory over France, and wasn't really called on again until the Balkans campaign in the spring of the following year, while it could be argued that, apart from its disastrous foray to Norway, the Kriegsmarine was yet to be tested. For the Luftwaffe, campaign had followed campaign, with its men and machines in constant demand as two captured Luftwaffe men acknowledged in a conversation their British interrogators secretly recorded:

> 'We've got an old observer in the Staffel, who's still flying, he's been in over seventy-five operations … and he's completely finished.'
> 'How old is he?'
> 'I believe he's only twenty-three or twenty-five, but he's lost his hair. He's practically bald, like an old man. He's hollow-cheeked, and looks terrible. He once showed me a picture of himself as a recruit, when he first joined up – he had a face full of character and looked so fresh. When you talk to him now he is so nervous, he stutters and can't get a word out.'
> 'Why does he still fly operations?'
> 'He has to.'[27]

And it wasn't just the stress of continuous operations that was taking its toll; it was the very nature of the job that was beginning to erode the basic humanity of the flight crews:

> On the second day of the Polish war I had to drop bombs on a station at Posen [current Polish city of Poznan]. Eight of the sixteen bombs fell on the town, among the houses, I didn't like that. By the third day I didn't give a hoot and by the fourth I was enjoying it. It was our before-breakfast amusement to chase single soldiers over the fields with machine-gun fire and to leave them lying them there with a few bullets in their back. Civilians too. We attacked the columns in the roads. I was in a *Kette* [flight of three aircraft] and our leader bombed the road and we bombed the

ditches ... You should have seen the horses stampede! I felt sorry
for the horses, but not sorry at all for the people.[28]

Dropping bombs has become a passion with me. One itches for it, it
is a lovely feeling. It is as lovely as shooting someone down.[29]

It would be these men that Hitler and Goering would fling against the
might of the Soviet Union, in a war that would become synonymous
with brutality and horror.

Just how horrific was presaged by the conference Hitler held in
early March 1941 for all the senior officers involved in planning and
carrying out Barbarossa, when the dictator held forth on how he
expected his own forces to behave in the coming battles:

The war against Russia will be such that it cannot be conducted in
a chivalrous fashion. This struggle is one of ideologies and racial
differences and will have to be conducted with unprecedented,
merciless and unrelenting harshness.[30]

He concluded by giving his infamous order stating that as Communist
commissars were standard bearers of the Soviet system, they were not
to be accorded the accepted treatment of other prisoners of war but
were instead to be murdered immediately on capture. Barbarossa, he
said, 'was a battle of extermination ... There is no question of the laws
of war ... commissars and members of the secret police are criminals
and must be treated as such [i.e. shot].'

Commissars were not going to be the only victims either, as General
Georg Thomas (he of the proud pre-war boasts on the growing size
of the German armed forces) made clear to the state secretaries of
various government ministries with whom he was working with on
the grotesquely titled 'Hunger Plan'. Thomas managed to get written
agreement from them all that the priority for the soon-to-be-occupied
territories in the east would be to firstly supply the Wehrmacht with the
food it needed, and then secondly to ship other essential agricultural
products, including grain, back to Germany itself. 'In doing so,'
Thomas's protocol laconically stated, 'umpteen million people will
doubtless starve to death, if we extract everything necessary for us
from the country.'[31]

The army wasn't the only service whose forthcoming role in state-
sanctioned murder was laid out by the Nazi dictator. Just before
Barbarossa was launched, the head of the Luftwaffe's air mission in
Romania met with Goering himself and then went back to Bucharest

and told his leading subordinates: 'The Reichsmarshall has clearly ordered that among Russian prisoners each Bolshevik functionary is to be immediately shot without any judicial proceedings.' There was little or no challenge to this extraordinary statement from Goering or the OKL. At a senior level both the Army and the Luftwaffe were quietly acquiescing to these utterly heinous policies.[32]

However, as these orders seemingly affected a minority of potential prisoners this could seem a detail, even though a murderous one, whereas in reality they were just a starting point, and in time they would help open the flood gates to a conflict, a wider war and an attitude to violence that made the ensuing Russo-German war one of the bloodiest in human history. What it would mean on the ground, and in the air as the armies clashed, would be slaughter without mercy. The Luftwaffe was about to enter a meat grinder.

Away from the politics of government-condoned murder, the Luftwaffe carried out the first ever extensive aerial reconnaissance of a seemingly peaceful foreign power with hundreds of overflights organised by the meticulous and dedicated Lieutenant Colonel Theo Rowehl and his specially designated 'Sonderkommando Rowehl'. Converted Dornier Do 215-B2s and Junkers Ju 88Bs and Ju 86Ps, capable of flying at up to 39,000 feet, streamed eastwards over the Soviet Union's borders to map out the new enemy; not an easy task when the area to be mapped covered 579,150 square miles – more than twice the size of France! What they found in that huge space should have given the military planners in Berlin significant pause for thought. The western districts of the Soviet Union were basically a gigantic armed camp, and among the mass of men and material no fewer than 2,000 airfields were identified, many of them packed with lines of standing aircraft. Major General Alexander A. Novikov's Leningrad District had 1,270 planes; his neighbour in the Baltic District, Major General A. P. Ionov, had slightly fewer at 1,140; while major generals I. I. Kopets and Y. S. Ptukhin in the Western and Kiev districts respectively had 3,144 between them. F. G. Michugin's Odessa District had the fewest at just under a thousand, and they were all backed up by Colonel Gorbatsevich's 1,346-strong long-range bomber reserve.[33]

The Soviets, though, were not oblivious to these German intrusions as one bewildered VVS man recalled:

We were in a very silly situation. We saw German spy planes fly over our positions every day, but we were not authorised to oppose them. We couldn't even request them to leave! A Ju-88 would overfly us early in the morning, heading deep into Soviet territory at high altitude. In the evening he overflew us again on the return flight ... on one occasion a pilot took off and chased a German plane. When he returned he was immediately arrested.[34]

As only bureaucracy can fathom, the pilot in question was not released on the advent of war; rather he was court-martialled instead – dictatorships do not like to be reminded they get things wrong.

With Rowehl's flights unearthing more and more military muscle, luckily for the Germans their fears were calmed by none other than their head of intelligence, Josef Schmid. Goering's personal appointment to head up Abteilung 5, the Luftwaffe's own intelligence branch, the arrogant Schmid, contemptuously nicknamed 'Beppo' by his many detractors, simply wasn't up to the task. Goering had plucked him from relative obscurity as a passed-over major and given him one of the most important roles in the Luftwaffe. By comparison, his counterpart in the British Royal Air Force was a full major general. Schmid himself had never bothered to learn to fly, didn't speak English or Russian and indeed had never been outside Germany. He was once memorably described as 'one of the most disastrous men in the Luftwaffe general staff ... a boxer's face, without wit or culture. An alcoholic, he started his career with factually false, optimistically exaggerated opinions ...' Erhard Milch said of him: 'The information he provided – it was dreadful. He made a report once and I thought "Never had I heard such rot." But Goering said, "You know nothing about it." Goering always had to have the last word.'

As it was, Schmid's view of Rowehl's reconnaissance was that the Soviets were deliberately inflating their strength to scare the Germans, and that at most only 10 per cent of the identified airfields were fully operational. Even having said that, one overarching conclusion was inescapable: the VVS had to be destroyed on the ground the moment Barbarossa was launched to try and nullify its numerical advantage, and so surprise would be all. The Air Ministry on Berlin's Wilhelmstrasse was buzzing with this news, and so, unfathomably, was the Kremlin. The German communist spy Lieutenant Heinz 'Harro' Schulze-Boysen, codenamed 'Starshina' (Sergeant-Major) by his Soviet handlers, was a planning officer on the Luftwaffe staff, and had sent back to Moscow detailed reports on the German intention to launch their invasion with pre-emptive strikes on the VVS's airfields. But Schulze-Boysen's reports were simply not believed by no less a dignitary than Stalin himself.[35]

Others in the Soviet hierarchy were not so sure of Berlin's peaceful intentions. Yakov Smuchkevich, the head of the VVS, was touring his airfields in the west and ended up visiting the 131st Fighter Regiment and its commander, Colonel Yemelyan F. Kondrat. One of the regiment's technicians remembers the inspection as hardly the unit's finest hour: 'According to the manual all 60 fighters were supposed to be ready for take-off in 20 minutes. In reality we only managed to bring four planes in two hours! The soil was so soft that planes bogged down, so men from each of our four squadrons had to carry a plane from the hangars to the runway on their shoulders ... I heard Smuchkevich say to Kondrat: "The war with Germany will start any time and you think this is just a game?" In short Kondrat was immediately dismissed.'[36] A few short weeks later Smuchkevich was arrested as part of the Purges.

The Luftwaffe dilemma was clear enough – how to achieve surprise.

Barbarossa was due to begin at precisely 0330 hrs on Sunday morning, 22 June. At that moment the German artillery batteries would open fire en masse, obliterating the forward Soviet defences and paving the way for the infantry and panzers. However, the targeted VVS airfields were all some 30–40 minutes' flying time away from the Luftwaffe's forward air bases, which would mean the Soviets would have ample time from the artillery strike starting to scramble their aircraft and evade the German raids. Jeschonnek's solution to this problem was daring in the extreme. The first wave of attackers would take off in the pitch darkness before 3 a.m., led by specially picked crews with significant night flying experience. They would then climb far higher than for normal bombing operations and head towards the sixty-six airfields selected as their targets. At 0315 hrs the 1,766 bombers and 506 escorting fighters would be over their objectives and would descend to attack height and begin their runs.

Darkness on the night of 21 June only lasted a few short hours, the air still warm and damp as the men manoeuvred the aircraft into position on their airfields. Stiff-legged, the pilots and crew marched purposefully over to the waiting planes – heads full of flight plans and last-minute details to try and blot out the enormity of what they were about to do. Strapping on parachutes, running through pre-flight checks and touching lucky charms, the engines were switched on and coughed noisily into life. The aircraft taxied off and took off in waves, hundreds of aircraft climbing higher and higher to reach their pre-planned positions and begin their journey east. On the horizon the sun was just beginning to rise, the land still cloaked in the semi-darkness of a short summer night. In the dim light of cockpit and navigator lamps, maps were checked and eyes strained nervously for any sign of fighter or anti-aircraft activity from their new enemy – there was none. The crews peered through the gloom, praying to see their targets, and then, suddenly, there they were below them. The Luftwaffe men struggled to comprehend what they were seeing, as one fighter pilot in the first wave described breathlessly what he saw: 'We could hardly believe our eyes. Every airfield was chock full of recce aircraft, bombers and fighters, all lined up in long straight rows as if on a parade. The number of landing strips and aircraft the Russians had concentrated along our borders was staggering.'[37]

With unalloyed glee the Luftwaffe pilots began their attack. Surprise was total. On the ground a Soviet border patrol sent a panicked signal back to their headquarters, 'We are being fired upon, what shall we do?' The reply would have been funny if it hadn't been so tragic: 'You must be insane, and why is your signal not in code?'[38]

On the Soviet airfields themselves, all was chaos. Ivan Konovalov, a fighter pilot, remembered, 'All of a sudden there was an incredible roaring sound. Enemy planes were overhead. Someone yelled "Take cover!" and I dived under the wing of my plane. Everything was burning, a terrible, raging fire. At the end of it all only one of our planes was left intact.'[39]

His compatriot Vitaly I. Klimenko was up with the 10th Fighter Regiment, based at Shaulai in Lithuania. Vitaly was due to take his pretty Lithuanian girlfriend to a nearby lake that day for some sunbathing and swimming, but instead, 'I flipped open my tent and saw planes with German crosses firing their machine-guns at us. "Guys the war has started!" – "Fuck you, what war?" – "It's a German air raid!" We jumped out of our tent, some of our neighbours had already been killed or wounded.'

The Soviets were caught totally unawares along the whole front.

> Our superiors had ordered no defensive measures, and at the airfields we had our planes parked next to each other, in neat, orderly rows. The Germans hit us hard. More than 800 planes were destroyed on the ground in those first few hours and another 300 were shot down soon after take-off. It was a total disaster. On the first day of the war we lost more than a thousand planes.[40]

Confusion reigned among Soviet commanders. At 0430 hrs, a full hour after the invasion began, and even as German artillery was hammering Soviet troop sites, the 26th Army's chief of staff, Lieutenant General Ivan Semenovich Varennikov, was telephoning Nikolay Popel, the lead commissar of the VIII Mechanised Corps based in the south on the River Dniester, and telling him, 'Do not fall for provocation. Do not open fire on German aircraft. Wait for orders!'

Popel duly waited, but before any orders came two waves of German aircraft appeared overhead. 'They bombed with precision; the railway station, the approach roads, the oil refinery, our barracks.'[41]

Vitaly Klimenko somehow managed not only to survive the onslaught but to get in an I-16 fighter and get airborne along with a comrade, Alex Bokach. The two of them flew west in search of their new enemy and found an advancing German column. 'Alex dived and I saw smoky bursts spitting from his plane as he strafed the column. I followed suit. We assaulted the column and it was impossible to miss, so dense was the mass of enemy troops on the highway ... We were the only ones from the entire regiment who fought back at the Fritzies without waiting for orders. But our losses were high – many planes and hangars were destroyed.' Klimenko and Bokach returned to base when their ammunition was gone, but instead of being congratulated the two pilots were taken in front of their regimental commander, who actually threatened them with arrest for provoking the Germans and attacking the troops of a friendly nation![42]

The Germans were under no such delusions.

In the skies above the new invasion front, the very first kill of Barbarossa went to the Staffel commander of I/JG 3 Udet, Robert Olejnik.

Everybody knew I was an early riser and liked to fly the dawn missions. So, shortly before 0330 hrs, I took off with my wingman to recce the Russian airfields along our stretch of the border. Everything seemed quiet in the semi-darkness below. It was not until we were returning to base, and flying back over the first airfield we had visited some 20 minutes earlier, that I spotted signs of activity. Two Russian fighters were preparing to scramble. As we circled 7–800 metres [2,300–2,600 feet] overhead, I saw the Russians start their engines and begin to taxi out. They took off immediately and climbed towards us, obviously looking for a fight. They were still some 300–400 metres below us when we dived to the attack. I caught the leader with a short burst on my first pass and he went down in flames. His wingman disappeared.[43]

Olejnik was not alone in chalking up a win in the air. Captain Wolf-Dietrich Wilcke of JG 53 managed to down no fewer than five VVS fighters in his first three sorties on the 22nd, making him the first 'Russian Front ace', and bringing his wartime tally up to eighteen. Fliegerkorps VIII's commander, Wolfram von Richthofen, wrote in his diary, 'The Russians that managed to get up in the air flew poorly, and we were able to bring most of them down.'

In total, German pilots and anti-aircraft crews claimed an unprecedented 322 victories on that first day,[44] but the real slaughter happened on the ground. The exact figures are heavily contested. The official Soviet record – *The Great Patriotic War* – not a work acclaimed for its historical accuracy, said, 'By midday of 22 June our losses totalled approximately 1,200 aircraft, including more than 800 machines destroyed on the ground.' The Luftwaffe pilots themselves claimed between 1,200 and 1,500,[45] a total that their boss back in Berlin thought utterly preposterous. Goering lambasted his pilots for over-claiming and instituted an immediate inquiry. As the Nazi spearheads overran the targeted VVS airfields, Luftwaffe specialists arrived in their wake to examine the evidence and determine the truth. Their report not only confirmed the pilots' version but went on to say that, if anything, the totals were understated!

As it was, the official German communiqué, like the Soviet record a news channel that on occasions only had a passing relationship with the truth, stated on 29 June that VVS losses to all causes on day one amounted to 1,811 planes (the Luftwaffe admitted to losing just thirty-five aircraft),[46] then 2,582 by the end of day two, and a mind-numbing 4,107 by the 29th itself. According to the bulletin, the Soviet air force had ceased to exist. The war in the air was over! The Luftwaffe were jubilant. Kesselring described the attacks on the VVS as a '*kindermord*', a 'slaughter of the innocents', and after just three days the Luftwaffe's primary mission was switched from eliminating the VVS and achieving aerial supremacy to one of close support for the Army. In this role, Germany's airmen began winning even more accolades. The handsome East Prussian Major Walter Storp led the Me 110s of Gruppe 210 (part of Albert Kesselring's Luftflotte 2) in over 1,000 sorties in the first month of the campaign, and claimed no less than 165 tanks, 2,136 vehicles and 60 locomotives (as well as 915 aircraft) destroyed. Storp's reward was a coveted Knight's Cross. The pace of operations was relentless, with fighter pilots averaging five to eight sorties a day, while their bomber colleagues chalked up anywhere between four to six. The prize, though, went to the Stuka crews, who seemed to spend more time in the air than on the ground as they were constantly called upon to support the Army with precision dive-bombing of anything from pillboxes and strongpoints to bridges, roads and even armoured trains. Outclassed and shown during the Battle of Britain to be seriously vulnerable against determined fighter opposition, the Ju 87s came into their own again in the Soviet Union. Reliable, needing a minimum of mechanical servicing and able to absorb pretty heavy punishment and still stay flying, the Stukas proved devastating. One Soviet counter-attack, launched near Bialystok and Lunna to try and slow down von Bock's men, was swamped by the Stukas of von Richthofen's Fliegerkorps VIII. Wave after wave of dive-bombers swooped on the Soviet armoured spearheads and by the end of the day some 105 tanks were left burning and shattered on the steppe.

As one panzer officer wrote:

> Our superiority in the air was quite obvious, both in quantity and quality. It soon became clear that the Russian air force had only obsolete machines at its disposal, but above all that the pilots did not function nearly as well as our own fighter and dive-bomber pilots, or the pilots of our Western opponents. This was naturally a great relief to us, and when Russian aircraft appeared we hardly bothered to take cover. In fact we often had to smile when, for want of bombs, thousands of nails rained down on us from their bomb bays. We soon came to realize that neither war at sea nor war in the air was suited to the Russian mentality. Russia had waged war mostly on land and her cumbersome military bureaucracy had obviously never given much thought to building up a modern air force.[47]

It seemed as if Goebbels's propaganda news reels were correct – the Soviets were finished. As Hitler had boldly stated, he had kicked the door in and the whole rotten structure was crashing down.

And yet. The Germans weren't getting it all their own way, and there were ominous signs for those with eyes to see that this campaign would be like no other the German Wehrmacht had fought. In Poland and France the pattern had become familiar; the enemy air force was overwhelmingly destroyed on the ground during the first few days of the campaign, and anything that was left was hunted out of the sky. They then had neither the time, space nor will to come back from their initial defeat. This was proving not to be true of the Soviets. Regardless of the cost, the Soviets were still taking to the air, attacking everywhere and refusing to capitulate. Some in the Wehrmacht had ominous forebodings, as relayed by the dashing twenty-three-year-old Captain Ekkehard Maurer of the Prussian 23rd Infantry Division:

> The morning of 22nd June 1941 my battalion commander and myself, I was his Adjutant at the time, were in our foxholes very close to the barbed wire and just before the artillery barrage began he whispered over to me something like "Don't ever forget 22 June 1941 at

three-fifteen in the morning." Then he paused for a moment and said "Well, I don't think I have to tell you not to forget because you won't forget it anyway. At this very moment the worst decline, the worst disaster in German history in many centuries, is going to begin."

Mauer would go on to win the German Cross in Gold for bravery on the Eastern Front and survive the war. His commander would not.

Near the border fortress city of Brest-Litovsk was Biala Polaska airfield, home base for the 77th Stuka Staffel. Even as the massacre on the Soviets' own airfields was in full flow, six Soviet fighters appeared over Biala and prepared to attack, but before they could, patrolling Bf 109s shot them all down in a matter of minutes. Then another twelve came in and were shot down too. Then another flight and another. But the Soviets just kept on coming. Kesselring said the Soviets seemed to have a wholly different concept 'of the value of human life'.

True or not, they had a different approach to resistance, as German pilots were confronted by the hitherto unknown phenomenon of the 'taran' – Soviet flyers deliberately ramming them to knock them out of the sky.

Sometimes I even wanted to ram German planes, never at low attitude of course that would have been suicide. But I remember trying to ram a German scout at Vyazma in the autumn of 1941. We'd begun a battle and the enemy I was chasing climbed higher and higher ... well he was obviously very experienced, as he first turned 90 degrees then shut down his internal engine and dropped like a stone ... I approached him at an altitude of 5–600m and thought, "There you are, you son of a bitch!" and prepared to ram him, but he disappeared into the clouds and that was it. Two scouts escaped me like this, I was very angry with myself.[48]

This fanatical act of resistance claimed its first German casualty on the 22nd over Grodno, when a Lieutenant Kuzmin flew his I-153 Chaika into the Bf 109 of Lieutenant Colonel Wolfgang Schellmann, a Staffel commander, Lipetsk graduate and twenty-five-score Knight's Cross holder. Kuzmin died in the impact, but Schellmann manged to bail out safely. His comrades saw him land, discard his chute, and head off in the direction of the German lines. He never made it. Captured by NKVD troops, the thirty-year-old Hessian was shot out of hand.[49]

Schellmann was just the first of a growing list of Luftwaffe Experten whom the VVS were slowly but surely claiming; thirty-seven-score Heinz

'Pietsch' Bretnütz, like Schellmann a veteran of the Condor Legion, died of his wounds after being shot down; another ex-Legion man, Hans Kolbow, score twenty-seven, hit by anti-aircraft fire, bailed out too low and died on impact; Erich 'Schmidtchen' Schmidt, hit by flak and never seen again, scored forty-seven; and Hubert 'Hubs' Mütherich, killed in a crash landing, scored forty-three. All were Knight's Cross winners, and now all were gone.

It wasn't just in the air that the Soviets demonstrated a will to fight on no matter the cost which seemingly defied all military logic. Down on the ground in the border city of Brest-Litovsk, the medieval citadel was attacked on that very first day by the Austrian-manned 45th Infantry Division. An experienced formation, it threw itself against the outnumbered defenders expecting a swift victory. Instead it got the fight of its life. It took Fritz Schlieper's men an incredible twenty days to smash major resistance, and even then some Red Army men refused to surrender and ended up being literally flushed out when the exasperated Austrians deliberately flooded the cellars over a month later. Hardly a single defender survived, and the butcher's bill for the Austrians included forty officers and 442 other ranks killed, and no fewer than a full 1,000 wounded.

One German soldier wrote home of his early experiences against the Soviets: 'It was incredible the way the Russians fought. They let us approach to within three metres and then mow us down … you wouldn't believe how fantastically the devils fought.'[50]

This seeming disregard for life, and willingness for sacrifice on an unimaginable scale, would be a hallmark of the Soviet war effort. As late as the autumn of 1943, with the Red Army liberating huge swathes of the Ukraine from Nazi occupation, enforced mass conscription was introduced for all males between the ages of nineteen and fifty. Nicknamed 'booty Ukrainians' by their new comrades, almost three-quarters of a million men were rounded up, issued a rifle, either a uniform tunic or trousers (rarely both), a pair of boots (usually US-made) and, if they were lucky, a steel helmet. They were taught to load and fire their rifle, no more than that, and then sent directly into battle. Needless to say, their chances of survival were slim in the extreme and most were dead within days. This was the Soviet way of war, and it was as ruthless as it was effective.

CHAPTER 6

Slaughter in the Air and on the Ground

It was clear to the whole German invasion force from day one of Barbarossa that this campaign was an altogether different animal from anything that had gone on before. Hitler and his Nazi cronies had whipped up a virulent propaganda storm that portrayed their Soviet enemies as akin to a disease that had to be extirpated. That meant the invaders had specific orders to murder, burn and pillage from the first moment the firing started. Language was distorted to depict a polyglot Soviet empire filled with 'sub-humans' devoid of intelligence, culture and humanity, and as the Germans advanced there were instances of atrocities that seemed to provide this lie with a veneer of truth. As early as the second day of the invasion, Major (later Colonel) Johann von Kielmansegg – an officer on the divisional staff of the 6th Panzer Division – reported an incident when his division tried to cross the Dubyssa River in Lithuania:

> During the night two platoons, totalling 50–60 men, established a bridgehead but were crushed by a Soviet counter-attack. The next day we found all the men shot, that is murdered, and atrociously mutilated. Eyes had been put out, genitals cut off and other cruelties inflicted. This was our first such experience, but not the last. I said to my general "Sir, this will be a very different war from the one in Poland and France."[51]

Von Kielmansegg also saw how the Soviets cleared a path through German defensive minefields. 'First they would herd cows through the minefields, and when they ran out of cows they used men linked arm in arm with machine-guns behind them, forcing them over our mines.'

Another officer, Lieutenant Leichtfuss, was with Army Group Centre and finding out just how different it would be: 'I found six of our men who had been nailed to a table through their tongues, ten more had been hung dead from meat hooks, and some more had been thrown down a well and stoned to death ... so when we captured a small detachment of Russians ... they were locked in a room and three or four hand grenades were flung in through the window.'[52] This eye for an eye approach to committing murder wasn't even limited to Red Army soldiers, as a recorded conversation between two German POWs highlights:

'The women fought like wild beasts.'
'What did you do with the women?'
'Oh, we shot them too.'[53]

Atrocity bred atrocity in a vicious downward spiral, and the Luftwaffe was far from immune to it at all. A downed pilot, captured by the NKVD secret police and interrogated by its specialist 7th Department, reported that, 'A pilot ... said that he participated in the execution of a group of Jews in one of the villages near Berdichev at the beginning of the war. They were executed as a punishment for handing over a German pilot to the Red Army.'

Officially at least, there was a total prohibition on members of the Luftwaffe committing such acts. Every member of the service had a pay book – a 'Soldbuch' – that doubled as their personal military ID, and on the inside cover were the '10 Commandments Governing the Conduct in War of the German Soldier'. Several dealt directly with the subject of war crimes:

Number 1 - The German soldier fights fairly to win victory for his people. Acts of cruelty and unnecessary destruction are unworthy of him.
Number 3 – Prisoners of war may not be mistreated or abused.
Number 7 – The civil population is inviolable. A soldier is not permitted to plunder or deliberately to destroy.

It was not inevitable that the men of the eastern Luftwaffe would commit atrocities; even soldiers of the Waffen-SS – often leading players in some horrendous war crimes – could decide not to pull the trigger. 'We took a man prisoner and the question arose as to whether we should shoot him. He was 45 years old. He crossed himself and murmured "ra ra", imitating murmured prayer as though he knew.

I couldn't shoot. I imagined him as a husband with a family and children probably. I said, "I won't do it." I went off, I could no longer look at him.'[54]

This was all a far cry from the invasion of Crete back in May when, as the British Royal Navy evacuated their Army comrades, the attacking Stukas studiously avoided bombing hospital ships, and men retreating towards the beaches under Red Cross flags were also left unharmed, with one Bf 109 even circling a British column to ensure its safety. The difference was that this was the east.

In the air, the war was different too. During earlier campaigns if the Luftwaffe hadn't completely destroyed their enemy on the ground, those that were left had put up sometimes ferocious resistance, and then had flown away to survive and fight another day. This was not the case with the VVS, and specifically its strategic bomber arm, the DBA. The DBA was an extremely important part of the VVS given the air force's doctrine, inspired by the Italian aerial warfare theorist Giulio Douhet, which emphasised destructive, mass bombing attacks on an enemy's heartland. In the dogma of the time, 'The bomber would always get through.' As was the case in the Soviet fighter regiments, the bomber units were in the process of being re-equipped with newer planes, but were still mainly equipped with old, outdated models, mainly SBs and DBs, when war broke out. These aircraft had nowhere near enough defensive armament or speed to survive long against the Jagdwaffe's Bf 109s. Just how defenceless they were was amply demonstrated at the German bridgehead over the Berezina near Bobruysk. The Soviets were desperate to crush it and restore their defensive line along the river, and sent in 125 bombers in waves to pulverise it. The 109s shot down 115 of them. Despite this aerial mayhem, the German fighter commander described the Soviet bomber pilots as 'grand flyers'.

At another bridgehead, this time near Ostrov on 6 July, it was the turn of Luftflotte 1's Hannes Trautloft and his JG 54 Grünherz to shoot down sixty-five out of seventy-three attacking bombers. Meanwhile his comrade, Günther Lützow, down in the south with his JG 3, found himself caught on the ground by a VVS bomber attack. Lützow and his men managed to get airborne and shoot down all the twenty-seven attacking bombers. Not that it all went the Germans' way; Captain Hermann-Friedrich Joppien, the commander of I/JG 51, who claimed five of the bombers shot down over Bobruysk, was himself killed in a flying accident over the battlefield on 25 August. A seventy-score Experte and Knight's Cross winner, his death was greeted with mixed feelings in the Jagdwaffe, as he had been castigated by no less a person than Werner 'Vati' ('Daddy') Mölders back in 1940 for strafing an English passenger train during the Battle of Britain.[55] Nor was it just the Germans who faced the DBA. Up in the far north the Finnish Air Force – the Suomen Ilmavoimat – was also called into the air to stop Soviet bombing raids. In their outdated Italian-made Fiat G.50 fighters, the Finns successfully repelled an attempted air raid on Helsinki on 25 June, shooting down some thirteen SB bombers, and leaving only two to make it home.[56]

Leopold Höglinger, a radio operator with the German 137th Infantry Division, wrote in his diary: 'Our offensive began with a long barrage of artillery fire, and squadrons of our planes flew overhead. There was no resistance from the enemy. A few hours later, as out troops began moving forward, some Russian bombers did appear – but they were immediately shot down. Soon the first prisoners started coming in.'[57]

Such was the slaughter, the DBA was in danger of collapse, but still they came, mainly in singles or pairs now rather than large groups, but nevertheless the bombers flew. Above the Romanian naval port of Constanza, Günther Rall – a man who would go on to become a legend in the Jagdwaffe – personally shot down eighteen VVS bombers during Barbarossa's opening stages as the Soviet crews repeatedly tried to bomb the port and its installations. But the Soviets were defending their homeland and accepted their duty. 'Yes, that was a hard time, but our task was clear. We knew that our Motherland depended on us, and we could endure anything.'[58]

Endurance was the word, as the Soviets continued to take a bloody pounding from the Wehrmacht.

Alexander Andrievich, a Supply officer with the Soviet 6th Army:

The German bombing of our frontier forces was merciless. The weather was ideal for their planes – with long, clear sunny days – and they rained bombs down on our troops as if they were conducting a military exercise. I came across the remnants of one of our units close to a forest. There were hundreds upon hundreds of dead. The German attack had been so rapid that most had not even had time to get out of their vehicles.[59]

General Ivan Ivanovich Fedyuninsky (a veteran of the Civil War and the defeat of the Japanese at Khalkhin Gol back in late 1939) was fighting around Kovel. 'Railway junctions and lines of communication were destroyed by German planes. Sometimes on narrow roads, bottlenecks were formed by our troops, artillery, motor vehicles and so on and then the Nazi planes had the time of their life.'[60] The human cost of the German pressure was all too apparent. At a field hospital near Smolensk, the medical orderly Very Yukina described the horrific scenes: 'The enemy's planes were bombing our military formations at will ... more and more wounded began arriving at the hospital ... We tried to evacuate some of them to hospitals further from the front, but although the trains were marked with the Red Cross the Germans methodically bombed them.'[61]

Little wonder that by 29 June Adolf Hitler was staring at a map of the Soviet Union and boasting to his cronies, 'In a few weeks we'll be in Moscow. Then I'll raze it to the ground and build a reservoir there. The name Moscow must be expunged.'

But, despite the Führer's vainglorious boasts, even at this stage the warning signs for the Nazis were there to see for anyone who cared to look.

Within ten days of the invasion, Moscow had issued orders for the mobilisation of an additional 5 million men called to the colours – a million and a half more than the Wehrmacht had in total for Barbarossa. Pilot training was cut again in the VVS academies, with time spent on learning to take off, land and little else. Formation and night flying, and even gunnery, were junked and new pilots began reaching their decimated regiments with only 8–10 hours' flying time. These novices were given obsolete aircraft like I-153 biplanes, which instead of being scrapped were now back in frontline service. 'The hardest thing was to get the novice pilots to maintain their position in combat formation. As soon as the Messers appeared they would close up tighter and trouble the formation leader. Instead of concentrating on the target you had to watch out not to collide with one of the new pilots.'[62]

Kesselring's '*Kindermord*' continued as a result, but there was no escaping the fact that in the aerial abattoir above the two armies, the Luftwaffe was paying its share of blood money too. By 19 July, less than a month into the invasion, the Germans had lost 1,284 planes destroyed or damaged, over half their original attacking force, and on that day their operational roster in the East consisted of just 906 aircraft. The Soviet war correspondent Vasily Grossman described a scene at an airfield near Gomel in Belorussia during the fighting: 'Finally, after a successful attack on a German column, the fighters returned and landed. The commander's aircraft had human flesh stuck in the radiator because the supporting aircraft had hit an ammunition truck that blew up when the leader, Poppe, was flying over it. Poppe was picking the mess out with a file. A doctor pronounced it "Aryan meat!" and everyone laughed, a pitiless time, a time of iron.'[63]

The Soviets were buying time with blood. They were also preparing for exactly the sort of long war that Nazi Germany, and the Luftwaffe in particular, was not geared up for in any way.

CHAPTER 7

The Chinese Example and Lend-Lease; Stalin's Dirty Big Secret

Back in 1937, Moscow had signed an assistance pact with Chiang Kai-Shek and his Nationalist Chinese government in their struggle against Imperial Japan. They had then supplied the Chinese with nearly 300 military aircraft, ammunition and other military aid worth some $250 million. Through this link, Stalin had seen for himself how Chiang Kai-Shek had relocated arsenals and key industries, and the 25,000 skilled workers to man them, away to the west and out of the path of the invading Japanese Imperial Army. As one Chinese factory owner put it, 'During the constant air raids my employees and I seized every minute to take apart and ship things. We put the machine parts in a wooden boat and camouflaged them with wood and sticks. Then along the way we were subjected to enemy air raids, so we hid in the reeds along the side of the river until we could come out and carry on.'[64] This material support had helped the embattled Chinese to stay in the fight and frustrate the more technologically advanced Japanese.

What Stalin then did in the summer of 1941 was to take this concept and upgrade it on a hitherto unimaginable scale. As the panzers streamed eastwards, and Belorussia, the Ukraine and western Russia fell under the heel of the jackboot, Stalin gave orders to dismantle a huge proportion of the country's industrial might and ship it out of danger. On 29 June alone some eleven aircraft factories began to be moved east. In total some 75 per cent of the Soviet Union's aviation industry would end up going the same way.

By Christmas 1941, 2,593 industrial enterprises had been put on 1.5 million railway wagons and evacuated. Almost 1,000 of them went beyond the Urals to Siberia, over 250 went to the Volga region, and another 300 to the Central Asian republics.[65] From Kiev alone,

197 factories went east. All their machinery, tools, infrastructure and the 350,000 workers who manned them climbed on board 450 trains and headed to towns such as Kuzbass and Magnitogorsk in western Siberia for a new life.

It wasn't just men either. The entire population was mobilised en masse; particularly women and teenage boys. By 1944 40 per cent of Soviet aircraft workers were women and another 10 per cent were boys under the age of eighteen – by the same date in Germany only 23 per cent of aircraft workers were female.[66]

However, the use of this initially unskilled workforce had its drawbacks – Viktor M. Sinaisky, a VVS aircraft technician, was testing a newly delivered Lavochkin fighter: 'The engine smoked like a train and it was obvious something was wrong with the gas distribution or ignition. It turned out that the ignition lead was installed at the correct angle but in the wrong direction. But what could you expect? These engines were assembled by kids of 14–15 years of age.'[67]

The VVS itself estimated that poor production quality was reducing the maximum speed of its Il-2 Shturmoviks by 25–30 miles per hour, forcing the pilots to operate the engines continuously at maximum power during combat flights, and thus rapidly wearing down the engines.

Flawed in some ways, this 'new' workforce would also achieve feats of production and endurance that defy description. They would arrive in the east, usually at night, with hardly anything prepared for them. Provided with the minimum of food and shelter, they were expected to unload their own trains, build their own factories and begin production as soon as possible. It was a human effort on a vast scale but it needed time to take effect. No matter how hard they worked, it would take months to get the production lines up and running at full speed and in the meantime the soldiers and airmen at the front still needed guns, tanks and planes – the question was from where would they come?

The answer was simple – the West, and more specifically, the United States of America. In the words of one observer at the time, the USA would provide the Soviet Union with everything 'from sheet steel to shoe leather; clothing, blankets, tents, radio sets, enormous quantities of tinned food (even fruit juice!), first-aid packs, and most important of all enough trucks to put the Red Army on wheels for the first time in its history'.[68]

The US was an industrial behemoth even before the war, boasting 28.7 per cent of total global output in 1938 (Germany had just 13.2 per cent),[69] but the war would supercharge the country, transforming it into a truly global power as Gross National Product more than doubled in just six short years.

The Soviet war machine would be transformed by its Western support – and the difference in the air war would be material. For example, all Soviet multi-engine bombers were already equipped with both transmitters and receivers, the Soviet-made RBS-bis being the standard model, but not fighters. American Lend-Lease changed all that, and the pilots themselves were grateful:

> The main thing about the Cobra was that it had an excellent radio ... When we received LaGG-3s not all of them had radios, so wingmen would get receivers, while leaders would get both receivers and transmitters. What did this mean in battle? Say I was a wingman and spotted the enemy, then how could I tell my comrades? But then when we flew I-16s there was no radio at all![70]

The Americans were already supporting the British war effort through the Lend-Lease Act of March 1941; the ex-Secretary of Commerce, Harry L. Hopkins, was President Roosevelt's point man to London. Hopkins, dubbed a 'godsend' by the British Prime Minister Winston S. Churchill, now lost no time in offering to extend America's support to the Soviets and flew to the Arctic port of Archangel to agree the extension of Lend-Lease to Moscow. This was a very delicate subject for the Soviet dictator, and indeed his Party and entire governmental system. To accept the offer of help from the Capitalist West would be to admit that Communism and the efforts of the Soviet peoples by themselves weren't enough to defeat the fascist invaders. It was a bitter pill for Moscow to swallow, and one the Kremlin was determined to keep as secret as possible from the mass of its people. So, aid would be accepted, but its impact would be downplayed and definitely not trumpeted. This reticence as to its source didn't stop Moscow from putting their hand out though – indeed, from putting out both hands and a bucket to boot! Their initial demands to Hopkins were jaw-dropping and included 3,000 fighters, 3,000 bombers, 20,000 anti-aircraft guns, 3 million pairs of boots (the US would actually send them 15 million pairs by the war's end), 10 million metres of woollen cloth, several thousand tons of bombs, flamethrowers, machine tools, wheat, meat, sugar and even submarine detection equipment. When the British were told of the Soviet demands they were visibly shaken. Eden, Churchill's Foreign Secretary, said: 'The Russians were avid in their demands: tanks, aircraft, raw materials, aluminium, they wanted it all, and I don't blame them for wanting, they were carrying the main burden of the battle in those days, but to get it all to them was a problem and our shortages were very real.' Eden saw it as the perennial problem between a land and a sea power, or as he put it, 'They didn't understand the problem of the elephant and the whale.'[71] Nevertheless Hopkins, an economic wizard and logistical genius, managed to arrange a conference for the three new allies in Moscow, where it was agreed that Britain and the USA would supply the Soviet Union with 400 aircraft, 500 tanks, 300 anti-tank guns, plus amounts of aluminium, tin, lead, cobalt, copper, zinc, phosphorous and toluene (1,250 tons of this precious additive to produce high-grade aviation fuel) – every month! London also offered Hurricane fighters (the Soviets wanted Spitfires but the British didn't have enough themselves, let alone any for export) and 200 US-built P-40C Tomahawks that were being retired from the RAF's Desert Air Force (247 were eventually handed over, 230 in 1941 and a further seventeen in 1942). Stalin was, initially at least, extremely unhappy with the offer made. President Roosevelt's Special Envoy to Europe, W. Averell Harriman: 'At first Stalin was very rough with us, he said, "The paucity of your offer proves that you want us to be defeated in the war." But after he'd finally gotten everything he could out of us he said, "This is very generous", and he ... gave us this big banquet.'[72]

This was just a first instalment though. By the end of the war the US would have channelled $50.7 billion dollars through Lend-Lease. Britain was far and away the largest beneficiary, receiving $31.4 billion worth of aid, with Moscow a distant second on $11.3 billion (Chiang Kai-Shek's Chinese Nationalists received just over 1 per cent of the aid sent abroad). That latter support to Moscow came in the form of 13,303 combat vehicles (including 7,500 tanks) 35,170 motorbikes, 14,795 aircraft, and an incredible 427,284 trucks, with 2.7 million tons of petroleum products to fuel them all, and 3.7 million tyres to keep them on the road (plus the Ford Motor Company's entire River Rouge tyre plant, which was dismantled in situ and shipped in totality to the Soviets). Knowing how dependent the Soviets were on their rail network as well, the Americans sent them 1,966 diesel and steam locomotives and over 11,000 rail cars. The US also became Moscow's supermarket, shipping 4,478,116 tons of canned meats, sugars, flour, salt, etc – it all equated to half a pound of concentrated battlefield rations for every member of the Soviet armed forces for every single day of the war.[73] Perhaps the most amazing aspect of this largesse was that it was still only a small fraction of what the States actually produced during the war in total, an astonishing arsenal which included 17,000,000 rifles, 2,434,000 motor vehicles, 315,000 artillery and anti-aircraft guns, 296,000 aircraft and 87,000 tanks. This from a nation that Goering contemptuously said 'could only produce cars and refrigerators'.

Nevertheless, Stalin never stopped wanting more. Even as the German Sixth Army was bleeding to death in Stalingrad, he sent a telegram to Winston Churchill pleading for more materiel. 'I have to inform you that the situation in the Stalingrad area has deteriorated ... The Germans have been able to concentrate great reserves of aviation in this area ... We do not have enough fighters for the protection of our forces in the air. Even the bravest troops are helpless if they lack air protection. We particularly require Spitfires and Aircobras.'

Churchill was flabbergasted at Stalin's gall, but couldn't help but admire his bravura.

The American President, and ultimate backer of Lend-Lease, Franklin D. Roosevelt, was extremely eager to justify this vast expense to his electorate. Repeatedly pressed in Congress and by the media, he said the Lend-Lease plan was akin to lending a neighbour a hose if his house caught fire. 'What do I do in such a crisis?' the President asked at a press conference. 'I don't say ... "Neighbour, my garden hose cost me $15; you have to pay me $15 for it" ... I don't want $15 — I want my garden hose back after the fire is over." One of FDR's opponents, the Republican Senator from Ohio Robert Taft, drily commented in response: 'Lending war equipment is a good deal like lending chewing gum. You don't want it back.'

FDR won through, though, and the American public broadly supported Lend-Lease, which was just as well as it was desperately needed by its recipients – no matter Moscow's official reticence as to its importance, particularly during that first winter. Just how desperately needed was demonstrated by the Soviet aviation industry. As the VVS was blown out of the sky during the summer and autumn, Soviet aircraft manufacturing plummeted from 2,329 planes in September to a measly 627 in November as the relocation programme disrupted production. This was exactly when shipments from the West were most needed, and soon they would be joined by the results of the monumental industrial effort of the Soviet peoples themselves. Aircraft Production Plant No. 295 in Voronezh was typical of the programme. It made Il-2 Shturmoviks, and in November of 1941 it was dismantled and moved en bloc to Kuybyshev in Siberia – a distance of over 3,000 km. One month later the very first Il-2 rolled off the new production line there from parts made earlier in Voronezh. By the end of January the following year the new plant, now renamed No. 18, was producing seven Shturmoviks per day.

Back on the ground at Smolensk, even as Very and her fellow medical staff desperately tried to deal with a torrent of wounded and maimed men, the panzer spearheads had raced deep into the Soviet rear and managed to encircle vast numbers of Red Army troops, but the German infantry – the *Landsers* (the nickname for the long-suffering infantryman in the Heer, the German equivalent of Soviet Ivans, British Tommies and American GIs) – who were needed to complete the victory and close the trap were dozens of miles behind, restricted as ever to how fast they could march on foot. Determined not to be thwarted and allow the trapped Soviets to escape, von Bock called in the Luftwaffe, demanding Kesselring do what his own soldiers could not and seal the pocket from the air. This was an impossible task, and despite valiant efforts and hundreds of sorties, the Luftwaffe crews had no chance. Realising their opportunity, over 100,000 Soviet troops fled east and managed to avoid death or capture.

They also fought back.

The Red Army, unconsciously at first, adopted the tactic of having every man pour as much fire as he could from every weapon at his disposal at any Luftwaffe aircraft sighted overhead. The use of ammunition was prodigious, but psychologically it made every soldier feel he was hitting back and wasn't defenceless, and it also worked. The majority of aerial engagements in the east were under 1,000 metres altitude, giving ground fire a very real chance of damaging an aircraft, or even bringing it down, as this story from the Red Army's official newspaper, the *Krasnaya Zvezda* (*Red Star*), reported on its front page:

A fascist aircraft appeared over the rifle detachment commanded by Lieutenant Pich. The soldiers immediately opened an intense rifle and machine-gun fire ... hit the target and the plane descended steeply. The soldiers saw the plane crash ... and forced the fascist airmen to surrender. The captured fascists proved to be inveterate wolves. The commander of the crew carried three Iron Crosses. *Oberfeldwebel* Lilienthal and *Unteroffizier* Stopf admitted that they had flown over most European countries, dropping bombs over peaceful cities.[74]

CHAPTER 8

Target Moscow; Operation Typhoon

With victory seemingly within his grasp, the Nazi dictator now decided the time was ripe to launch bombing attacks on the Soviet Union's two greatest cities, Moscow and Leningrad, and he issued Führer Order No. 33, telling Goering that he wanted 'no inhabitants left that we will have to feed during the winter'.

Was this change of tactic a mistake? The previous year, in the campaign against Great Britain, the turning point of the battle according to most observers came with Hitler's order to switch the Luftwaffe from hitting the RAF's crucial airfields and hunting down its fighters to instead launch massed raids on London. Dreadful though this was for Londoners, it allowed Hugh Dowding's Fighter Command to recover and begin to take a very heavy toll of the German bomber arm. Was the order to start bombing Moscow and Leningrad the same fundamental error of strategy? In principle, it would seem not. Moscow was the political and administrative centre of the entire Stalinist regime. It was a major transport hub, both east–west and north–south, and home to major industries vital for the war effort. It was also a considerably smaller city than London, so potentially a lot easier to destroy. As for Leningrad, it was much the same; an industrial centre, it dominated the north of the Soviet Union.

The problem was not the intent. The problem was the execution. The Luftwaffe was just not up to the task. The mainstay of the German bomber fleet was still the Heinkel He 111 and Junkers Ju 88 – both twin-engine medium bombers that in 1939 and 1940 were among the best aircraft of their type in service anywhere in the world, but with limited range and payload capacities of 2,000 kg for the Heinkel and even less for the Junkers, they were not strategic bombers in any sense. Nevertheless, the order went out, and on the evening of 21 July some 200 bombers – well over a third of all the eastern Luftwaffe's operational fleet – appeared in the warm night skies over the Soviet capital, and rained destruction down on the city and its people.

Ivan Sokolov, a member of the city's well-organised air defence service, witnessed the raid: 'It was a sea of fire, there were flash bombs, incendiaries and bombs which emitted a terrible sound as they hurtled through the air. They were designed to create a sense of terror.'[75]

But even that effect was limited, as the physicist Andrei Sakharov's aunt proudly said to him in an air raid shelter: 'For the first time in years I feel like a Russian again!' The physical impact was limited too. To flatten the city the raids needed to be repeated night after night, but the Luftwaffe only managed to send 115 bombers the next night, and just 100 on the third, as serviceability rates dropped and aircraft were redeployed to attack Leningrad. The grand bombing offensive against Moscow petered out within days, and thereafter the numbers of planes involved fell dramatically to fifty, thirty and finally a bare handful of aircraft. Within a fortnight the attacks were no more than nuisance raids, and were no match for Major General Mikhail Gromadin's air defence system – the *Moskovskaya Zona PVO* – with its almost 600 fighters, belts of searchlights and some 1,044 anti-aircraft guns of all types. As the anonymous German aviation insider 'Hauptmann Hermann' (a *nom de guerre* the unknown author adopted as he wrote his work in exile) wrote, 'as Leningrad began to be attacked Moscow was let off and the bombing had all but stopped. Evidently the Luftwaffe was no longer capable of fighting on a large scale in more than one place at a time'.[76]

As for Leningrad, it did indeed begin to feel the explosive power of the Luftwaffe bombers. Some of the first raids targeted the city's main food storage warehouses at Badayev in the south-west of the city. The Tsarist-era wooden buildings, all built within a few metres of each other, were full of meat, lard, butter and sugar, and were sitting ducks. The Junkers in the first wave dropped forty-eight high-explosive bombs ranging from 500 to 1,000 pounds each. The whole area, covering several acres, went up in flames. The smell was overpowering: a mixture of burning sugar and meat carbonising in the heat. In one night virtually the entire city's food reserves were turned into ashes. In that first attack, 3,000 tons of flour was lost, as was nearly 2,500 tons of sugar, which poured into the Neva River in a molten flood that polluted the very water itself. Vasily Churkin, one of the city's defenders, wrote in his diary: 'Columns of thick smoke are rising high. It's the Badayev food depots burning. Fire is devouring the six-months' food supplies for the whole population of Leningrad.'[77] Another Leningrader, Elena Skrjabina, wrote in her diary: 'The destruction of the Badayev warehouses can already be felt. The daily ration has been lowered to 250 grams [the daily ration for non-working dependants]. Since there is almost nothing else besides this bread, the decrease is felt most strongly.'[78] That quantity of bread is about six slices of a medium-sized loaf, and provides around 500 calories. Recommended daily intake for a man is 2,500 calories, 2,000 for a woman and over 1,000 for a child – hunger and starvation had come to Leningrad.

Horrifyingly, the Luftwaffe also found the time and resources to pick up where they had left off in earlier campaigns and specifically target civilians, and not just any civilians in Leningrad's case but child evacuees. Thousands of mothers and their children had been hurriedly sent out of the city in the late summer, only to find themselves sent accidentally into the path of the Wehrmacht spearheads. They were piled onto a train to be sent back to the city for safety when the Luftwaffe bombers found them at the station at Lychkovo. One of the young boys being sent back, Ivan Fedulov, grimly recalled the attack: 'Someone was shouting, "Bombers, Bombers!" A plane flew right over us and along the length of the train, dropping bomb after bomb, with terrifying, methodical precision. There was a huge explosion, and when the smoke cleared carriages were scattered everywhere, as if they had been knocked off the track by a giant hand.' Fedulov gathered some surviving children and led them into nearby potato fields to try and escape. Above and behind him he heard the drone of aircraft engines. 'A plane circled and came back, then it began machine-gunning the fleeing children. It was flying so low that I could clearly see the pilot's face – totally impassive.'[79]

Mistakes occur in war, and Luftwaffe veterans loudly proclaim their innocence of attacks such as Lychkovo, but the weight of evidence – even their own words when secretly recorded as POWs – strongly suggests that some of them at least not only knew exactly what they were doing, but felt it was part and parcel of their duty. They were indifferent to it at best, and some even took a perverse enjoyment from it.

However, as with Moscow, the Germans were finding it increasingly difficult to maintain their bombing assault on Leningrad and its environs in the face of continual demands for close support from their needy Heer comrades, and soon most of the bomber Staffeln were back operating at the front. Increasingly the Luftwaffe wouldn't play a strategic role in the East; 'instead it was used on the battlefield itself, at least most of the time, as a purely auxiliary weapon, in a way as an ersatz for artillery'.[80]

The British agreed with this view. Their Air Ministry's study *The Rise and Fall of the German Air Force*, written after the Battle of Britain, discussed whether the Luftwaffe was used tactically or strategically against them in 1940, and it rather shrewdly suggested, 'The Germans were not clear themselves, and became confused in the extreme.'

As the Wehrmacht continued to drive eastwards, the Luftwaffe now totally dominated the skies above, and the victories multiplied.

On 9 July the Minsk-Bialystok Pocket was wiped out, and with it went 3,332 Soviet tanks destroyed or captured. The stubborn defence of Smolensk finally collapsed on 5 August; the bag this time contained 3,205 tanks. Next came the Uman Pocket just four days later – 317 tanks, and then the great Kiev Pocket on 26 September with a further 884 tanks. Remember, the Germans had invaded with fewer than 3,500 panzers, and here was their enemy losing almost 8,000 in just three months, and yet they were still standing. Fliegerkorps V's chief of staff, Hermann Plocher, wrote in his diary, 'The equipment of the Red Army amazes us again and again.' He wasn't the only one to be dumbfounded by the Soviets' seemingly limitless reserves of both men and equipment. The Chief of the OKH General Staff, Franz Halder, wrote half in admiration and half in dread: 'The Russian colossus ... has been underestimated by us ... whenever a dozen divisions are destroyed the Russians just replace them with another dozen ... At the outset of the war we reckoned on about 200 enemy divisions. Now we have already counted 360.'[81]

The Soviets were also capable of giving their invaders a bloody nose at times.

Colonel Viktor I. Davidkov [of the 131st Fighter Regiment, later the 32nd Guards Fighter Regiment] asked, "What's going on?" A scout pilot, Sigov, said, "The Romanians are marching with a brass band and banners flying. They're in columns like in peacetime, have they lost their minds?" "I don't know, but we will come down on them! Load RS missiles!" [Probably RS-82s weighing about 7 kg with less than half a kilo of high explosive, an incredibly inaccurate weapon brought into service in 1940.] Twenty fighters were armed – a total of 160 missiles – and Davidkov led them. They flew in low, fired their missiles and then continued the slaughter with machine-guns. Our fighters hunted the Romanian cavalry for two days, on the third day we relocated on U-2s and had to fly over the massacre, but couldn't fly lower than 300 m due to the stench of rotting bodies. Lieutenant General Korneets visited us later and said, "You have destroyed the 5th Romanian Cavalry Corps, the enemy breakthrough has been eliminated."[82] [There was no Romanian 5th Cavalry Corps at the time; the unit involved was probably the 5th Cavalry Brigade, which together with its sister formation the 8th comprised the Romanian Third Army's Cavalry Corps.]

Victories like this against von Runstedt's Army Group South were few and far between for the VVS. Despite his chronic alcoholism and contempt for Hitler – 'the Bohemian corporal' as he supposedly called him in private – the old Prussian field marshal was pushing his men forward and driving deep into the Ukraine. Reaching the great Dnieper River, Europe's fourth largest, he sent the Hanoverian 22nd Infantry Division charging across it at Berislav. The division's engineers threw a pontoon bridge over the 750-yard-wide flowing waters only to see their efforts blown to pieces by a VVS bomber strike, which killed and wounded sixteen of their number. Undeterred, the men from Oldenburg repaired the bridge, only to see it hit again. The call went out for air support, and no less an Experte than Werner Mölders himself appeared with a Bf 109 Staffel to provide round-the-clock cover. In two days the German fighters shot down seventy-seven Soviet bombers, and the guns of the Luftwaffe's 1st Battalion 14th Anti-Aircraft Regiment and 1st Battalion 64th Anti-Aircraft Regiment brought down another thirteen. The bridgehead survived and the Germans streamed across and headed towards the Crimea.

Runstedt also successfully lobbied Hitler to have most of von Bock's panzers assigned to him, and swung them south to achieve the Cannae-like victories at Uman and Kiev. Löhr's Luftflotte 4 played a leading role in these huge battles. At Kiev, von Greim's Fliegerkorps V alone flew 1,422 sorties, dropped 567 tons of bombs, destroyed sixty-five Soviet aircraft in the air and forty-two on the ground, as well as fifty-two trains, twenty-eight locomotives, twenty-three tanks, 2,171 motor vehicles, one bridge and eighteen railway lines, all for the loss of just seventeen aircraft and nine men killed. Their VVS opposite numbers knew they were being bested and resented it massively. 'As for the Germans ... they were awesome. For example, we'd be defending some town and a message would come, "Russian soldiers, we will capture this town at such-and-such a time. Do not waste your energy, surrender! You will not be able to do anything anyway." Then, as promised, they'd capture the town at the appointed time – bastards! It was a bitter blow to our morale.'[83]

To the north, it was a different theme but the same story. Von Leeb's Army Group North was blessed with neither large panzer forces nor a mass of aircraft. That isn't to say that Keller's Luftflotte 1 didn't play its part. Firstly it helped smash up a major Soviet counter-attack spearheaded by 200 tanks near Siauliai in Lithuania and then it protected the German bridgehead over the Velikaya River at Ostrov in early July, knocking down sixty-five VVS bombers in a further haemorrhaging of the already depleted DBA strategic bomber arm. Indeed, towards the end of August, Keller reported that his men had destroyed some 2,541 Soviet aircraft with another 433 'probables' since the launch of the invasion. No mean feat, and one that helped pave the way for Army Group North to reach Leningrad, its final objective for Barbarossa, at the beginning of September.

Hitler decreed the city would not be stormed but would be starved out instead. To surround it, the Germans needed to capture the town of Schlisselburg, about twenty miles east of Leningrad at the head of the Neva River on Lake Ladoga. That mission was entrusted to Paul Laux's 126th Infantry Division, and specifically Colonel Harry Hoppe's 425th Infantry Regiment. The 425th was a proud regiment, its Westphalian recruits devoted to their much decorated commander. Born Arthur Hoppe, the young Braunschweiger changed his first name by deed poll to Harry when a young man, but was forever nicknamed 'Stan Laurel' by all who knew him due to his uncanny resemblance to the famous English comedian and actor. When Laux gave Hoppe his objective, he also confirmed he would be supported by elements of both Fliegerkorps I and VIII. Armed with this knowledge, Hoppe and his men reached the outskirts of the town in the early hours of 8 September. Hoppe pushed out reconnaissance patrols, and Sergeant Becker of the 3rd Battalion reported back that he had found few defenders in the town – it could be taken by storm if the regiment acted swiftly. The problem was that Hoppe had anticipated Schlisselburg would be heavily fortified and had agreed an air strike to hit at 0900 hrs that morning. Communications with division were down and Hoppe had no way of letting the Luftwaffe know of any change of plan, but nevertheless he took the risk and led his men into the attack at 0700 hrs. The Westphalians raced up the near-deserted streets and by 0740 hrs it was more or less over. A Sergeant Wendt grabbed a big swastika flag used by the troops for air recognition, and climbed the main church steeple, hanging it out the belfry to try and warn the incoming flyers off. Below, Hoppe's signaller desperately kept on transmitting, 'This is Group Harry, Schlisselburg already stormed, the Stukas must be stopped, have you got that?' The reply was only static, but the message had got through and the Stukas had turned back to base – all except for a single Staffel who at 0845 hrs appeared overhead. The dive-bomber crews ignored the frantically waving infantrymen, the swastika panel, and the white Very signal lights and banked into the attack, ready to rain death on their fellow countrymen – only for the leader to pull up at the last moment and drop his bombs into the Neva as the abort message finally got through.[84]

With Schlisselburg taken, Leningrad was cut off from the rest of the country and the city was forced to settle into what would become the longest siege of the entire war. Moscow ordered that its 2 million inhabitants and 200,000 defending troops would be supplied by air. This would be an airlift whose ambition would dwarf the far more famous Stalingrad attempt a year later, but would end with the same result – total failure. At Stalingrad the Luftwaffe's deficiency in air transport capacity and expertise would be laid bare, and Leningrad was the same for the VVS. With a shorter distance to cover and the benefit of large and permanent air bases to both take off from and land on, the Soviet air bridge was never anything more than a gangplank, and a creaky one at that. In the fortnight between 14 and 28 November, as winter closed in and the demand for food and fuel, let alone ammunition, climbed rapidly, the VVS managed to fly in just 1,200 tons of supplies at an average of a pretty paltry 86 tons a day. For some sort of comparison with an airlift that actually worked, in the winter of 1948/49 when Stalin imposed a blockade on West Berlin in a vain effort to get the West to surrender it to Communism, the 2.5 million inhabitants were initially airlifted 4,500 tons of provisions a day, with this figure steadily climbing to a staggering 10,000 tons a day at its height. West Berlin didn't fall, needless to say.

Belatedly, the Nazi high command realised that capturing Moscow offered them their last best chance to win the war in the East in 1941. Their summer blitzkrieg campaign, designed to destroy the Soviet Union in a matter of weeks, had failed despite an endless stream of victories, the like of which the world had never seen. Now, as summer turned to autumn and October dawned, Berlin believed they had enough time for one huge thrust from Army Group Centre that would reach the capital and doom the Soviets to defeat. As von Richthofen noted in his diary, 'In order to achieve success before the onset of winter we must move forward with our maximum strength. We only have a short time to pursue this attack.'

Von Bock was reinforced with the bulk of all the panzers and artillery pieces still in working order along the front, which enabled him to mass a formidable force composed of the Second, Fourth and Ninth Armies, plus the 2nd, 3rd and 4th Panzergruppen of Guderian, Hoth (Hans-Georg Reinhardt took over command from 5 October) and Hoepner respectively. He now had over a million men, over

1,500 panzers and 14,000 guns – the only panzer force of any size not committed to Typhoon was von Kleist's Panzergruppe 1, which was down south leading von Runstedt's advance towards Rostov. On paper it all looked pretty impressive, but on the ground the reality was less so. The men had been marching and fighting non-stop for over three months and were tired and footsore. Panzer serviceability was low, as tracks, gun barrels and engines wore out and supplies weren't getting through in the quantities needed – ammunition and fuel were a particular problem. Kesselring's Luftflotte 2 typified the situation. His Staffeln could only muster about a third of the aircraft they had at the beginning of Barbarossa, and even after the bloodletting they had inflicted on the VVS during the summer, they would go into Typhoon still outnumbered by two to one in the air. The men were constantly moving airfields as they advanced east; most of the strips they flew from were just grass fields with no infrastructure to speak of. The flight and ground crews slept in tents next to hurriedly dug slit trenches to protect them from the nightly raids by U-2 '*Nähmaschinen*', 'sewing machines', that wore down the men's nerves and deprived them of the sleep they desperately needed:

> We were witness to another form of Soviet aerial warfare; night harassment … One night as we were just about to retire to our quarters we heard the sound of a ratchety aircraft engine from somewhere overhead. This was the distinctive noise made by a Russian U-2. These antiquated biplanes – nicknamed 'sewing machines' for obvious reasons – were armed with small 2kg bombs and used by the Soviets to attack our lines and rear areas during the hours of darkness. Although indiscriminate and causing little material damage, these nuisance raids were part of the Soviets nocturnal war of nerves.[85]

Lieutenant Georgiy Pavlov flew such night missions in old UT-1b trainers. 'This aircraft was armed only with two ShKAS machine-guns and four RS-82 rocket projectiles. Our task was simply to deprive the Germans of their sleep. We flew at night and made our attacks randomly, such as against the headlights of a car, or against a searchlight on the ground.'[86]

The tactic was remarkably effective, as one German infantry soldier grudgingly admitted: 'We lie exhausted in our holes waiting for them.' One official report detailed how it impacted the men. 'The Russians' unchallenged air superiority at night has reached an unbearable level, the troops get no rest and their strength will soon be dissipated.'

Morale was still high, though, and when the orders came to advance, the panzers again headed east under a sky seemingly swept clear of Soviet aircraft. The Saxons of Walther Nehring's 18th Panzer Division even rigged up loudspeakers to play Tchaikovsky as they drove. 'In the weeks before our attack we constantly saw Russian bombers and fighters, but now they seem to have blown away. Either the enemy is frightened or he hasn't got any planes left, and the last few are being held for the fellows in the Kremlin's towers.'[87]

Once again the Soviets were caught out, and the bitterness of the troops shone through: 'History has never witnessed anything like this defeat ... We haven't seen a single one of our aircraft in the last few days. We are giving up cities with practically no resistance.'[88]

Orel was one such city. Guderian's panzers entered it on the morning of 3 October, their leading vehicles passing trams trundling along the streets, full of locals on their morning commute into work. The passers-by all waved and cheered the panzers, believing them to be their own army arriving to defend the city. Panic and confusion soon erupted, and within hours the city had fallen. In fact Moscow was so oblivious to what was happening, and the collapse at the front was so swift, that it was only when Hitler himself made a national radio broadcast two days later speaking of a 'final decisive offensive' that the Kremlin realised something major was afoot. In response, reconnaissance aircraft were scrambled to try and find out what was going on. One of the crews was detailed to fly over the Smolensk–Moscow highway – the main metalled road that would almost certainly be the primary axis of any German advance. As they climbed over Moscow and headed west, the observer peered through the broken cloud, searching for any signs of activity. The miles flew by with nothing out of the ordinary; it was all so normal. There was the usual Soviet military traffic and farmers with their horse-drawn wagons going from *kolkhoz* to *kolkhoz* (a *kolkhoz* was a Communist collective farm), and then something ... motorbike outriders, armoured cars, panzers! Swastika air recognition panels covered the vehicles' engine cowlings, and then came the first bursts of anti-aircraft fire. The VVS crew flew on, bravely trying to glean as much information as possible. Was this an isolated unit, a raid perhaps? Within minutes the answer was clear – the German column was twenty-five kilometres long; this was no raid, this was a major offensive. Dodging the flak, the Soviets turned and headed home as fast as they could. On landing they immediately reported the sighting to their headquarters. The Kafkaesque reply came back – the NKVD were on their way to arrest them as 'panic mongers'.

Such wishful thinking couldn't stop the panzers as the three Soviet Fronts holding the line against Typhoon were ripped apart. 'We were racing ahead … we saw a column of Russian tanks and artillery rumbling along in the opposite direction, heading towards the front … our commander summoned an air strike against the enemy … plane after plane swooped down on the forest, bombing the helpless Russians – and their tank brigade simply disintegrated before our eyes.'[89]

In Belev, on the road to Tula, the soon-to-be-famous Soviet war correspondent Vasily Grossman wrote, 'Lots of mad rumours are circulating, ridiculous and utterly panic-stricken. Suddenly, there is a mad storm of firing. It turns out that someone has switched on the street lights, and soldiers and officers opened rifle and pistol fire at the lamps to put them out. If only they had fired like this at the Germans.'

Within days von Bock's blitzkrieg had enveloped the defenders and shoved them aside into two gigantic pockets; the one based on the city of Bryansk contained three Soviet Armies, while the other around Vyazma had four. As usual the Luftwaffe pounded the trapped Soviets from the air, as they in turn desperately tried to escape east. Bruno Loerzer's Fliegerkorps II alone destroyed 579 Soviet vehicles and one train, smashing eight cavalry and twenty-three infantry attacks, and somehow took 3,842 POWs to boot! The carnage on the ground was horrific. Von Richthofen himself flew over the collapsing Vyazma pocket. 'There are horrific scenes of destruction in the places where Red Army soldiers have made unsuccessful attempts to break out. The Russians have suffered a total bloodbath. Piles of bodies, heaps of abandoned equipment and guns are strewn everywhere.' Von Richthofen was euphoric: 'The Russians can now be finished off militarily, if everybody makes an all-out effort.'

It seemed von Richthofen was right. The Soviets had started Typhoon with 1.25 million men in the line, equipped with 1,500 tanks and 7,600 guns; the Bryansk – Vyazma Pockets cost them 663,000 of those men, 1,242 tanks and 5,412 guns. Surely it was only a matter of time before Moscow fell.

Boris Baromykin of the Siberian 32nd Rifle Brigade remembered:

The Germans kept trying to finish us off … their artillery was constantly shelling us, and their planes hovered overhead, bombing and machine-gunning our retreating columns … The retreat was a living nightmare. Human guts hung from the trees where soldiers' bodies had been blasted by the sheer force of the explosions. The

ground around us was soaked red with blood ... To slow the German
advance we set light to everything so that the enemy would not have
it. We were determined not to let them through.[90]

This scorched earth policy was a particular nightmare for the Luftwaffe
and its daily requirement for around 14,000 tons of fresh supplies. In
previous campaigns it had relied on capturing enemy airstrips together
with their facilities and supply dumps, and then using them to make
up for the deficiencies of their own logistics. Now, as Boris and his
comrades retreated, leaving only ashes in their wake, the already
stretched Luftflotte 2 began to struggle, and then the first snows fell.
Within hours it had melted, but it turned the Russian earth into the
dreaded '*rasputitsa*' – the word is almost untranslatable but it can be
rendered as 'quagmire season' or 'the time without roads' – all too
true in a country where the vast majority of roads were made from
packed earth, with only a tiny 64,000 kilometres of metalled road.
As the Germans sank knee-deep into the mud, the Soviets rejoiced:
'I don't think anyone has seen such terrible mud, there's rain, snow,
hailstones, a liquid, bottomless swamp of black paste mixed by
thousands and thousands of boots, wheels and caterpillar tracks. And
everyone is happy once again. The Germans must get stuck in our
hellish autumn.'[91]

The famed and celebrated nineteenth-century German strategist von
Moltke the senior had written that 'an operation cannot be based on
the weather, but it can be based on the season', and the Germans were
about to understand the truism of that statement.

Only tracked vehicles could move in the glutinous mess, forcing
panzers to pull five or six trucks behind them as a sort of 'supply
train' that both guzzled fuel and wore out transmissions. Goering had
once said that the key to winning the war in the Soviet Union was just
'a problem of the necessary supply organisation'. But as Von Richthofen
wrote in his diary, 'Supply is for us the greatest difficulty in this war,'
and indeed it got even worse. Luftflotte 2's improvised grass airstrips
turned into mud flats, totally unusable by aircraft, and the 1,000
sorties a day being flown by the Germans at the dawn of Typhoon fell
dramatically to less than 300 from the 9th onwards, with serviceability
rates dropping to less than 60 per cent for fighters and an alarmingly
low 40 per cent for the bombers von Bock's troops needed so badly.

Still, the advance ground forward, but every mile gained felt like ten
to the tiring Germans. The hurriedly constructed Mozhaisk defensive
line was reached and breached after two weeks of desperate fighting
against its 90,000 Soviet defenders. The Germans now spent the last

two weeks of October regrouping their forces and preparing for one last final push to take Moscow. It was a gamble. Only one third of Army Group Centre's entire motor vehicle fleet was still functioning, and the frontline infantry divisions were all down to a third or a half of their establishment. With the Wehrmacht's logistics system unable to cope, fuel and ammunition were prioritised, and there was no room for any winter clothing or specialist anti-freeze oils and greases – even if they had been pre-ordered by the OKW, and they hadn't. Anthony Eden, the urbane and aristocratic British Foreign Secretary, was on a mission to Moscow for Churchill and after intensive lobbying was allowed to go near the front to see what was going on. Along with his escort he came across some captured German prisoners, 'mostly from the Sudetenland':

> the most pathetic thing I'd ever seen because it was ice-cold and none of them had a decent overcoat at all, hardly even a pullover of any sort, and they were dragging their shirt cuffs down over their hands to try and keep warm ... it made you realise how unprepared the so-called perfect Hitler machine had been for a winter war in Russia, and I remember saying to Winston when I got back, "They can't be all that good because I can't believe we would have sent divisions into Russia at this time of year without ... some form of overcoats."[92]

Well, that wasn't quite true for all the German forces. For once the Luftwaffe High Command had thought ahead and Hans-Georg von Seidel – the Luftwaffe's Quartermaster General – had, under direction from Milch, ordered adequate winter clothing (especially woollen underwear and fur boots) for all the several hundred thousand Eastern Front Luftwaffe personnel, prior to the launch of Barbarossa. Milch had served in the east during the First World War, as had many on the vaunted German General Staff, but this experience had seemingly not lodged strongly enough in their minds to remind them of the specific needs dictated by a Russian winter, and their men paid for it as one officer acknowledged. 'My company was mechanized; we had large lorries and these lorries stuck in the mud – they were frozen the next morning, they could not move at all. Within a period of 2–3 days we had to improvise mobility by requisitioning horses and wagons.'[93]

Lieutenant Heinrich Schmidt-Schmiedebach was an artilleryman. 'The mud froze to irregular hard waves and we had horses ... At first it was not so bad, perhaps 15 or 20 degrees below zero and our weapons were fine. But suddenly at a certain point the rifles didn't shoot anymore. This was the turning point in the winter war I think, and it was the worst point for our soldiers.'

As the weather worsened, Soviet resistance stiffened, and the advance slowed even further. 'The German attacks began with heavy artillery and mortar fire, supported by air attacks. Bombers circled overhead, diving in turn and dropping bombs on our infantry and artillery positions.' But the Soviets fought back and didn't give ground. 'I began to believe that the Germans might not reach Moscow.'[94]

It wasn't just the Red Army that was fighting back; so was the VVS. Private Graf Castell of Gustav Fehn's Silesian 5th Panzer Division wrote, 'Enemy fighters and bombers are increasingly active, and they have found where our tanks and armoured support vehicles are located, making low altitude flights over our lines with guns blazing, regardless of the risks to their own planes.'[95]

Events back in the Reich didn't help Typhoon either, as two of the Luftwaffe's greatest heroes died in quick succession in mid-November, causing minds to wander when they should have been focused on Moscow.

CHAPTER 9

Udlinger and Vati

Ernst Udet had been on a downward spiral for months. His drinking, always heavy, had become chronic. His old comrade Goering had turned on him, blaming him for everything that was wrong in the Luftwaffe: the programme disasters of the Heinkel He 177 heavy bomber and the Messerschmitt Me 210 twin-engine fighter, the stilted production lines, and the failure of the aviation industry to keep the front-line forces up to strength. The worst thing for Udet in all this was that deep in his heart he agreed with Goering. He knew that the cost to the German aircraft industry in wasted money, raw materials and production capacity of the Me 210 debacle alone was somewhere between 600 and 1,000 planes lost – something the Luftwaffe couldn't afford. The 210 wasn't the only failing that could be laid at his door. His pre-war obsession with dive bombing led to the Junkers Ju 88 – originally designed to be an extremely lightweight, ultra-fast medium bomber which didn't require fighter protection – to be fitted with dive brakes and increased its all-up weight from just 6 tons to 13! One of its pilots, Peter Stahl, called the new plane 'a diva' and said 'she was capable of carrying out surprising things all by herself, she was particularly prankish during take-off'. Junkers' General Manager, the moustached and extremely serious Dr Heinrich Koppenberg, despaired at 'the horrendous number of changes, some 25,000 in all' foisted on the plane by Udet's office. The result, as Milch described it, was to make the Ju 88 'a flying barn door which was only capable of becoming a bird again after it had dropped its bombs'. Obviously Udet was not solely to blame for these manifest failings; he had to share that burden with his boss, the man who had, despite all the advice to the contrary, put a dazzlingly unqualified ex-daredevil fighter pilot in charge of the very productive lifeblood of the Luftwaffe. Unsurprisingly, Goering didn't see it that way and with him giving Udlinger the cold shoulder, all of the Reichsmarshall's cronies dropped him like a wet rag too, and Udet – ever the bon viveur and centre of attention – now found himself friendless and openly derided.

On the night of 16 November it all became too much for him and he sat alone at home, drinking himself sober with two bottles of cognac. As dawn broke he picked up the phone and dialled Frau Inge Bleyle – his young and beautiful mistress. When she answered he blurted out, '*Ingelein* [his nickname for her], I can't stand it anymore, I'm going to shoot myself. I wanted to say goodbye to you. They're after me.' Bleyle said afterwards, 'In vain I pleaded with him and begged him to wait. I told him I would be right there. I heard the shot over the telephone. When I got there he was dead. His bed was covered with notes, brief letters of farewell.'[96] According to his biographer, Udet had scrawled, 'Reichsmarschall, why have you deserted me?' in red on the headboard of his bed.

It was a sad end for a fundamentally decent man who had let himself be fooled by the monsters around him into becoming part and parcel of the Nazi project.

However, Udet's death gave the Nazis something of a problem. A suicide like his just wasn't acceptable, heroes were meant to die a glorious death 'for Volk, Fatherland and Führer', not sprawled across a dirty unmade bed surrounded by empty bottles of booze. So the Nazis hushed it up. The story was put out that the Old Eagle had died while test-flying a new plane. An elaborate funeral was planned in Berlin and the cream of the Luftwaffe's hierarchy was called upon to attend, among them the first ever *General der Jagdwaffe* – twenty-eight-year-old Werner 'Vati' Mölders. Adored by pretty much everyone who knew him, Mölders had emerged from obscurity while serving in the Condor Legion in the Spanish Civil War. While there he had become an ace and then went on to become the first pilot in history to claim 100 kills – all the more remarkable considering he had almost never made it as a pilot in the first place due to debilitating air sickness. His first flight physical had ended in failure when he threw up during the spin-chair test, but the young Mölders had practiced again and again until he mastered the chair and passed it. Even then he suffered from air sickness for months after graduating from Alfred Keller's Bomber School in Brunswick before becoming a Stuka pilot and then finally a fighter pilot. His final score would be 115 and Guderian would write of his prowess as a fighter pilot, 'Wherever he showed himself the air was soon clear.'

Mölders wasn't just a great pilot, though: he was an original thinker, and as well as flying he began to completely rethink German fighter tactics. The Jagdwaffe's Kette and Schwarm systems of flying and fighting that had proved to be hugely successful in the war so far were down to him and his compatriot Günther Lützow, as recognised by his fellow Experte Günther Rall: 'He was a marvellous tactician. My admiration for him was boundless, he had a great wit and great personality. He was the most highly principled man I ever met.'

Nicknamed 'Vati' – 'daddy' – by his men, who knew just how much he looked after them, he was visiting the fighter Staffeln in the Crimea when the summons arrived on the 22nd; Mölders jumped into an He 111 and set off for Berlin, ignoring the pilot's advice on the bad weather systems they would have to fly through. The weather was indeed terrible, and the plane took a battering as it flew on north-west across the continent. On nearing the eastern German city of Breslau, one of the Heinkel's two engines failed in the storm. Ordering the pilot to land at the Schmeidefeld air strip on the edge of the city, the other engine stalled on the final approach and the bomber smashed into the ground. Ground crews rushed to the scene only to find Mölders, sitting in the co-pilot seat, dead of a broken neck and crushed ribcage from the impact. The aircraft's mechanic, Sergeant Hobbie, was also dead but the pilot – Lieutenant Knobe, a Condor Legion veteran like Mölders – was still alive and was rushed to hospital, as were the radio operator, Sergeant Tenz, and Mölders' personal aide, Major Dr Wenzel. The latter two lived, but Knobe didn't survive the ambulance journey and was pronounced dead on arrival. Mölders' death was a body blow for the Luftwaffe in general, and the fighter arm in particular, and realistically was more significant militarily for the future of the Nazi air force than Udet's. Along with Adolf Galland, Mölders was by far the best tactical thinker in the Jagdwaffe and his loss would be keenly felt as the Luftwaffe came under increasing pressure from both east and west.

As it was, Udet was buried, with all due pomp and ceremony, next to the grave of Manfred von Richthofen in the Invalidenfriedhof Cemetery in Berlin. Mölders was interred alongside them both, and in a typically ill-judged gesture given Mölders' devout Roman Catholicism, Goering ended his eulogy by declaring, 'You will arise in Valhalla!'

The deaths of Udet and Mölders were a distraction at the very worse time for the faltering Typhoon offensive. With Berlin's eye off the ball, not enough attention was given to the increasingly concerned reports from the front as the Wehrmacht's lack of preparedness for the winter season became more apparent every day. Blinded by just how close they were to Moscow, the OKW did not want to see that the great assault on the Soviet capital had now degenerated down to a few pitifully weak units trudging forward slowly and painfully, measuring their advance in metres. Hasso von Manteuffel, a colonel at the time and a man who would go on become one of the *Panzerwaffe*'s finest generals, said, 'My division ... was the only unit that crossed a bridge within thirty miles of Moscow ... we could ride the tram to Moscow ... I heard no troops came after my division, and because we had no reserves we had to retreat.'[97]

By now the thermometer was plunging as winter arrived in earnest. The panzer general 'Fast Heinz' Guderian was appalled by what he saw. 'Only he who saw the endless expanse of Russian snow during this winter of our misery and felt the icy wind that blew across it can truly judge the events that now occurred.'[98]

With no anti-freeze, engines needed to be thawed out for several hours before they could be started. The artificial rubber – *buna* – that the Germans used in so much of their equipment became friable and took on the consistency of wood. Weapon sights misted over and recoils jammed as grease and oil froze. Cases of frostbite became an epidemic – Guderian noted that there were 400 in each of Friedrich Mieth's 112th Infantry Division's three regiments by the end of November. He also noted that men were freezing to death on sentry duty and even when relieving themselves as their anuses froze over while in the act.

By contrast the factories of Moscow were pumping out winter gear for the Red Army: some 326,700 pairs of Russian-style felt boots and 264,400 pairs of fur gloves. It wasn't just the boots and gloves, either; it was the men to wear them. One of the divisions closest to Moscow was the 2nd Motorised Division 'SS-Das Reich'. One of its artillery officers wrote to his mother:

> These Russians seem to have an inexhaustible supply of men. Here they unload fresh troops from Siberia every day, they bring up fresh guns and lay mines all over the place. On the 30th [November] we made our last attack – a hill known to us as Pear Hill, and a village called Lenino. With artillery and mortar support we managed to take all of the hill and half of the village. But at night we had to give it all up again in order to defend ourselves more effectively against the continuous Russian counter-attacks. We only needed another eight miles to get the capital within gun range – but we just could not make it.

In Heinz Hellmich's veteran 23rd Infantry Division – nicknamed the '*Grenadierkopf*' – Colonel Adolf Rägener reported that two of the battalions in his 9th Infantry Regiment absolutely refused to advance any further. Desertion, never before a problem in the German army, reared its head. The artilleryman Gerhard Bopp witnessed the field execution of one poor soul who had been recaptured. 'An execution squad of nineteen men is about to shoot a German soldier for running away from his unit ... The man stands upright, his eyes downcast ... the officer gives the command "Fire!" and a volley of shots ring out, the soldier falls slowly backwards ... He is then buried in a hollow, without honour.'[99] The Soviets too were merciless in their treatment of any soldier who was deemed guilty of cowardice in the face of the enemy. When Marshal Gheorgy Zhukov was asked by his American counterpart Dwight D. Eisenhower about reports that Red Army men were shot for cowardice, Zhukov replied by saying, 'In the Red Army it takes a very brave man to become a coward.' Zhukov knew what he was talking about. That first winter, the NKVD may have executed as many as 100,000 of their own men. Another 13,500 would be shot during the Battle of Stalingrad a year later.[100] Deserters were sometimes shot in front of an audience of a couple of hundred fellow soldiers from their division – *pour encourager les autres* – but more usually the condemned man was led off by an NKVD squad to a spot behind the lines. There he was told to strip naked before being shot. His uniform and boots were then issued out to another conscript.

It was little different in the ranks of the VVS.

> The rule was that if you disengaged without a reason SMERSH [literally meaning 'Death to spies', SMERSH was the counter-intelligence department of the NKVD secret police] would investigate you immediately. Many pilots were under scrutiny. One was my friend from the Academy, Privalov. He was a bit scared and they wanted to court-martial him, but I supported him as I knew he could defeat his fear ... I took him with me and gradually he got used to combat, He did well and finished the war with a chest full of decorations.[101]

Privalov was by no means the only Soviet flier who almost fell foul of SMERSH. Arkadiy Kovachevich, a MiG-3 pilot, had carried out an escort mission for a bombing raid by Pe-2s but had fallen behind as his high-altitude fighter couldn't keep up with the speed of the bombers as they hugged the deck on the homeward flight. Caught short for speed, Kovachevich had to watch helpless as a group of Messerschmitts attacked the Pe-2s and shot down five of them.

As I landed the whole unit already knew what had happened. A car with three men from the counter-espionage organisation, SMERSH, arrived. They seized me and started to interrogate me. They accused me of treason and sabotage and threatened to have me transferred to a punishment battalion. Only when the unit leader of the Pe-2s, a Captain, arrived and confirmed the superior speed of the Pe-2s during the return flight, were the accusations against me dropped.[102]

Sometimes, though, even fellow pilots thought the harsh counter-measures were justified. 'As for cowardice, yes it existed ... I remember one pilot was executed in front of his regiment for deliberately shooting himself in the hand.'[103]

With discipline beginning to crack it was clear that Typhoon was done. Von Bock's Army Group Centre had reached what the nineteenth-century military theoretician Karl von Clausewitz had called its 'limit of strategic consumption'.

At this critical point, when von Bock needed every plane he could get hold of, Hitler decided to almost halve his air support by withdrawing Bruno Loerzer's Fliegerkorps II and sending it to the Mediterranean after a period of rest and recuperation away from the front. Before leaving, Loerzer himself sent out a valedictory note to his men lauding their achievements since the launch of Barbarossa, which included completing over 40,000 sorties; dropping 23,150 tons of bombs; destroying 3,826 aircraft (2,169 in the air), 789 tanks, 14,339 vehicles, 159 complete trains and a further 304 locomotives; and not forgetting his signallers, who had laid 3,000 kilometres of telephone wires and transmitted 40,000 radio and 30,000 teletype messages.

In truth, Loerzer's command was exhausted, but the timing couldn't have been worse for the Germans. Now, their only air support came from Von Richthofen's Fliegerkorps VIII.

Why did Hitler do it? Overconfidence would seem to be the answer. Not for the first time, he believed the Soviets were finished. He had seen the reports stating the Soviet government had decamped for Kuybyshev in the east, and that the NKVD and Red Army had abandoned the streets of the capital to mobs of bewildered Muscovites. In his mind the capture of Moscow was a foregone conclusion, and then the Wehrmacht could march onwards to its final victory at the Archangel–Volga line.

At the front, his horrendous miscalculations were coming home to roost. The German artilleryman Gerhard Bopp, from Rudolf Freiherr von Roman's 35th Infantry Division, wrote on 2 December that his unit was twenty miles or so from Moscow when 'a Russian fighter swooped low over our position, firing wildly. Others followed and we ran for cover'.

The next day, Horst Lange of Karl von Oven's Saxon 56th Infantry Division was near Tolstoy's famous estate at Krasnaya Polyana and the Moscow–Volga Canal when, 'Enemy planes are in the sky above us and more and more of their tanks are appearing ... Our assault has been called off, instead we are laying mines and trying to dig trenches in the middle of a snowstorm.'[104] Close by, Georgi Osadchinsky of the Soviet 35th Rifle Brigade was on a reconnaissance patrol and came across a field of dead Germans. 'We found wrecked German tanks and the corpses of their soldiers covered in snow. They had been caught in one of our air attacks.'[105]

Von Richthofen wrote in his diary: 'Kluge's Fourth Army suffered a serious setback yesterday ... What a grim day! Our efforts to drive home the offensive on Moscow have failed.'

CHAPTER 10

The Moscow Counter-Offensive

With the Germans frozen in the snow, and Typhoon a failure, the Soviets struck.

On the morning of 6 December they launched their own counter-offensive. Thirteen Soviet Armies, comprising eighty-eight infantry divisions, sixteen of cavalry and twenty-four tank brigades, were flung against von Bock's worn-out sixty-seven divisions. The frozen Landsers reeled backwards, and the call went out along the front – 'Where is the Luftwaffe?' The truth was that they were in as bad a condition as their Army comrades. The men themselves may have been issued with winter equipment but the aircraft hadn't been. Fritz Hübner described it: 'Our planes – on forward airfields with little protection from the elements, were no longer able to start their engines – and at a stroke we were deprived of all protection from the air.'[106]

'Eighty percent of the aircraft park of the Luftwaffe was paralyzed' and the daily sortie level had dropped by over two-thirds. A report from JG 52 stated: 'Due to the sudden cold spell, hardly any aircraft could be made serviceable, since there was no heating equipment available. II/JG 52 lost its entire technical equipment, and a large part of its aircraft park at Klin.'[107] Serviceability rates plummeted, with the Stuka Staffeln at just 50 per cent; the fighters were even lower at 46 per cent, and the bombers at just one in three able to fly. Von Richthofen was distraught, and wrote in his diary, 'Because of the bad weather and the short winter days we have been unable to make many flights and as a result have had little effect on things. Our troops are unable to hold their ground and there are no more reserves.'

The VVS, despite its losses, had somehow managed to concentrate 1,376 aircraft, and now they were all up in the sky pounding the shivering Germans below them. Flying an average of 480 sorties a day from all-weather airfields around Moscow, it was now the VVS that had the upper hand at last. At first the VVS itself didn't understand why this was the case. Arkadiy Kovachevich, flying in the Moscow zone at the time, said: 'Suddenly there were only small groups of enemy aircraft in the air, and this puzzled us because our air reconnaissance had reported large concentrations of German planes at Klin and other airfields.'[108]

Kovachevich later saw the reasons himself when he inspected several captured German aircraft at Klin airfield after the Soviets had retaken it. 'We captured several German aircraft there, all of them intact but with their engines frozen. The desperate Germans had even attempted to thaw out the engine of a Bf 109 by wheeling the nose into a house!'

Desperation was the word, and panic was another. The fear of an impending disaster spread through the higher echelons of the Nazi leadership like wildfire. Von Richthofen was at Hitler's headquarters when he wrote in his diary: 'Everyone here is quite overwhelmed. What shall we do now? There is a terrible sense of anxiety. If the frontline soldiers are not able to hold their lines everything will go to the dogs ... If one looks at the bigger picture, it is clear we are facing an imminent catastrophe.'

That catastrophe was unfolding for Horst Lange as he and his comrades of the 56th retreated west in a near-rout: 'The Red Air Force is swooping down on us, their fighters raking the village with their machine-guns. The bombers will soon follow. No German aircraft are to be seen, and apparently our flak guns have seized up.' Lange was taking shelter in a house when it was attacked by the VVS.

I fell off my chair in shock and in the moment of falling saw bright, pin-point lights of tracer fire smash through our window. My hand and sleeve were covered in blood and I tried to bind it up, but there was no pain. Then I realised the blood was not mine. Others called out "They got Max!" There was the sweet smell of blood, oozing and sticky – and Surkowski [the platoon leader] lying on the floor, quite still. He had been shot in the head.

More air attacks followed as Lange and his comrades carried on running. 'I saw the muzzle flashes of their machine-guns. There are only 100 metres to the shelter of the forest, but now bombers are coming ... The psychological effect of these air attacks is considerable. They take us by surprise, in a state of utter helplessness ... The enemy's planes seem to move around at will.'[109]

After months of Red Army soldiers cursing the Luftwaffe and asking where the VVS was, the boot was now firmly on the other foot, as the Soviet air regiments hammered away at anything German. 'In the battle-scarred ruins of the village we are in there are just a few undamaged buildings which we can use ... The enemy air force is a frequent visitor and our own planes are scarcely to be seen.'[110]

The army had gotten used to air superiority, and having flights of Stukas, 109s and bombers at their beck and call, but that was a thing of the past for the first crucial weeks of the Soviet attack. Hans von Luck with the famed 7th Panzer agreed. 'Russian planes would appear behind our retreating columns, strafing the infantry and bombing the horse-drawn supply and artillery units. Soon the narrow roads were choked with the corpses of men and horses. Those that escaped the carnage were usually finished off by Russian ski patrols.' Von Luck's description of the misery being inflicted by the resurgent VVS was repeated up and down Army Group Centre's disintegrating front; Reinhardt's Panzer Group 3, on von Bock's northern flank near Klin and Livny, was cracking up. Reinhardt recalled, 'The road is under constant Russian air attack, and those being killed by the bombs are no longer being buried ... the Panzer Group is in a dismal state.'

Luftwaffe crews themselves could see what their enforced absence was contributing to on the ground, including the Ju 88 pilot Peter Stahl.

> It was a truly harrowing picture. Long columns of our soldiers floundered through the snow. Abandoned vehicles were everywhere. As we flew over these men, at low altitude, we saw that most were almost unconscious with fatigue. They paid no attention to us whatsoever. Villages were burning – the entire horizon was filled with columns of black smoke. What a pitiless war![111]

Army Group Centre was melting away in the snow. Heavy weaponry and broken down vehicles were abandoned, the dead and soon-to-be-dead were left to be covered over by the next blizzard. Divisions were now only that in name only; Johann Kielmansegg's 6th Panzer didn't actually have any serviceable panzers left, and had just 350 grenadiers fit for duty. Hans von Luck's 7th Panzer was in an even worse state, with a bayonet strength of just 200.

Hitler responded in three ways; first, he sacked the Army's commander-in-chief, Field Marshal Walther von Brauchitsch, and took over direct command himself.

Second, he realised there was no way von Richthofen's depleted force could hope to provide the Army with the support it so desperately needed, so in a huge volte-face, he ordered Fliegerkorps VIII reinforced with a bomber Geschwader from the west, plus three more newly activated bomber Geschwader, a twin-engine fighter Geschwader from the Reich night-fighter force, plus an air transport Geschwader from the south, and four more from the Reich. The transports would be used to ferry forward fuel, ammunition and other supplies to the beleaguered divisions, which were now subject to his third major decision: his famous 'Stand Fast' order. There would be no further retreat. The army would stay where it was, dig in and fight it out.

The problem this posed for the Luftwaffe's transport command was that there weren't nearly enough of them to go round, so these reinforcements for Von Richthofen came straight from the training schools, which were pretty much emptied of instructors and specialist crews. These irreplaceable men were now put in immense danger, and if casualties were high then the transport fleet could be crippled for the future.

CHAPTER 11

Mass Murder and the End of Barbarossa

As Army Group Centre bled to death in front of Moscow, one of the worst mass atrocities of a war that would see so many was occurring behind the German lines – the starvation and murderous neglect of the millions of Soviet POWs captured during the summer and autumn, in what was deliberate Nazi policy.

There was history here. Back in the First World War, the fighting on the Eastern Front had been savage and confused. Droves of conscripts from both sides had surrendered en masse and ended up dying in horrific circumstances as their Russian, Austrian and German captors had signally failed to cope with the sheer numbers involved. Men had starved, disease had been rampant, and some 472,000 POWs from the Central Powers of Imperial Germany and Hapsburg Austria-Hungary had died as a result. The number of Russian dead had been even higher.

But now the scale was of an altogether different size. The Wehrmacht would take anywhere between 5.3 million and 5.7 million Soviets prisoner – the number couldn't be accurately determined as the Germans never made any serious attempt to register and count them – of whom it was estimated at least 2.5 million, and maybe as many as 3.3 million, died, the majority by the end of that first winter.

Much has been made over the years by apologists for the Wehrmacht that this slaughter was the result of nothing more sinister than a lack of planning on the Germans' part; that the army in particular had not foreseen the capture of so many prisoners, and so no camps, transport, shelter or food had been prepared for them, and thus when the long columns of prisoners came marching in the system was overwhelmed. This version of events is in no way supported by the facts.

As early as August, after hosting a dinner for some of his generals, Hitler waxed on about what conquering the Soviet Union meant to him:

What India is for England, the territories of Russia will be for us. If only I could make the German people understand what this space means for our future! We must no longer allow Germans to emigrate to America, on the contrary, we must attract the Norwegians, the Swedes, the Danes and the Dutch into our eastern lands. The colonists will live on handsome farms, German services will be lodged in marvellous buildings, the governors in palaces, and around the cities, to a depth of 30–40 kilometres, we shall have a belt of handsome villages connected by the best roads. What exists beyond that will be another world in which we will let the Russians live as they like, it is merely necessary that we should rule them.

Goering was even more explicit when he talked with Ciano (Galeazzo Ciano – the Italian Foreign Minister) about the issue in November of 1941. Ciano reported back to his father-in-law Mussolini that Goering had told him, 'In the camps, Russian POWs have begun to eat each other. This year between 20–30 million people will die of hunger in Russia, but perhaps that is how it should be, certain peoples must be decimated.'

This claim of cannibalism may seem far-fetched but it was widely reported at the time by German troops themselves: 'When one of the prisoners died the Russians often ate him while he was still warm, that's a fact.'[112]

Goering was not only prepared to gossip about it with foreign diplomats; he also thought it a subject suited to macabre humour, as one of his subordinates attested.

Goering told me that hunger among the Russian prisoners had reached such an extreme that in order to start them toward the interior it is no longer necessary to send them under armed guard; it is enough to put a camp kitchen at the head of the column which emits the fragrant odour of food, and then thousands and thousands of prisoners will trail along like a herd of famished animals.

It wasn't just the Nazi hierarchy who knew what was happening either; it seemed it was common knowledge among many servicemen at the front, including Luftwaffe personnel. A captured Luftwaffe NCO told a fellow prisoner, 'There were 50,000 Russian POWs in the citadel at

Templin ... At the time there was an outbreak of typhus. A sentry said to us "We've got typhus in the camp, it'll last another fortnight, and then the Russian prisoners will all be dead, and the Poles too, and the Jews."[113]

News of the massacre of Jews by the advancing Wehrmacht was even printed in the pages of the Soviet propaganda newssheet – *Pravda* – in an article purportedly written by a Luftwaffe pilot who had defected to the Soviets:

I, the son of Sebastian Freitag's family in Reising, have gone over to the Russian side in order to struggle against the rapacious robbers from Germany ... I have witnessed the horrible scenes in Kharkov, where innocent Russians were hanged from balconies. *From what I have heard I understand that they are executing all the Jews* [author's emphasis]. Germany is carrying out a murderous war against Russia and halts at nothing, using derision and torture of prisoners. There is no doubt that the Russians will achieve victory. One only has to get acquainted with the Russian people – everywhere you are met with an exceptional cohesion and confidence in victory. I have met with Russian airmen, and we understand each other perfectly. During one of our discussions we talked about the inevitable fall of Hitler.[114]

As millions of benighted Soviet POWs literally rotted to death behind Nazi barbed wire, 1941 came to a bloody close on the Eastern Front. The German tide had reached its high-water mark in front of Moscow, and now the Soviet counter-offensive was rolling back Army Group Centre and killing huge numbers of Germans into the bargain. Soon, Stalin would suffer from the dictator's constant companion – hubris – and widen that offensive out along the entire front line to try and beat the Wehrmacht in the spring of 1942 and win the war – he would fail spectacularly.

For Adolf Hitler and the Nazis, Barbarossa had been a disaster. The short, sharp summer campaign that would kill the Russian bear and fulfil the Nazi dream of an immense empire in the East had deteriorated into the opening gambits of a protracted war of attrition – exactly the type of conflict Nazi Germany was least suited to winning. Army Group Centre alone had lost 3,643 cars, 4,351 motorcycles and 7,319 lorries in the retreat from Moscow – the vaunted German mobility was gone. Berlin was now faced with a two-front war, and to cap it all Hitler had declared war on the United States of America after the sneak Japanese attack on Pearl Harbour on 7 December. The Führer loudly declared he had no choice morally and was only fulfilling his Tripartite Pact agreements with Tokyo, but observers couldn't help but notice that the Japanese seemed in no hurry to reciprocate and declare war on the Soviet Union. Khalkhin Gol had been a salutary lesson to the Japanese Imperial General Staff.

In Wilhelmstrasse the Luftwaffe high command was struggling to come to terms with a year that had started so well and ended so badly. The air force was now spread worryingly thin across not two fronts but four. Her main strength was still concentrated in the east, but there were still significant forces facing Great Britain and the Mediterranean was sucking up resources while, lastly, British RAF night bombing raids were beginning to necessitate more home-based fighter defence. One of her senior leaders and the darling of the press, Ernst Udet, was dead, as was her first ever Inspector of Fighters, and inroads had been made by the VVS into the core of her irreplaceable Experten. The new year would have to produce either a swift final victory or a revolution in the way the service was structured and resourced.

In the east the men themselves had performed superbly: for the loss of 2,093 aircraft (almost half in accidents), with another 1,361 damaged, the Experten and their wingmen had destroyed 15,500 Soviet aircraft, 57,600 vehicles, 3,200 tanks, 2,450 guns, 1,200 locomotives, 650 trains and innumerable strongpoints and pillboxes. However, it is important to note that the Soviet records dispute these figures.

However the cost, beyond a simple toll of aircraft lost, was considerable.

Of all the three services, the Luftwaffe was designed and geared towards a series of small, short, contained campaigns, with rest gaps in between to replenish front-line strength. To cope with the forward flow of the battlefield in the Soviet Union, mobility was all. The relatively cheap victories in the west had helped provide the Luftwaffe with that crucial mobility, but now the vast captured vehicle parks of the French army were now lying littered and broken across the western Soviet Union. Their two-wheel-drive trucks and cars were perfectly fine for the metalled roads of Western Europe, but wore out all too quickly on the dirt roads and tracks of the Soviet Union. The result was that the eastern Luftwaffe had lost 85 per cent of its 100,000 motor vehicles by the end of the year. She was also losing an average of 741 aircraft and 318 specialist ground-crew killed a month by the end of the year, her resupply and logistics system was failing and the losses weren't being replaced by the industries and depots back in the Reich. The Luftwaffe was in grave danger of being hollowed out.

Hermann Plocher's verdict was a warning: 'By the winter of 1941–42 the effects of the war were beginning to tell heavily upon the Luftwaffe organisations in Russia and in other theatres as well. It was the beginning of the death of the German air force.'

Hundreds of miles away on the streets of Dresden there was a subtle change noticed by the German Jewish diarist Victor Klemperer, who wrote acidly, 'A few weeks ago the Russians had been officially "annihilated", now they are to be "annihilated later". Instead the Wehrmacht is to hold on "absolutely" to what it has already conquered, and the Army is now "heroically resisting".'

Aircraft from the VVS flew over the German lines dropping sacks of Christmas cards. Each card had a message inside offering the Wehrmacht season's greetings from their Soviet comrades. The picture on the front cover was of a snow-covered field full of crosses topped with German helmets. The caption simply read: 'Living space in the east.'

PART FOUR

1942

During the 166 days from 22 June to the end of 1941, the Germans had advanced 800 miles (1,290 km) into the Soviet Union and now stood on a front line that was almost 1,000 miles long from north to south. They had inflicted crushing defeats on Stalin's forces, destroying the entire pre-war Red Army in the western Soviet Union 1.3 times over and almost the whole VVS. The Soviet Union's second city, Leningrad, was under siege, Kiev had fallen, and the Wehrmacht was in the Crimea. But Barbarossa had failed. The German attempt to capture Moscow had ended in near disaster and the Soviet December counter-offensive had almost caused the Wehrmacht's most powerful formation; Army Group Centre, to disintegrate. The German Army in the East, the Ostheer, *had lost 80 per cent of its armour (3,486 panzers from a starting force of just 3,350, with only 873 replacements arriving), half its horses and 40 per cent of its guns from its pre-invasion inventory. Motor vehicle numbers had collapsed, with 75,000 lost during the winter battles alone, and munitions stocks were at one third of June 1941 levels.*

Franz Halder recorded on 25 March that a full 33.5 per cent of the Barbarossa invasion force had become casualties since the offensive began: 32,485 officers and 1,040,581 NCOs and men, with losses worst in combat units where regiments were lucky to still have 50 per cent of their original establishment.

1942 would be a vital year for the Third Reich and the Soviet Union. The Soviets had bought time with blood during 1941, and now needed to stay in the war, build their strength, and use attrition to win the long game. For Nazi Germany time was against them: they needed to finish the job and win quickly.

CHAPTER 12

Moscow Overreaches

Sitting in his office in the Kremlin, Stalin was sure he could scent victory. Army Group Centre was in tatters, Fedor von Bock and almost forty other senior German officers had been relieved of their commands, the whole German line was tottering.

'Now the moment has come to launch a general offensive along the entire front!' the Soviet dictator told his highest military council, the STAVKA. The man who had lead Moscow's recent Houdini-like escape from capture, Gheorgy Zhukov, vehemently protested, saying the army was in no position to launch such an ambitious assault after the calamities of the late summer and autumn. A clearly annoyed Stalin growled, 'Does anyone else want to speak on this matter?' When no one backed Zhukov up, the dictator slapped the marshal down: 'With this, I regard the matter as settled.' The Red Army and the VVS went over to a general assault on 5 January to drive the Wehrmacht out of the Soviet Union and win the war by the summer.

Stalin would have perhaps not been so confident had he heard one of his own fighter pilots, Alexsandr Pokryshkin, who was called to a meeting with many of his other comrades to be lectured by an engineer on why the MiG-3, the I-16 and even the totally obsolete I-153 biplane were all superior to the Bf 109. 'I could not see the reason for this lecture, after all the audience was made up of experienced airmen who had met the Messers and Junkers on several occasions, and who knew how good these aircraft were.' Pokryshkin then made the mistake of pointing this out at the meeting, only to be berated by a senior officer who was also present. He was then placed under suspicion of having an 'unpatriotic attitude' for having the temerity to speak out.

Pokryshkin wasn't the only VVS pilot unconvinced of the imminence of Soviet victory. Lieutenant Petr Kulakov, a pilot with the Soviet Red Banner Baltic Fleet, had already downed a Finnish SB before mistaking a brand-new Pe-2 bomber for a Luftwaffe Bf 110. He attacked, shot it down and killed the radio operator. Arriving back at base, he was arrested, tried, convicted and sentenced to eight years' forced labour, suspended until after the war. With his sentence hanging over him, he had carried on flying and been shot down three times and wounded once before deciding enough was enough and that the best course of action was to switch sides, so, cramming his wife into the cockpit with him, the couple took off from his air base and flew over to the Germans. A report by the Navy Commissar, Ivan Rogov, into the incident reported that:

> Kulakov took off together with his wife in an I-16 in broad daylight and flew over to the enemy. This occurred due to insufficient organisation of the airfield and an absence of orders and military discipline. It is incredible that the technicians who prepared the aircraft for the flight, the duty officers, and the flight officers, were all unable to see that a woman was entering a combat aircraft.

Interrogated after landing, Kulakov was almost certainly currying favour with his new friends but nevertheless his words can probably be taken at face value.

> The mood among the old flyers is very negative. In any case, there are very few of them left. Most pilots are young novices who have arrived at the front directly from the schools. Some of them only flew their first sorties in '41. The old pilots evade combat with the Messers, and the word 'Messerschmitt' is banned amongst us. The attitude among the younger pilots is quite different. They are fanatical and naïve, very narrow and incapable of realising the seriousness of the situation.[115]

In truth the VVS weren't the only ones unimpressed by their new comrades. Lieutenant Hans-Ekkehard Bob of JG 54 Grünherz wrote in his unit log that, 'Our novice pilots give us less pleasure. *Unteroffizier* Höger crashed his aircraft during landing, and it is a miracle that he managed to survive.' Not all of the Experten felt the same, though. Hermann Graf was leading a flight of new boys to help acclimatise them to the situation at the front when he saw a formation of Ju 88s come under attack. Without hesitation he led his charges into action to protect them.

> My kids intervened with great enthusiasm, and I helped them by streaming tracer over the Russians in order to disconcert them. But then I saw how a Rata got on the tail of one of my wards, it would be seconds before he was shot down. Moments later I had positioned myself behind the enemy aircraft and immediately dispatched him ... I needed the beginners help to explain myself to my commander.

However, the VVS was still a shadow of its former self, while the Luftwaffe by contrast was adapting quickly to the Russian winter. 'Aircraft engines that had been stopped overnight in the extreme cold were difficult, if not impossible, to start. Warming ovens and all sorts of expedients were devised in an effort to solve this problem. Planes on standby were often placed with their noses in 'alert boxes' – heated shacks, which kept the engines warm enough to start at short notice.'[116] The result was that as Stalin's offensive got underway, the Experten were back in the skies in force. Men like Sergeant Leopold 'Poldi' Steinbatz, an Austrian Bf 109 pilot with JG 52 down in the south, who wrote gleefully to his wife, 'Today was my lucky day. Early this morning we took on a free hunting mission and we actually spotted three Soviets.' Steinbatz shot down all three; two fighters and a bomber. 'I came in [to the bomber] very close and then I shot him in flames with a few rounds. Burning, he crashed into a village. The crew had no chance to bail out since they had been flying at an altitude of no more than 450 feet.' These kills took him to a score of forty-two for which he was awarded the Knight's Cross.[117]

Lieutenant Vladimir Goncharov of the Soviet Thirty-Third Army was advancing west towards Vyazma when it was hit by the resurgent German flyers. 'The Luftwaffe has reappeared in strength and is inflicting substantial damage. The advance has slowed considerably – the enemy is holding his line more firmly and we are running low on ammo and food. Our soup tastes like water now.' Goncharov would be killed less than a fortnight later trying to stem the renewed German assault.

In Army Group Centre, Walther Model had replaced von Bock and had brought with him a new offensive spirit to his tired troops, and with the Luftwaffe once more overhead it was now the Germans' turn to attack once again. 'Our Stukas smashed the Russian positions, and then our panzers broke through and joined us. The motor highway is jammed with military traffic and our planes are flying overhead.'[118]

Up to the north on the Volkhov River the story was the same, as noted by Johannes Trautloft in his diary: 'The bombers created total chaos among the columns, which brought considerable relief to our infantry.'

It wasn't all roses for the Luftwaffe though. Captain Erich Woitke's JG 52 Staffel was left with just six unserviceable Bf 109s as the Soviets advanced. With no planes left to fly, the men were sent into the trenches as infantry on the orders of Model himself. It wasn't long before they came under attack.

> Woitke received a telephone call warning him of a Russian breakthrough and instructing him to man the defensive positions. But he was so drunk he didn't pay any notice. The result was a disaster. The Russians killed several pilots and members of the ground-crew during this ice-cold night. The injured adjutant [the eighteen-score Experte Lieutenant Carl Willi Hartmann] was abandoned during the retreat. Later we found him dead. Woitke was court-martialled, and the verdict was demotion and a conditional sentence.[119]

Not that turning to the bottle was solely a German issue. 'Did we drink before flights? It happened sometimes. I only drank once before a flight ... I felt so sick ... After that I didn't drink a single drop of alcohol before a flight ... Among our group was Hero of the Soviet Union Ivan Novozhilov. If he flew sober he was a chicken and not a pilot. If he flew drunk he was a great fighter pilot.' This was VVS fighter pilot Alexander E. Shvarev, who then explained how Novozhilov's drinking eventually did for him as he crashed drunk while showing off to a watching crowd. His fellow pilots, including Shvarev, went to see him in hospital where he was being treated for concussion and loss of consciousness. 'He was shouting "Nurse, give me vodka!" They wouldn't give him vodka but instead gave him water. He gulped it down and said "Good vodka but a bit weak." Such a story! He was the only one of us who drank before flights, but he drank too much, he survived but never flew again.'

Novozhilov and Woitke weren't alone. This testimony was from VVS fighter pilot Ivan D. Gaidenko:

> Those who liked to drink just drank. We had one guy, Peter Aksentievich, I remember we had one day with bad weather so no flights and we were in our dug-out preparing for a dancing party. We were flying in

padded pants and Canadian flight jackets and I couldn't go dancing like that, but where were my smart uniform trousers? I couldn't find them anywhere. So I went to see Aksentievich who issued pilots with replacement kit. 'Peter Aksentievich, have you seen my trousers?' 'What do they look like?' 'Smart dark blue ones.' 'Ah, do you remember I bought half a litre of vodka two days ago? Those were your trousers.'[120]

Another VVS pilot who drank was Leonid Nikitovich Khrushchev, son of the future Premier. As a bomber pilot he took part in the Winter War against Finland before converting to fighters. According to reports, he accidentally killed a comrade in a drunken accident, trying to shoot a bottle off his head in horseplay that went terribly wrong. He and his YaK-7B fighter were reported missing presumed shot down after a sortie in the spring of 1943.

All along the front, the Soviets were beginning to unravel.

In the north, Stalin had ordered General Andrei Vlasov's 2nd Shock Army to attack across the Volkhov River and help relieve the pressure on Leningrad by taking Army Group North in the flank. Keller's Luftflotte 1 was still the eastern Luftwaffe's poor relation, but Colonel Pavel Lopatin of the 4th Guards Infantry Division, fighting near Lyuban, testified to its effectiveness nevertheless. 'The enemy's planes dominate the sky. Our infantry attack without success, our artillery are running low on shells and we do not have enough tanks.' A week later he wrote in his diary, 'The enemy's planes are now very active. They are bombing the villages all around us.' Another Soviet officer in the 2nd Shock wrote:

> The damned Germans have gone really seriously into bombing us ... and where are our airmen? I have endured for so long, but now I can feel that my nerves can't take this any longer. For how long are we going to starve and remain without tobacco, whole allowing the cursed Prussians to drop their bombs on us? ... We are told that a terrible number of people have been killed at Myasnoy Bor. We are like trapped hares, we're starving and eating horse-flesh ...[121]

The 2nd Shock was cut off and annihilated. Abandoned by Stalin and the STAVKA, Vlasov was eventually captured and joined the Germans in an attempt to overthrow Communism. As for Lopatin, he managed to survive the battle and get back to his own lines. As the mirage of a quick victory began to disappear in front of his eyes, the Soviet dictator busied himself with micro-management of his forces and meddling in his generals' affairs, sending one of his commanders the following 'helpful' missive:

> I noticed the 108th Tank Division got encircled and lost lots of tanks ... You shouldn't send a division into the offensive on its own without giving it air cover. If aircraft can't fly because of bad weather you must cancel the offensive ... The *Shturmoviki* can even fly in bad weather if the cloud is above 100 to 150 metres.

With the ground carpeted in targets of all kinds, the Luftwaffe's Bf 110 *Zerstörer* (destroyer) Staffeln came into their own. The 110, once a great white hope for the Luftwaffe, had been thoroughly outclassed by the single-engine Hurricanes and Spitfires of the RAF and had suffered dreadful casualties in the Battle of Britain in 1940. Reclassified as a ground-attack aircraft for Barbarossa, the 110, with twin 20-mm cannon and four 7.92-mm machine guns mounted in its nose, packed a terrific punch against infantry and soft-skinned vehicles, as attested to by Lieutenant Johannes Kiel of ZG 26:

> There were Soviet troops on all the roads, and they were unable to take cover, because these 'roads' were nothing but narrow tracks that had been created by snowploughs, with huge mountain walls of snow rising on both sides of them. Congested like flocks of sheep, tightly squeezed between vehicles and other equipment, entire battalions were often caught without any chance of survival from our air attacks. There was no escape from these ravines of death. Flying at low level we mowed them down on road after road, and saw the snow becoming stained red by all the blood.

Kiel spoke of another mission: 'The Bolsheviks had no idea from where death appeared. As though struck by lightning an entire company lay flat in the snow, none would ever rise again. We continued our deadly flight, and two horse columns became our next targets where we tore the horses apart with machine-gun fire.'

These attacks weren't risk-free for the 110 crews, as Kiel as his companions discovered after the latter attack when they were jumped by two VVS fighters, who shot down one Bf 110 before Kiel claimed one of them. 'As the two birds of prey attempted to disengage I took a short cut and overtook one of them. I got the climbing fighter right in front of my nose guns and my bullets ripped large parts away from its fuselage and wings – gone and out!'

Unsurprisingly, the Bf 110s soon became high-value targets for the Soviets and were avidly hunted. Bf 110 Gruppe commander and Knight's Cross holder Captain Rolf 'Schlitzohr' Kaldrack was leading an attack on a Soviet supply column near Toropets when five MiG-3s roared into them. The Bf 110s desperately manoeuvred to escape, and it looked like they would get away, but a determined MiG pilot then flew straight into Kaldrack's machine, killing himself and the entire German crew.[122] The VVS continued to do all it could to support their army comrades. 'We carried out intensive air operations. Each crew never flew less than three sorties per day, sometimes even four or five. We suffered losses on almost every mission, mostly through enemy fighters. The Messer pilots showed very high self-confidence ... I lost several close friends, all of them experienced men and good people.'[123]

Down in the south, JG 77 was fighting hard against its VVS rivals. Herbert Ihlefeld was the Geschwader's leading light – a veteran of the Condor Legion, Poland, France and the Battle of Britain, he was credited with shooting down more RAF Spitfires than any other German pilot. He scored heavily in Barbarossa and became only the fifth Jagdwaffe pilot to reach 100 kills in April 1942. Under his command were a bevy of other high-scoring pilots, Wolf-Dietrich Huy, Kurt Ubben and Emil Omert among them, each vying with the other to be 'top dog'. The twenty-four-year-old Omert achieved his fortieth kill on a sortie he described rather laconically in his diary: 'Low-level attacks against Russian field positions. Air combat with an I-15 and an R-5 during a fighter sweep. I shot down the I-15 and was credited with a probable victory against the R-5.' As for Huy, he ended up on the receiving end in a dogfight against Lieutenant Mikhail Avdeyev, a VVS ace. 'Everything happened very quickly. Before I had time to put myself in a firing position another Russian took a shot at me and hit my engine, which stopped abruptly and then began to emit smoke.' Huy belly-landed and walked away unscathed.[124]

Combat fatigue started to bite on both sides. The experienced German bomber pilot Hansgeorg Bätcher remembers: 'Those of us who were young didn't pay much attention to this during those days, we thought, "OK, things can go wrong, but so what!" But to the older officers, those of around 35–40 years old it was absolutely terrible. They had great difficulties coping with those sorties.' German nerves weren't helped by the ever-present threat of being deliberately rammed by their VVS enemy, the dreaded 'taran', as Bätcher acknowledged. 'Generally they attacked nose-to-nose, but because of the high closing speed in such attacks they were never able to score more than a few hits. On occasion they also attempted to ram us, but I never saw any occasion when they succeeded in this.'

Having mastered the vagaries of the weather, and with the VVS overextended as it tried to support Stalin's over-optimistic general offensive, the Jagdwaffe's earlier dominance of the skies began to reassert itself.

> The Germans blocked our airfields ... They flew in pairs near our aerodromes ... but our commander took no active measures to counter the blockade ... and we paid a high price for poor command. On one of those days I witnessed the death of Captain Tikhomirov over the airfield at Gremyachevo. He was returning to base after completing a mission and was out of ammunition when the hunters fell upon him. Tikhomirov was a very skilful and experienced pilot, but without any ammunition there wasn't much he could do against the Me-109 hunters.

So successful was this tactic that the VVS emulated it – with a twist. Hermann Graf and his Katschmarek, Alfred Grislawski, were based at Zuerichtal, where local partisans kept watch, alerting the VVS to German activity. 'We called her the "Egg Lady", because we imagined that she was sitting somewhere with her radio-transmitter hidden in an egg basket, reporting our take-offs and landings to her compatriots. Time after time we had barely touched down before our "rivals" came buzzing in.' Grislawski came up with an idea to turn the tables on the Soviets and a few days later they put it into action.

> Once again we heard the Egg Lady telling her stories about us, she definitely informed the Russians that we were about to land ... we made a wide turn and went down as if we were about to land, and then took off again. Having done this four times and still no sight of any Russian, I finally decided to land. I was just a few metres above the ground when I heard Grislawski cry out that they were coming. Stick backwards, retract the landing gear, adjust the propeller pitch and up we go!

Grislawski took up the story: 'We pursued the MiGs, Yaks or LaGGs all the way back to Sevastopol, shooting them down one by one. Only one of the Russian pilots survived. He bailed out and his parachute got stuck in a pine tree in the mountains east of Sevastopol.'[125]

The spring thaw now set in, turning the ground into a sea of water, mud and swamp that rivalled the rasputitsa of the previous autumn and causing the operations of both sides to grind to an exhausted halt. For both the Luftwaffe and the VVS, the respite couldn't come quick enough. Armin Köhler of JG 77 wrote in his diary: 'Each day there is an uninterrupted stream of sorties. We are unable to sleep at night. If this carries on much longer our nerves will soon be worn down.' The Austrian Experte Gordon Gollob was of the same opinion:

> The pilot situation looks bad, partly because of losses in aerial combat and injuries, and partly because some pilots have to be relieved from frontline service. Far from everyone is able to stand the enormous physical and mental strain. The most reasonable – and most human – thing to do is to release those pilots who have lost their perseverance from first-line service before they contaminate other pilots or get killed.

The Soviet SU-2 light bomber pilot Lieutenant Alexsandr Pavlichenko, serving down in the southern area of operations, said: 'The veterans of my unit, 210 BBAP, sat together in the underground shelter at our air base. We counted our losses and found that only twelve crews had survived since June 22 1941, out of a total of fifty crews!'[126]

The Germans licked their wounds too. One ground crew member from JG 52 wrote, 'Towards the end of February 1942 we were withdrawn from the front and relocated back to Königsberg, where we received new equipment. We had entered combat with 142 men, and now there were just thirty-seven of us left. The rest were dead, wounded or in the hospital with frostbite.'

By the beginning of April 1942 the Luftwaffe had lost almost 5,000 aircraft destroyed or severely damaged in the East since the launch of Barbarossa. Their total serviceable combat strength facing the VVS was estimated at just 650 planes of all types.

What both sides were in dire need of was reinforcements, and not just a drip-drip of planes and crews, but a massive and sustained inflow of the very latest aircraft and well-trained personnel. 1942 would be the year of the production battle, where success at the front would be hugely affected by what was happening hundreds, if not thousands, of miles away in the factories, mines, mills and workshops of industry, and the classrooms of the flight training schools.

CHAPTER 13

The Production Battle

'Germany's own aircraft production at best ensures maintenance of the present strength. Expansion is impossible either in personnel or in material.' This was the stark warning contained in a document issued by the Luftwaffe General Staff on 15 November 1940. Considering that Germany barely had 4,000 combat planes in service at the time, this was definitely not good news for Hitler's plans for military conquest and was a damning indictment of the incompetence of the Udet era. But that era wasn't quite finished back at the end of 1940. Udet's total mismanagement of the aviation industry would mean 1941 would be another 'lost year' for the Nazis, with Germany producing just 2,992 fighters and 4,007 bombers throughout that critical time. In comparison, the Soviets built 10,565 planes in 1940 and another 15,735 in 1941, even as they were under attack and shipping most of their aviation industry east. Little wonder that the anonymous Hauptmann Hermann believed that the German failure to develop a long-range strategic bomber fleet, to invest in production, repair and servicing and to gamble all on a short war would be the Nazis' undoing in the air. Writing in 1942, he boldly stated: 'The Luftwaffe is doomed. The weapon of which the Nazis have been so inordinately proud, the weapon they thought would conquer the world for them, has been shown up as a failure.'

What the Nazis needed to avoid this fate was nothing less than a revolution in production and, beginning on 8 February 1942, they got one. On that day, Hitler's Armaments Minister, the affable and optimistic engineer Fritz Todt climbed aboard his plane at the Wolf's Lair – Hitler's headquarters near Rastenburg in East Prussia – and was promptly killed as it crashed shortly after take-off. The man who should have been his co-passenger but had cried off a few hours previously, Hitler's architect Albert Speer, was immediately made the new Minister of Armaments and War Production by the Nazi dictator himself, despite Speer's own assertion made years later that Goering raced to Rastenburg on hearing of Todt's death to try and secure his own appointment to the now-vacant post.

What the new minister found behind the propaganda was an economy coasting along at a stately pace, seemingly without regard for the needs of the war effort. There was little real control of production – five so-called 'Supreme Authorities' had jurisdiction over separate elements of the armaments sector – consumer goods were still being produced at almost the same levels as in peacetime, absorbing huge amounts of raw materials and masses of workers, there were relatively few women in the industrial workforce and factories were still operating on a single shift basis. Soon after his appointment Speer visited an armaments factory in Berlin one evening only to find it totally deserted – the entire workforce had finished for the day and had gone home.

Almost alone among Hitler's ministers, who were usually, and in no particular order, lazy, incompetent and greedy, Speer was a square peg in a square hole. The debonair Württemburger proved himself a near-genius in the command and control of an economy, centralising enormous power in his own office and totally reordering the traditional German political/industrial structure. Armed with Hitler's authority ('Speer, I'll sign anything that comes from you') he created a central planning committee, headed by himself, which brought Germany's entire armaments capability under his aegis. The armaments sector was divided into specific departments for each weapon system with experts rather than civil servants given control of each. No department head was allowed to be over fifty-five and no deputy older than forty – in Speer's view youth encouraged innovation and vigour, while age encouraged 'routine and arrogance'. Speer's word soon became akin to law, with the minutes of a conference at Wehrmacht High Command in March stating, 'It is only Speer's word that counts nowadays. He can interfere in all departments. Already he overrides all departments.'

Speer's appointment as armaments supremo coincided with the highpoint of Erhard Milch's career, and the two men formed an extremely effective partnership that transformed German aircraft production in 1942.

Speer knew a transformation was vital. Not long after his Berlin armaments factory drop-in, he had gone to visit the major Junkers plant in Dessau and had met with the firm's General Manager, Dr Heinrich Koppenberg. The sixty-two-year-old Koppenberg was a senior, well-respected figure in Germany's aviation industry. 'He took me into a locked room and showed me a graph comparing American bomber production for the next few years with our own. I asked him what our leaders had to say about these depressing figures, and he replied, "That's just it, they won't believe it," whereupon he broke into uncontrollable tears.'[127]

By 1942 Erhard Milch had shed none of the controversy that had accompanied his earlier career. Disliked and admired in almost equal measure, he was still one of the most able senior commanders in the Luftwaffe. Kesselring – no fan of Milch by any stretch – said of him, 'Milch, next to Goering, was the decisive personality, and despite his youth proved to be extraordinarily useful in the establishment of the Luftwaffe.' One of his other peers, Lieutenant General Klaus Uebe, said of him, 'Taken in the right way and assigned to the right position he was a motor without equal.'[128] The praise seemingly always had a 'but' attached to it, and that was Erhard Milch to a tee. Before he and Udet had fallen out, a common factor in Milch's career, the two men had introduced what was loosely called the 'Milch system', in the run up to the war. This 'system' was predicated on the Luftwaffe fighting the succession of small campaigns with long rest periods in between that everyone in the high command anticipated. As such, large-scale investment in repair facilities and stockpiled spare parts was deliberately negligible, with a culture inculcated in the service of throwing anything away when it was broken and replacing it with new – a policy that could only work for short periods of time with an aviation industry able to maintain frontline strength. With Speer's elevation, the two men realised that a major change of direction was needed, and Speer felt confident enough in the Luftwaffe man to give him a free hand to deliver it.

Milch's first move was to present a plan in March to Goering and Jeschonnek to increase fighter production exponentially: 'Herr Reichsmarschall, your total demand is for 360 new fighter aircraft per month. I fail to understand. If you were to say 3,600 fighters, then I would be bound to state that against America and Britain combined even 3,600 are too few! We must produce more.'[129]

'I do not know what I should do with more than 360 fighters!' Jeschonnek exclaimed to a bemused Milch.

Goering was caught in the middle of his two chief subordinates, and opted as usual to back neither completely but to try and mollify both and thus maintain his own supremacy, regardless of whether it was the right thing to do for the Nazi war effort or not. The result was a new production plan called, rather sycophantically, the 'Goering

Programme'. It called for far-reaching changes in Germany's aviation sector in order to significantly increase total aircraft production. There was a lot of room for improvement; between 1939 and 1941 the number of workers involved in the sector had increased by fully 50 per cent to some 1.85 million (by 1944 this number would have risen again to 2.3 million), and yet total aircraft production had only risen by 15 per cent, while an average of half a ton of high-grade metal was lost in machining every single aero engine made, and in the desert the Luftwaffe was using valuable aluminium to build sunshades for ground crew. The result was that in 1941 the entire German aircraft industry only produced around 600 fighters and bombers per month when losses on the various fronts were running at over 750 a month from July onwards.[130]

Not that all the blame could be laid at the doors of Junkers, Messerschmitt, Dornier and Heinkel, however. The Air Ministry itself seemed determined to make a bad situation worse, constantly interfering with demands for relatively minor adaptations and additions that hindered mass production. For example, the main fighter with the Eastern Front Staffeln was the proven Bf 109. From the beginning of the war up until 1944 it underwent three major evolutions, from the 1940/41 E 'Emil' model to the more advanced mid-1941 F 'Friedrich' and then the final G 'Gustav' version from 1942 onwards; however multiple Ministry missives meant there were no fewer than sixty sub-types of the E, F and G series, with an estimated cost of up to 20 per cent of total possible production lost.[131]

Milch would revolutionise it all. He was a human dynamo, constantly touring factories and facilities and meeting and cajoling executives and managers. Co-ordination with the wider industrial base would become the norm and modern manufacturing techniques and ways of working would be adopted wholesale. Chief among the changes he introduced was the sweeping away of the previous laissez-faire attitude towards the manufacturers that dominated production, with control centralised in the Ministry: the status quo, which was once memorably characterised as the manufacturers being the lions and the Ministry the lion tamers but without whips or stools, was done away with overnight. From now on firms would be given targets and resources directed towards those who achieved their objectives. Plants would be concentrated on single manufacture and others would be merged. Hoarding of key raw materials such as copper and aluminium would be punished and craft-style production consigned to the bin. A big advocate of flow production – a high-volume production methodology focused on round-the-clock manufacturing – Milch forcibly introduced it, firstly into Willy Messerschmitt's company and then BMW, Heinkel, Henschel and Junkers. The standard forty-eight-hour week was replaced by shift work and skill levels were reduced, enabling small numbers of highly skilled workers to oversee far greater numbers of semi-skilled workers and so increase production overall. The effects were dramatic; for instance, at Junkers between 1941 and 1942 aircraft production rose by 42 per cent. By 1944 there was a 53 per cent saving in production time for a Bf 109, with man-hours halved and raw material use reduced by a quarter – hugely significant given that 34,000 109s were made, coming second only in terms of numbers built to the Soviet Il-2 Shturmovik during the war. Between 1941 and 1944 the amount of metal required to make each of the 28,000 jack-of-all-trades BMW 801 radial engines dropped from just over 5 tons to less than 3, while the man-hours needed to build one plummeted from 3,260 down to 1,250.

Overall, the impact of Milch's Goering Programme was little short of a manufacturing earthquake. Production shot up in 1942 to 15,556 aircraft built – including 5,228 bombers and 4,583 fighters – an increase of almost 4,000 planes on 1941, while actually using 15,000 fewer tons of aluminium.[132] Production did not plateau there, though, and 1943 saw 9,601 fighters and 6,601 bombers built, and even more in 1944 before the Anglo-American bombing offensive on the Reich wrecked it all.

There were some downsides to this story for the Luftwaffe. To increase numbers, Milch not only streamlined production; he also ordered the mothballing of almost all new aircraft designs to focus on existing models. This didn't mean that Nazi Germany wouldn't still experiment – the Me-262 jet and Me-163 rocket fighters were proof of that – but what it did mean was that while the Western Allies and the VVS would end the war with whole inventories of new models, the Luftwaffe would only bring into general service one new aircraft during the war – the Focke-Wulf Fw 190 fighter, powered by the ubiquitous BMW 801 engine. Goering himself had been to Bremen to see its designer, Kurt Tank, back in 1940 and told him to 'turn these new fighters out like so many hot rolls' and turn them out he did, no fewer than 20,068 by the war's end.

The 'Speer effect' throughout Nazi Germany's armaments sector was just as dramatic as what Milch achieved for the Luftwaffe. Production of everything from panzers, guns, mortars and shells rocketed, even as the RAF night bombing offensive began to ramp up and overall industrial output only rose sluggishly; steel production only went from 31.8 million tons in 1941 to 34.6 million tons in 1943, and coal from 258.3 to 266.9 million tons in the same period. However, the key inputs for aircraft production, synthetic rubber (the famed *buna*), aluminium and synthetic oil, bucked the trend and rose considerably from 1941 to 1943 – buna from 69 million tons to 117 million, aluminium from 230,000 tons to almost 260,000 and synthetic oil from 4,000,000 to 5,700,000 tons.[133]

Output could have grown even more, but curiously the Nazis were loath to institute the sort of war economy that their major competitors, the Soviet Union, the United States and above all Great Britain, had. Dr Paul Samuelson, a member of the US War Production Board, conducted an investigation into the Nazi economy after the war and was incredulous at what he found. 'We all thought the Nazis were very good organisers of the economy, but after the war we found out that they didn't even know what their gross national product was. They were never even on a two-shift basis in their factories.'

Haunted by the near-revolution of the civilian population back in 1918, Hitler and his cronies constantly sought to somehow shield the people from the economic effects of the war – hence the continued production of consumer goods such as fridges – and this was nowhere seen more clearly than in their attitude to the employment of women in the labour force.

> In 1942 the great difference between Great Britain and Germany was that in the former, women were mobilised to a very high degree. I tried to get women in war production but it was opposed by Goering and Sauckel (the Bavarian Fritz Sauckel, de facto Minister of Labour and Nazi Party functionary). Hitler also said no, women must be preserved, they were for family.[134]

So deeply was this attitude ingrained in the Nazis that they even introduced the 'Cross of Honour for the German Mother' to be awarded to *Frauen* who stayed at home and gave birth to as many future Aryan soldiers as possible.

Goering, as the Plenipotentiary for the Four Year Plan, had an alternate vision to transform the German economy and solve the labour crisis: 'It used to be called plundering, but today things have become more genteel. In spite of that I intend to plunder and to do it thoroughly.'

He wasn't joking.

On a personal level, Goering conducted what he euphemistically called 'shopping trips' to some of Europe's most famous galleries,

helping himself to whatever took his fancy and having it all shipped
to one of the many properties he had collected over the years –
most, like Carinhall itself, paid for from years of extortion and
outright theft.

On a policy level, it meant encouraging tens of thousands of
foreigners to come and work in the Reich and when there weren't
enough volunteers, they were taken by force to be sent to Germany as
little more than slaves. Sauckel – a man of very little imagination or
obvious talent except for his willingness to blindly carry out orders –
said of the practice at a Central Planning Board meeting, 'Out of five
million foreign workers who have arrived in Germany, not even two
hundred thousand came voluntarily.' He later repeated this statement
at his trial at Nuremburg and unsurprisingly was convicted of war
crimes, sentenced to death and hanged. Large numbers of these
workers were from western Europe, 274,000 Dutch, 223,000 Belgians,
and 764,000 French, with many of the latter conscripted under Vichy
France's *Service du Travail Obligatoire* (STO – Compulsory Work
Service) regulations, but by far the majority were from the Soviet
Union, Eastern Europe and the Balkans: 230,000 Yugoslavs (Serbs,
Croats, Slovenes, Bosnians and Montenegrins), 851,000 Poles and
almost 2 million Soviets. Rounded up at gunpoint, torn from their
families and friends and transported west like livestock, their existence
was at best miserable, and often downright wretched. Whole villages
in Belorussia, the Ukraine and western Russia were sealed off by
SS units, their inhabitants seized, divided up and carted off to the
Reich, as Himmler declared:

> The Führer has decided that the partisan-infested areas of north
> Ukraine and central Russia are to be evacuated of their entire
> population. The whole able-bodied male population will be assigned
> to the Reich Commissioner for Labour … the female population
> will be assigned to the Reich Commissioner for Labour … and all
> orphaned children will enter our reception camps.

Units such as SS-Sonderbataillon Dirlewanger – commanded by the
convicted sadist and paedophile Dr Oskar Dirlewanger – carried out
these gruesome orders under the fig-leaf justification of 'anti-partisan'
operations. In one such series of operations in 1943, Dirlewanger's
unit killed 15,000 'bandits' for the loss of ninety-two men killed,
and 'seized 213 work-fit persons for shipment back to the Reich'.
Fewer than 1,500 weapons were recovered during the operations.
The obvious conclusion to be drawn is that the vast majority of the

so-called 'bandits' were just unarmed civilians, and the object of the mission was the seizure of slave labour and plain murder.[135]

Such a press-ganged labour force was never going to do anything more than what was strictly necessary to get by and survive and industrial sabotage soon became a major headache for the Nazis, but forced labour was not the only mistaken policy adopted through short-sighted arrogance and a sense of racial superiority.

The pre-war French aviation industry was one of the most powerful in Europe, having undergone a major modernisation programme in the 1930s, buying in large amounts of the newest American machine-tools and reforming working practices. With the country falling quickly, there was relatively little damage to this industrial infrastructure, but the German response to this gift horse falling into their lap was inspired by Goering's plundering philosophy. Those same machine tools, production lines and industrial plant were boxed up and shipped back to Germany to lie rusting in freight yards. Little was done to capitalise on existing facilities and expertise. Finally, in July 1941, Vichy France did sign the '*Programme aeronautique commun franco-allemand*' which detailed a twenty-four-month, 15-billion-francs agreement whereby the remaining French aviation industry would not be dismantled and taken to Germany but instead would produce engines and planes for Germany, as well as its own small air force, and indeed 11,219 aero engines and 3,606 planes (primarily transport aircraft) were delivered to the Luftwaffe[136] and the renowned Latécoere factory in Toulouse was used to develop the four-engine Ju 488. However, just before D-Day there were still only 95,000 workers engaged in the French aviation sector supplying the Luftwaffe, while 100,000 had been conscripted and sent to Germany. What France ended up producing was a fraction of what the Luftwaffe could have gained had Nazi policy not taken its lead from their own Reichsmarshall's looting philosophy.

An American journalist wrote in 1941, 'Like Americans, the Russians admire size, bigness, large numbers. They take pride in building a vast army of tanks – some of them the largest in the world – armoured cars, airplanes, motorized guns, and every variety of mechanical weapon.'

The influential US defence consultant of the 1970s and 1980s and director of the Allied Interdependence Programme at the Centre for Strategic and International Studies, Thomas A. Callaghan Jnr argued repeatedly at the time for massively increased spending on the military, coining the phrase in 1979 'quantity has a quality all of its own' – this quote, often attributed to Stalin during the war, may not have been his words but it was still a pretty accurate description of the Soviet view of production. Their pre-war air force had more or less been destroyed on the ground or slaughtered in the air in 1941, with much of their remaining inventory being obsolete models pressed back into service from the near-scrapheap in desperation. Lend-Lease was a godsend, supplying 4,355 aircraft when they were most needed as their relocated aviation industry found its new footings in the east of the country.

Not that the VVS was necessarily overawed by the Western imports they received: 'Those Kittyhawks and Aircobras are damned good – not like last year's Tomahawks and Hurricanes – which were pretty useless. But here we mostly use Soviet planes, especially low-flying Shturmoviks which scare the pants off the Germans...'

The Aircobra, also called the Cobra, was quite well liked by its new owners: 'The Germans were going for Murmansk and we were defending the city from the sky. At first the Germans used old models of Me-109s and 110s. The Cobra was superior and we beat them up good ... I removed the wing machine-guns from my Cobra and it was a perfect plane, even in vertical flights. The Germans were no match for us!' [137]

Alas, British Hurricanes were at the other end of the scale and hugely disliked by their Soviet pilots. Major Gheorgy Zimin said of them, 'It was an excellent aircraft for tourist flights above a picturesque country, but unfortunately we were forced to appraise it from another position.'

Meanwhile his fellow flier Lieutenant Igor Kaberov said, 'This aircraft was far from being a hurricane, it was slow to gain height and was not good in a dive.'[138]

In an echo of the air combats over the Kent countryside more than a year previously, Hurricanes once again found themselves up against Bf 110s. Sergey Kurzenkov recalls:

Suddenly our commander called out, 'Watch out! Above ... enemy aircraft!' ... Two of our aircraft emitted smoke ... They lagged behind and made desperate attempts to defend themselves. Kravchenko managed to shoot down a Me-110 with a well-aimed burst of fire from close distance. Two fascists concentrated their attacks on him. Suddenly his aircraft broke apart right in front of our eyes. The Kuban Cossack, Mozerov, was barely able to evade the enemy's attacks. Orlov raced to assist him, but it was too late. Several fascists surrounded him, the engine in his aircraft was hit and the plane turned into a blazing, red torch. Why didn't Mozerov bail out? Had he been killed? No, he was still alive. He pulled up his aircraft for the last time and rammed a Messerschmitt from below.

Minutes later, Kurzenkov was shot down himself. 'I landed my airplane on its belly, and the next moment everything seemed to crash. I can't remember anything else.'[139]

Soviet industry did, however, perform miracles of production, given the circumstances. As the year went on the number of aircraft churned out steadily grew until it almost hit 5,000 in the month of December and overall through the year more planes came off their assembly lines than the Germans'. The Soviets had no scruples about the role of women in the war effort either and they increasingly manned the factories, making up 40 per cent of the aircraft production labour force. Some 8 million were also conscripted into military service of some sort – many as anti-aircraft crews. The famous Stuka Experte Hans-Ulrich Rudel wrote of them: 'In those days we always said, "Today we're going to meet the women's anti-aircraft artillery." There was nothing derogatory about this comment. Everyone knew how accurately they aimed their fire.' The VVS even formed several all-women combat units such as the 585th Fighter Wing, the 587th Dive Bomber Wing and the 588th Night Bomber Wing, even though their male counterparts at first had their doubts about them, as mentioned by one of their number, Mariya Kuznetsova: 'From the very start, the male regimental commander didn't believe we were good pilots.' To test their skills a mock combat was arranged. 'Belyayeva and Budanova flew, and the male squadron commander and the wing commander took off. When Belyayeva was in her cockpit she said, "I will approach their aircraft from the rear," and she did it and won the attack.' From then on the women were accepted as valuable reinforcements.[140]

A German prisoner described to his Soviet captors what they thought of the women pilots. 'When the women started bombing our trenches we had a number of radio nets, and the radio stations on this line warned all the troops, "Attention, attention, the ladies are in the air, stay in your shelters."'

The all-female bombing unit was soon nicknamed the 'Night Witches' by the Germans.

The Nazis had had ample warning of what the Soviet aviation industry was capable of, and it shouldn't have come as any sort of surprise. Back in April 1941, a high-powered German delegation was invited to conduct a week-long tour of Soviet factories to see for themselves – Moscow thought it would act as a sobering reminder to Berlin of what any aggression would be up against. The delegation was headed by the German Air Attaché to Moscow, Colonel Heinrich Aschenbrenner, and contained two leading Luftwaffe engineers as well as representatives from Daimler-Benz, Henschel, Mauser and other major industrial concerns. Hosted by Artem Mikoyan, the Armenian designer of the famous MiG fighter series, they visited plants in Moscow, Rybinsk, Perm and elsewhere in a hectic schedule. At the end of the trip Mikoyan told the delegates rather indelicately, 'You have now seen everything we have and are capable of. Anyone attacking us will be smashed.' Mikoyan should have known what he was talking about; not only was he the brains behind the MiGs but his brother, Anastas, was the People's Commissar for Economic Affairs. Aschenbrenner did indeed make a report to the Air Ministry, pointing out that just one of the aircraft engine factories they had seen was bigger than Germany's six principal engine plants combined. Wilhelmstrasse refused to believe the report; Goering was furious, accusing Aschenbrenner and his team of 'defeatism'; and Beppo Schmid dismissed it all as complete rubbish, declaring the delegation had been the naïve victims of an elaborate Soviet hoax.

CHAPTER 14

The Spring: Transport, Attrition and Restructuring

The end of the winter may have brought a respite for both sides in terms of major operations, but it didn't mean the war got put on hold; far from it. Fighting continued up and down the front, leeching away at the Luftwaffe's strength in particular, and especially at its vital air transport capability.

Always a bit of an unloved orphan in the Luftwaffe, the service had suffered from Goering's disparaging view that it wasn't important as it didn't kill the enemy. As far as he was concerned the only real use for it was as a training ground for multi-engine crews – the majority of whom would go on to bombers afterwards, or at least heavy fighters like the Bf 110. It was a truism in the Luftwaffe that, as with most other modern air forces across the world, the best pilots and crew went to bombers as the level of technical skill and expertise required was far higher and training about twice as long. Multi-engine crews needed to be able to master bad weather flying, exact navigation, and night operations – never popular among many pilots:

'I don't like night flying do you?'
'No, I swear by day flying, I detest night flying, it's that uncertainty, you may get it in the neck any minute, you can't see the enemy.'[141]

Many of the Luftwaffe's better pilots were dismayed at being denied entrance to the Jagdwaffe as one of them, Hansgeorg Bätcher, recalled when he protected the decision to his commanding officer and got this sarcastic response: 'Bätcher, now you are a soldier, and since when have soldiers been free to choose?'

The Luftwaffe's answer was to double up their transport arm with multi-engine training, so the bomber schools were mostly staffed by expert transport instructors and their aircraft, mainly the old, reliable Junkers Ju 52. The flaws in this structure are easy to pick out. As long as losses in transport crews and planes at the front could be adequately replaced, and there was no requirement for a sudden capacity surge, the system could more or less stay in balance, but if casualties rose, or a major concentration of assets was needed, the training schools would be forced to close down as their staff and aircraft were hived off. The folly of relying on the best of all circumstances had already showed itself to be misplaced the previous May when the decision had been made to launch Operation Mercury to capture the Greek island of Crete with an airborne invasion – the first of its kind in military history. Innovative and ultimately successful though it was, Mercury was a major blow for the Luftwaffe's air transport arm, which lost 121 aircraft destroyed and a similar number damaged and 438 trained aircrew killed in the space of a couple of weeks.

The onset of Barbarossa not only ensured there was no time to fill these gaps, it would also dramatically increase the workload for this unglamorous but vital function, as was demonstrated that first winter and spring at Kholm and Demyansk.

Both located in Army Group North's area of operations, Kholm and Demyansk were wholly unremarkable towns that became focal points for some of the bitterest fighting of the Russo-German war so far.

The Kholm Pocket was formed in late January as advancing Soviet forces from the 3rd Shock Army swept up to and around the town. Trapped inside were some 5,500 soldiers under the command of Major General Theodor Scherer. Mainly older reservists from the 218th Infantry Division, they were ordered by Hitler himself to hold out until relieved. The only option to keep them supplied was via the air, even though there wasn't an airstrip in the Pocket and not enough room to build one. Keller's first attempt at resupply was a tragic farce. He ordered that seven transports should land between the lines, and throw their onboard cargo out as they taxied to take off. The hare-brained scheme was a disaster and five of the seven aircraft were destroyed. This meant that everything had to be dropped in and the wounded couldn't be flown out. Relays were established to take in ammunition, food and fuel, with a designated air corridor set up that the Red Army gleefully placed dozens of anti-aircraft guns along to wreak havoc among the lumbering, low-flying transports. Somehow the Pocket held out for 105 days, until finally relieved on 5 May. By that time 1,200 of the defenders had been killed and another 1,500 were lying wounded and sick in makeshift field hospitals.

About 100 miles to the north-east of Kholm, the Demyansk Pocket was a much larger affair. Surrounded by strong Soviet forces from the beginning of February were the 96,000 men of General Count Walter von Brockdorff-Ahlefeldt's II Corps. Refused permission to break out and retreat by Hitler – who wanted to hold on to the position and use it as a jumping-off point for future offensives in the region – the Corps would be sustained by an airlift, much the same as with its much smaller 'brother' at Kholm. The differences were of scale, with the needs of the garrison estimated at 300 tons of supplies a day. Even though there were two rudimentary airstrips in the Pocket to land on, conditions for the transport crews were perilous, with poor weather and heavy Soviet anti-aircraft fire. 'More often than not our planes either could not take-off due to the abnormal temperatures, or if they did manage to get airborne, there was the constant danger of icing over and eventually crashing.'[142]

Colonel Fritz Morzik, the Luftwaffe's Chief of Air Transport, then arrived to take charge of what would become the first mass airlift operation in history. Morzik was an extremely capable officer but found himself not only battling the VVS but also Keller, who was upset at having control of the airlift taken away from him. Keller's petty reaction was to refuse to provide fighter escort to the transports, despite their lack of defensive armament. It was true that some of the aircraft concentrated for the operation had up to three machine guns fitted, but those sent from the training schools usually had none and were to all intents and purposes defenceless. Morzik's solution was not to send in single planes in a conveyor-belt approach, but to organise the lift instead into waves of 20 to 30 aircraft at a time. This not only 'scared off' the VVS fighters – who, according to many accounts, lacked aggression – but also maximised the few hours of daylight available for flying in the winter.

The VVS did make its presence felt though as described by one of the Waffen-SS trapped in the Pocket:

Almost every evening one of the Russians' slow, old-fashioned planes, known as Ratas and nicknamed by us 'sewing machines', somehow managed to take-off and circle our positions, hiding behind low cloud and emptying sackfulls of hand grenades, scrap iron and long nails that would drop like darts, penetrating ones's helmet and going straight through a man's body. Yet through all this the majority of our lads still managed to crack jokes.[143]

The arrival airfields were veritable ants' nests of activity as aircraft landed, unloaded their precious cargoes and took on board wounded or sick men who were flown out for treatment. By the time the Pocket was relieved and a ground supply route established at the beginning of May, Morzik had flown in 65,000 tons of supplies at an average daily delivery load of 302 tons. Some 34,500 men had been flow out and 30,500 flown in as replacements. Even some forage for the Corps' 30,000 horses had gone in, although many of them had ended up in the landsers' 'giddy-up soup', which, nevertheless, was not enough to stave off dire hunger among the men: 'Our encircled unit depended for absolutely everything on air supply ... Everyone was on the verge of starvation ... At times six men had to share one loaf of bread, which had to be chopped into pieces with an axe.'

Seemingly, the operation was a triumph and Morzik and his crews had indeed wrought miracles, but it was far from an unqualified success. 'Even though 100 to 150 aircraft were committed, flying two to three daily missions, the supply situation deteriorated rapidly, leading to symptoms of malnutrition among the exhausted troops. The use of ammunition, particularly by the artillery, had to be limited to a minimum, which resulted in increased losses.'[144]

The cost was also calamitous for the Luftwaffe: 30 per cent of the Luftwaffe's entire transport fleet was lost – 262 aircraft – along with irreplaceable experienced crews. Back in the Reich, multi-engine training had almost stopped and the bomber Staffeln were now being starved of replacement personnel. The air transport arm was decimated and worse was to come later in the year as the failed Stalingrad airlift tolled the death knell for Luftwaffe transport.

Elsewhere along the front the aerial war continued.

The twenty-seven-score Experte Lieutenant Kurt Schade, out flying with his JG 52 comrade Hermann Graf, was shot down over the southern sector that spring.

I'm on fire! I bail out 30 km behind the front! ... I land in one metre deep snow, there are Russian soldiers in the nearby hamlet and so I'm captured. Day and night there are interrogations, including beatings. 'Special treatment' – not quite according to the Hague War Convention! From April 1 1942 I'm locked into the notorious Lubyanka in Moscow, then Oranki POW camp, Yelabuga, Kazan, and Stalingrad ...[145]

His Luftflotte 1 comrade, the hugely popular Captain Franz Eckerle of I/JG 54 Grünherz, fared even worse. Shot down during a dogfight near Turyshkino outside Schlisselburg, Eckerle managed to bail out and according to reports landed safely. Several days later interrogations with captured Red Army men who had been in the area at the time revealed that Eckerle had been captured unhurt by Soviet soldiers who marched him into the nearby forest and lynched him. Horrified as his Gruppe were, many thought he had fallen foul of the 'just back from leave' syndrome that seemed to claim many pilots lucky enough to have got a few days' break back in the Reich. The Luftwaffe (and the VVS) didn't operate a rotation policy like the RAF or American USAAF did, so home leave was rare, but the stories did the rounds of the flight messes that it could be a virtual death sentence if lady luck was against you on your return to the front.

Back down south, another Jagdwaffe Experte who seemed to fall foul of the 'home leave curse' was another friend of Hermann Graf's and a member of JG 52, Lieutenant Gerhard Köppen. He reached seventy-two kills and was summoned back to Hitler's headquarters to receive the Oak Leaves to his Knight's Cross and take a few days leave. He returned, shot down thirteen more Soviets in just six days and then took off on a mission to attack a camouflaged VVS airfield on the northern Crimean coast. The mission had been a failure, but on his return flight Köppen, according to Graf's diary 'engaged a couple of Pe-2 bombers and … was shot down. His plane slid down into the Sea of Azov. His Me-109 had disappeared below the surface after only a few seconds. My men observed as Köppen started swimming for the coast, then they saw Russian artillery open fire on the crash site … Will we ever hear from him again?' Graf was distraught – Köppen was one of his best friends – and the answer to his question would be no. Twelve days before his twenty-fourth birthday, Gerhard Köppen was listed as missing and was never heard from again.

This superstitious fear of leave was typical of how many pilots from both sides felt. A lot had lucky mascots; rabbit's feet, pictures or mementoes like a scarf you had to wear, or a pre-flight ritual that had to be done, as two Luftwaffe men mentioned to each other:

'In our Gruppe there is the superstition that senior sergeants are always shot down.'
'That's funny, we have exactly the same superstition.'[146]

It was just as prevalent in the VVS: 'Did we have superstitions! Some did. For example some pilots wouldn't shave in the evening, and some were scared of the number 13.'[147]

Luck or not, it wasn't just VVS flyers who were successfully bleeding the Luftwaffe; the ordinary soldiers of the Red Army were getting in on the act too. Their immediate response back in the previous summer of firing every weapon they had at any German plane they saw was now more or less official military procedure and it worked, as attested to by Corporal Siegfried Wittmer, a radio operator in a Ju 88 bomber from KG 54:

> We dropped our fragmentation bombs from low level. The Soviet soldiers lay flat on their backs and opened fire against us with rifles, submachine guns and machine-guns. Suddenly our left engine was on fire. My pilot [Lieutenant Johannes Griessler] managed to pull up above a small forest. I jettisoned the canopy. We were down to only 120 feet. After another half mile we bellied in on the snow-covered ground. I destroyed the radio equipment. The aircraft burned up, and armed with a submachine gun we started to walk.

After four days the exhausted Wittmer and his crew reached German lines and safety.[148] Wittmer's Ju 88 was just one of the 1,170 aircraft the Luftwaffe lost in the East in the first five months of 1942.

The VVS weren't having it all their own way, though. Reinforcements were slow to arrive. Lend-Lease and Soviet-manufactured aircraft were enough to drip-feed the front line aviation regiments, but not enough to enable them to build up their strength. The academies were still sending masses of relatively untrained pilots forward, only for them to be clawed out of the air within days by the Luftwaffe's Experten, or lost to the accidents that their inexperience made them prone to. A report from a VVS war diary at the time reads as follows: 'We engaged a large formation of German fighters, approximately forty. Our formation disintegrated during the course of the combat. The battle was conducted by single planes, each against three or four enemy aircraft.' Only a single VVS fighter survived the encounter undamaged.

Lieutenant Mikhail Satalkin, a Tomahawk fighter pilot, wrote in his diary in January:

> Today I lost three comrades; Lieutenant Golovach was forced to return from a reconnaissance mission due to engine malfunction. But he wasn't able to reach the airfield and crashed into a dense forest. The engine was separated from the fuselage and his dead body was recovered from the burnt-out wreck. Lieutenant Vasiliy Kharitonov had to make a forced landing, but his aircraft stood on its nose. He was sent to the hospital. In the evening Lieutenant Ilya Shishkan crashed in his aircraft, suffered a jaw fracture, and was also hospitalized.[149]

During this period, as the VVS sought to husband its resources as much as possible, the Luftwaffe's top flying killers were just as determined as ever to keep their scores climbing. The Experten had become used to scoring more or less at will in skies packed full with poorly trained opponents, but now they were being starved of targets as the VVS drastically reduced the number of sorties they were flying and their frustration at this lack of kill oppurtunities was growing. Many tried fairly unorthodox ways of continuing to build their tallies, none more so than Hermann Graf. Tall for a fighter pilot, Graf was the goalkeeper for the leading Luftwaffe football team, *Die Roten Jäger* (the Red Hunters), whose coach, Sepp Herberger, would go on after the war to hold the same post with the post-war West German team.

Graf, desperate to coax the unwilling VVS into the air to be slaughtered, came up with an idea.

> One day we tried something that was rather uncommon. We made up a parcel with chocolate and cigarettes, tied it to a small parachute, added an invitation to the Russians, and dropped it over the Russian fighter airfield south of Rostov. It read: 'Comrades from the other side, we invite you to a dogfight over the Don delta south of Rostov tomorrow, Wednesday, at 1200 hours, altitude 4,000 meters. We guarantee that we will come with only eight machines, you can bring as many as you like! Horrido! In sincere friendship, your enemy.' However we waited in vain.[150]

Graf, later to become the first fighter pilot in history to reach the 200 kill mark, was showered with medals, awards and promotions for his exploits in the air, as were all the Experten. Successful VVS aces were also honoured, although these men were not always popular with their fellow pilots. In March a VVS force of DB-3F bombers with an I-16 escort were despatched to hit the Bf 109 air strip at Sarabuz near the Kerch Peninsula. The attack was a success with two Bf 109s caught on the ground and destroyed. Lieutenant Anton 'Toni' Hackl was airborne at the time with seven other Bf 109s from his 5/JG 77 and they were vectored in to intercept the returning flight. Lieutenant Anatoliy Ivanov, one of the I-16 pilots, recounted how the Germans were twice beaten off before the escorts saw one Messerschmitt flying away, seemingly in trouble: 'We could see one of the German fighters disengaged in a steep dive, but there were no signs it had been damaged, neither smoke nor flames. Previously we had seen how the Germans had used this method to trick our fighters into leaving their escort task, but normally we remained with the bombers and paid it no attention.'

However, this time a VVS pilot, Lieutenant Viktor Radkevich, could not resist the temptation and 'completely ignoring his task as wingman for our commander, he left our formation'.

What happened next was nothing less than bizarre. Radkevich pounced on the Bf 109 and shot it down. It belly-landed and he landed next to it, jumping out of his cockpit and chasing after the unhurt German pilot, who was running away. Radkevich takes up the story: 'I fired several shots into the air, but the German officer did not halt. Finally, after a pursuit of two miles, I managed to overtake him, and I commanded "Hands up!" Several soldiers who had heard my shots came running and I handed over the captured air pirate to them.' Radkevich had scored his first kill, and had captured Lieutenant Heinz Froese, one of Toni Hackl's most promising young pilots. However, back in the air, Ivanov was furious.

> Radkevich's action left only five of us against seven fascist fighters, and although he was without his wingman's cover, Terpugov [Captain Lev Terpugov, the commander Radkevich was tasked to cover] continued to lead us in combat. The Germans quickly regrouped for a new attack and came in against the bombers from the rear in pairs. As soon as they noted Terpugov was without his wingman they immediately hurled themselves against him.

In the ensuing dogfight four of the bombers were shot down, three by Toni Hackl himself. As Ivanov bitterly noted, 'Radkevich's victory cost us dearly!'[151]

The whole scoring system – so beloved by the Luftwaffe Experten in particular – could be controversial and there was always the issue of over-claiming. For example, on 26 March 1942 in the Ukraine over the Slavyansk area, there were two separate German formations in the air: a lone Ju 88 reconnaissance plane and six Stukas escorted by a flight of twelve Bf 109s from Herbert Ihlefeld's I/JG 77. Seven Yak-1s from 296 IAP, led by Captain Boris Yeryomin, saw the latter and attacked.

> We attacked the bombers and ripped their formation apart, and then I made a head-on attack on the Messers. I managed to hit one of the fighters on my first pass, and it fell to the ground like a flaming torch. Almost simultaneously Lieutenant Aleksey Salomatin set a second Messer burning – it went down not far from the first – and Lieutenant Aleksandr Martynov shot down a third, while a fourth was set on fire by Sergeant Dmitriy Korol.

The Soviets also claimed a Stuka too. However, according to I/JG 77 records no losses were filed that day at all. Not that the Germans weren't just as bad. They claimed a single Yak destroyed that day but VVS records show it was only hit in the radiator and was successfully nursed back to base by its pilot and quickly repaired. Elsewhere, in June, the pilots of JG 5 in the far north filed 127 claims that month, with their opposite numbers in the VVS reporting losses of just fifty-six, including those lost to the Finns. The VVS pilots in turn claimed they'd shot down thirty-four German fighters that same month, while JG 5 actually reported the loss of just two Bf 109s and a single Bf 110. Anomalies like this weren't confined to the Eastern Front, nor to just the VVS or the Luftwaffe; all air forces were prone to it. Over in the West, during the Battle of the Bulge in the Ardennes during the winter of 1944/45, an official report from General Omar Bradley's 12th Army Group into US air force kill claims for German panzers stated that, 'It is obvious that Air Corps claims must be exaggerated, otherwise the Germans would be without any tanks at all, whereas our reconnaissance indicates plenty of them.'[152] A British after-action investigation into the same battle concluded rather more prosaically, 'The three Allied tactical air forces claimed the destruction of a total of 413 enemy armoured vehicles, but a subsequent ground check carried out confirms this figure is at least ten times too large.'

The Shturmovik pilot, and later major general of the VVS, Alexander E. Shvarev, denied over-claiming was an issue; 'Were there cases of cheating? Devil knows! We didn't have it in our regiment. Why? Because we were good friends. If someone tried to brag or lie he would immediately be reminded of his place. Everyone understood we had to work as a team.'

In reality it was incredibly difficult for any pilot to accurately record what happened in an aerial combat, with aircraft tumbling, diving and banking everywhere at incredibly high speed. A pilot might shoot at an enemy plane and then see it burst into flame without seeing the two or three other fighters also firing at it, while an aircraft that trailed smoke and lost height might look like a kill but was only damaged and made it home to fight another day. All of these circumstances sometimes made scoring subjective and open to error, but the loss reports filed by both the VVS and the Luftwaffe themselves were horrendous enough.

As the VVS husbanded its strength in early 1942, it also underwent a major restructuring.

First up was the old long-range strategic bomber force, the DBA, which had suffered near-annihilation in 1941. A young and energetic VVS major general with dark, movie-star good looks, Aleksandr

Yevgeniyevich Golovanov was promoted to head up the redesignated ADD (*Aviatsiya dal'nego deystviya* – Long-Range Aviation) arm, which would now comprise some eight Air Divisions, equipped primarily with a total of 356 Il-4s (also called DB-3Fs).

Golovanov threw himself into his new role, so impressing Stalin that the Soviet dictator promptly offered him the job of VVS commander-in-chief, the previous occupant – Pavel Zhigarev – having been swiftly shuffled off to command the VVS in the Far East for what Stalin perceived to be the air force's failings during the winter. Golovanov hesitated to accept, wary perhaps of what had happened to the last few incumbents of his new post. As far as Stalin was concerned, Golovanov's hesitation was enough to disqualify him from the running and instead he turned to the VVS northern front commander, Lieutenant General Aleksandr Novikov. He was an inspired choice. Short, with a youthful appearance that belied his forty-one years, Novikov had started life as an infantryman and so understood what air power meant to the footslogger down on the ground. He was also a graduate of the prestigious Frunze Academy and an accomplished staff officer with a clear vision of where the VVS needed to go to help win the war. Novikov had watched with admiration how the flexibility of the Luftwaffe's command and control structure allowed it to shift and concentrate forces on the main points of focus whenever needed and that was what he wanted to mirror in his own reorganisation of the VVS. The old Front Air Forces and Army Air units that were tied to separate Army commands were dissolved and all units centralised into eight brand-new Air Armies (*Vozdushnye Armii* – VA); 1 VA (the old Western Front), 2 VA (old Bryansk Front), 3 VA (old Kalinin Front), 4 VA (old Southern Front), 5 VA (old North Caucasus Front), 6 VA (old North-western Front), 7 VA (old Karelian Front) and 8 VA (old Southwestern Front). This was the first consolidation of a force that by the end of the year would number over a dozen Air Armies as the VVS grew in size and stature.

In the next tier down in the front-line air regiments, overall establishment was reduced from sixty to thirty aircraft to give commanders the chance to learn the ropes with smaller formations that were easier to handle. The same was done in the army, with the creation of 170 rifle brigades with a complement of 4,000 men each, to be used in effect as 'on the job training' for new leaders.

Stalin also continued his drive to turn the war into one of national, Russian survival, instituting medals and awards named after heroes of Russia's Tsarist past: Alexander Nevsky, marshals Suvorov and Kutuzov – victors against the Teutonic Knights, Ottomans and Napoleon. Symbols

Above left: 1. Hermann Graf (left) and the legendary aircraft designer Willi Messerschmitt. Graf, a former blacksmith's apprentice and local authority clerk, became the first ever pilot in history to achieve 200 kills. He was transferred to Home Defence, flying with JG 11 against the formidable Viermots. He survived the war with a final tally of 212 kills.

Above right: 2. The Austrian Experte Walter 'Nowy' Nowotny on 19 October 1943, on the occasion of being awarded the Diamonds to his Knight's Cross. Nowotny was killed in action flying an Me 262 jet fighter on 8 October 1944. By then his score was 258, of which 255 were from his time with JG 54 in the East.

Below: 3. Two of the Jagdwaffe's finest Experten chatting with colleagues. In the centre is the third-highest-scoring flyer of all time, Günther Rall, and on his left is Walter 'Graf Punski' Krupinski, who ended the war on 197 victories. This photo was taken on 29 August 1943 after Rall shot down his 200th victim.

Top: 4. Three Luftwaffe fighter aces, from left to right: Gerhard Barkhorn, 301 kills, second only to Erich Hartmann; Wilhelm Batz, 237 kills; and lastly Otto Fönnekold. Fönnekold reached 136 kills before being shot down and killed by US fighters on 31 August 1944.

Left: 5. Stalingrad, the afternoon of 23 August 1942. In the foreground, binoculars covering his face, is Wolfram von Richthofen, commander of Luftflotte IV. Behind and above him with the spectacles is the commander of 16th Panzer Division, Hans-Valentin Hube. It was direct co-operation like this that helped make Von Richthofen such a superb provider of close air support.

Above left: 6. Barbarossa – summer of 1941. On the banks of the River Desna, men of the German 197th Infantry Division advance eastwards past dejected Soviet prisoners. Intermingled with the German infantry men are Soviet 'Hiwis', or 'willing helpers' – ex-prisoners carrying ammunition and supplies.

Above right: 7. A clearly uncomfortable Otto Kittel posing for the camera in April 1944, on the occasion of being awarded the Oak Leaves to his Knight's Cross. Kittel scored 267 kills before being shot down and killed over Courland on 14 February 1945.

Below: 8. The Germans capture the town of Slutsk in late June 1941, with Heinkel He 111s bombing Soviet fuel dumps and providing close air support to the advancing panzers.

9. The Soviets mobilised everyone for their war economy, including children, thousands of whom worked in the aviation industry.

10. Germany was utterly devastated by the Anglo-American bombing offensive. This is Hamburg after the firestorm raids of July 1943.

11. VVS fighter pilot Alexander F. Khaila. Khaila survived the war, suffering terrible burns when shot down in April 1945. He flew 149 sorties, took part in thirty-nine dogfights and scored nine individual and five shared victories. Despite this he was treated with suspicion by the Soviet authorities for being an ex-POW.

12. VVS pilot Vitaly I. Klimenko. Klimenko was one of the few VVS pilots to survive the surprise Luftwaffe attacks on the first morning of Barbarossa, get airborne and fight back. On landing he was almost arrested for his courage by a paranoid senior officer who thought he might have provoked the Germans.

13. VVS pilot Alexander E. Shvarev. Made a Hero of the Soviet Union for his wartime exploits, Shvarev went on to reach the rank of major general after the war. He passed away in 2006 at the age of ninety-two.

14. A squadron of Yak-9 fighters lined up on a VVS airfield. The Yak-9 was produced in greater numbers than any other Soviet fighter of the war.

15. The commander of the 19th GIAP (Fighter) Regiment, Georgy I. Reifschneider, poses in front of his Lend-Lease supplied Aircrobra in 1942.

Above left: 16. A Soviet airfield under bombardment. What makes this photo interesting is the fact that it was taken by Field Marshall 'Smiling Albert' Kesselring from his observation plane.

Above right: 17. The first chief of the Luftwaffe General Staff, Walter Wever. Wever was a strong advocate of the need to develop a long-range bomber. When he died in a flying accident in 1935, so did the concept of the 'Ural bomber'.

Below: 18. 'Beppo' Schmid (centre), the Luftwaffe's Head of Intelligence, was a conspicuous failure in his crucial role.

Top Left: 19. On the right is Field Marshall Erhard Milch. A consistently controversial figure, he was responsible for much of Nazi Germany's increased aircraft production in the latter half of the war before incurring Hitler's wrath over the Me 262 programme. To his right is Field Marshall Walter von Reichenau.

Left: 20. Wolfram Freiherr von Richthofen in 1941 whilst commanding Fliegerkorps VIII. He would eventually die from a brain tumour on 12 July 1945.

Below: 21. The command staff of Luftflotte 4 in 1941. Fourth from the right in a white tunic is the air fleet's commander, the Austrian Alexander Löhr. The tall thin officer second from the right is the very capable Kurt Pflugbeil who commanded Fliegerkorps IV. Löhr would be executed by the Yugoslavs after the war for war crimes. Pflugbeil survived the war and spent nine years in Soviet captivity.

Above: 22. On the left is Ernst Udet, a hugely successful fighter ace in the First World War and a total disaster as head of the Luftwaffe's aircraft production programme. Next to him is Werner Mölders, who was killed in a flying accident en route to Udet's funeral.

Below left: 23. Hans Jeschonnek. As Chief of the Luftwaffe General Staff he failed to stand up to either Goering or Hitler, or indeed build up the Luftwaffe's strength in the East. He committed suicide in August 1943.

Below right: 24. Günther Korten. A successful staff officer, Korten would go on to succeed Hans Jeschonnek as Chief of the Luftwaffe General Staff. He died from injuries suffered during the failed assassination attempt on Hitler in July 1944.

25. The Ostheer is often portrayed as a technologically advanced force; in reality it was a mainly horse-drawn and foot-born force that had to struggle along Soviet Russia's inadequate road network.

26. The famous Avro Lancaster, the mainstay of the RAF's night bomber force from 1943 onwards. As the Lancasters pounded Germany the Luftwaffe had no choice but to strip pilots and aircraft from the east to try and protect the Fatherland.

27. The Allies decision to attack Nazi Germany's aircraft production plants was a fateful one that hugely impacted the Luftwaffe's ability to compete with the growing VVS. This picture was taken from one of the USAAF's 100-strong B-17 force which destroyed the Focke-Wulf factory at Marienburg on 9 October 1943.

28. By the winter of 1942 the Luftwaffe had learned its lessons about coping with the harsh Russian winter. This Stuka has parked with its engine inside a protective hut to keep it warm.

29. When the Luftwaffe launched Barbarossa it faced no fewer than 1,549 of these obsolete I-153 biplane fighters, most of which they destroyed in the first few months of the campaign.

30. Fighter pilots from JG 5 based up in the Arctic North flying over Murmansk and Finland. From left to right: Hans Döbrich, the Experten Theo Weissenberger, Heinrich Erler, Rudolf 'Rudi' Müller, and on the far right is Albert Brunner. Erler was still flying with Weissenberger in April 1945 when he was killed ramming an American B-24 Liberator bomber over Germany. His last radio message was, 'Theo, Heinrich here. Have just shot down two bombers. No more ammunition. I'm going to ram. Auf Wiedersehen, see you in Valhalla.'

31. Hans-Ulrich Rudel's Stuka armed with underslung 37 mm tank-killing cannon.

32. The USAAF's extremely capable commander in Europe, Carl 'Tooey' Spaatz. Spaatz was the architect of the critical bombing offensive against the Third Reich's oil industry, which deprived the Luftwaffe of the fuel it needed to fly and fight.

33. A battery of 105 mm guns opens up against an RAF night raid. The Luftwaffe's flak arm absorbed vast amounts of scarce resources which perhaps could have been used to better effect with the night-fighter arm.

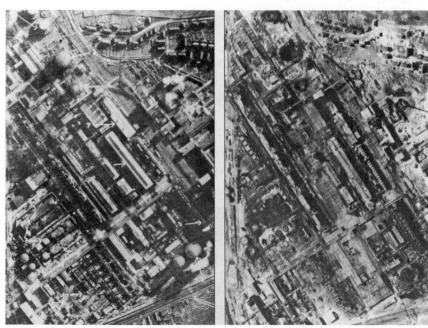

34. These aerial photos were taken before (left) and after (right) the bombing raids of June 1944 on the Gelsenkirchen synthetic oil production plant. The impact was clearly devastating.

Above left: 35. A squadron of Focke-Wulf Fw 190s lined up on their airfield. Heavily armed and armoured, the 190 increasingly took over from the Me 109 as the Jagdwaffe's mainstay fighter in the East from 1943 onwards.

Above right: 36. An Me 109 pilot on the Eastern Front paints another victory mark on his tail fin.

Below: 37. The German answer to the British Lancaster and American B-17: the Heinkel He 177 Greif. The He 177 was a disaster and was never produced in any numbers. This one was captured and is shown in British markings.

Above: 38. Hermann Goering (centre) talks to two of his most talented fighter commanders: Werner Mölders on the left and Adolf Galland on the right. Galland fell out with Goering later in the war as he saw his beloved Jagdwaffe ground into dust.

Below: 39. Werner Mölders on the Eastern Front with two of the Jagdwaffe's best unit leaders. On the left is JG 54's Johannes 'Hannes' Trautloft, and on the right is JG 3's Günther Lützow; both would be key players in the 'Fighter Pilot Mutiny' against Goering.

40. The most successful fighter ace of all time, Erich Hartmann (standing), with another Experte, Josef Priller, seated on the left.

41. The impact of the infamous Russian rasputitsa on a Stuka field. With conditions like these operational readiness rates took a hammering.

Right: 42. An excellent shot of a Ju 87 Stuka just as it releases a bomb on a target on the Eastern Front.

Bottom Left: 43. The VVS made extensive use of female personnel, including this armourer who is loading 20-mm ammunition belts into an La-5's twin nose-mounted cannon.

Bottom Right: 44. Two members of the famed 588th 'Night Witches' Regiment pose in front of their U-2 light bomber. The Regiment won twenty-three Hero of the Soviet Union awards during the war.

Above: 45. The Heinkel He 111 was the workhorse of the Luftwaffe bomber arm during the war. This one has managed to return to base in the East with extensive damage to its right wing.

Below: 46. The final victory of the VVS! Il-2 Shturmoviks fly unchallenged over the ruins of Berlin.

Above: 47. This propaganda shot, taken as the survivors of the Sixth Army surrendered at the end of January 1943, was intended to show the chasm between the well-fed, well-equipped Red Army and the terrible state of their German opponents – in reality in was pretty close to the truth.

Below: 48. The Germans forced Soviet POWs to load and unload the Ju 52s arriving at Stalingrad's Gumrak airfield during the battle.

Above: 49. This photo, taken in January 1942 at the height of the Red Army's winter offensive, shows advancing Soviet troops well-equipped for the harsh Russian winter.

Below left: 50. In contrast to Soviet troops kitted out in warm felt boots and white camouflage smocks, these miserable Germans, captured during the Soviet winter offensive of 1941, are clearly totally unprepared for the rigours of a Russian winter.

Below right: 51. During the Stalingrad airlift the Luftwaffe ground crew used heating kits to enable the frozen engines of the Ju 52 transports to start up.

Above: 52. A Ju 87 Stuka attacks Soviet positions on the Volga River just north of Stalingrad during Case Blue.

Below: 53. German troops relax amongst the rubble of the Maxim Gorky Fort at Sevastopol, which had been bombed into submission by massive Luftwaffe assaults.

54. Although better than the fighters the VVS faced the Luftwaffe with in 1941, the MiG-3 fighter was difficult to handle and proved itself inferior to the German Me 190 and Fw 190.

55. Nazi Germany's allies made contributions to the air war on the Eastern Front. This is a Dornier Do 17 manned by Croatian personnel in the winter of 1941/42. The Croats were withdrawn home in January 1942 after suffering heavy losses.

56. On this MiG-3 airfield in the far north the Soviet ground crews used local reindeer as the favoured form of transport.

57. The Me 109 was the mainstay of the Jagdwaffe on the Eastern Front for much of the war. This one has been shot down and is being guarded by the Red Army prior to investigation.

58. As the war ground on the VVS became more and more adept at striking back at the Ostheer. This German supply column has been hit near Voronezh by Shturmoviks during the fighting in 1943.

59. By the summer of 1944 the Germans had lost air superiority over the Eastern Front. As the Soviets launched their Bagration offensive the Ostheer became more and more reliant for air cover on flak guns like these 37 mm-equipped half-tracks.

Above: 60. One of Goering's many awful decisions during the war was the establishment of the Luftwaffe Field Divisions made up of underemployed ground crew and staff. These men of the 6th Luftwaffe Field Division were based near Vitebsk in the summer of 1944 and were utterly crushed by the Soviet's Bagration offensive.

Below left: 61. As the Ostheer retreated ever backwards from the autumn of 1943 the Ju 52 transports became vital to airlift out wounded personnel. Here, a flight engineer watches over injured men being taken out of the Cherkassy Pocket in January 1944.

Below right: 62. The JG 77 fourteen-kill German fighter pilot Horst Bochmann is interrogated by Soviet intelligence officers after being shot down on 1 August 1941.

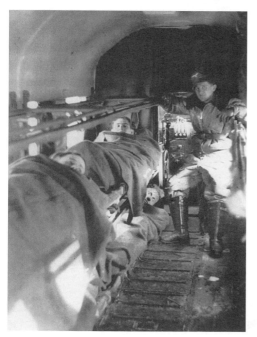

Above left: 63. As Case Blue rolls across the southern Soviet steppe in the summer of 1942 this picture gives some impression of the endless nature of the 'green ocean' and the importance of air power as an Me 110 flies over a German armoured column.

Above right: 64. In stark contrast to the war economies of Great Britain and the Soviet Union, where women were encouraged to play a full role in the war effort, in Germany the government attempted to shield women from the realities of war as this photo spread from the wartime Signal Magazine shows.

Below: 65. A German aircraft production line. Great Britain, the United States and the Soviet Union were soon churning out more aircraft between them than the Third Reich could ever produce.

Top Left: 66. Captain
Anatoly Kuznetsov of
the Red Fleet's 4th GIAP
(Fighter) Regiment is
readied for a sortie with
his I-16 at Vystav airfield
in the summer of 1942.

Left: 67. The Romanian
Stuka pilot Andrei Tudor
is shown here posing in
front of an Me 109 on
the Eastern Front in the
summer of 1941.

Below: 68. An Me 109 of
JG 3 Udet on its Russian
grass airfield in the
summer of 1942.

Top: 69. A Hungarian 'Heja' fighter on an airfield in the Soviet Union.

Middle: 70. These Ju 88s of KG 51 Edelweiss were originally designed as ultra-fast bombers but lost much of their technological edge after Ernst Udet insisted they have dive-bomber capability built in.

Bottom: 71. German soldiers pose on the wreck of an Il-2 Shturmovik in the summer of 1941.

Above: 72. From left to right: Johann Fieber (Missing in Action 30 May 1943), Willi Buchner (Missing in Action 10 August 1942), Albin Wolf (Killed in Action 2 April 1944), Heinz Wernicke (Killed in Action 27 December 1944), Hermann Schleinhege, Karl Sattig (Killed in Action 10 August 1942), Hans Beisswenger (Missing in Action 6 March 1943), Karl Klopp (Missing in Action 3 September 1942), Johannes Runge (Missing in Action 22 May 1943) and Unteroffizier Nickel – such was the fate of the eastern Jagdwaffe.

Below: 73. The pilots of the VVS's 299 ShAP (ground-attack) squadron pose in front of one of their Il-2 Shturmoviks.

Top: 74. Soviet industrial production rocketed from the middle of 1942 onwards. Here a factory relocated east is churning out Il-2 Shturmoviks.

Right: 75. These aircraft wings are stacked in an American production plant ready to be shipped across the Atlantic.

Bottom Right: 76. The Battle of Britain. Luftwaffe casualties were extremely high and deprived the Germans of the time they needed to build their forces in preparation for Barbarossa.

Above: 77. Adolf Hitler with some of his original Luftwaffe Field Marshals. From left to right Erhard Milch, Hugo Sperrle, Adolf Hitler, Hermann Goering and Albert Kesselring.

Below left: 78. A Soviet propaganda poster highlighting the importance of industrial production in defeating the Nazis.

Below right: 79. A German poster extolling National Air Day in 1937. The Nazis put an enormous effort into glorifying air power.

Above: 80. Major Vasiliy Naydenko flew Western-supplied Curtiss P-40s for 126 IAP (Fighter) until a dogfight against Me 109s in September 1942 saw him shot down and badly injured. Despite losing a leg Naydenko returned to combat duty and ended the war with ten personal and twenty-nine shared kills.

Right: 81. Blitzkrieg in the West, 1940; the aftermath of a Luftwaffe air strike on a French supply column.

Below: 82. On the right is the Soviet fighter pilot and renowned ace Boris Safonov. He is talking to two RAF flight sergeants from No. 151 Hurricane Wing.

Above: 83. The Luftwaffe was especially adept at hitting enemy ground targets. Here, a Soviet railway station burns after a German air raid.

Below: 84. Ju 87 Stukas – the Luftwaffe's formidable 'flying artillery'.

of Russia's military past were also brought back, including the creation of new Guards units for those formations that distinguished themselves in action, and the arch-dictator even allowed a modest revival of the hitherto suppressed Orthodox Church. He would even go as far as ending the dual-command structure in the military with the role of the politruk – the infamous commissar – downgraded to one of political education only rather than practical military decision making. As one soldier wryly remarked, 'They've invented the Orders of Kutuzov and Suvorov, now they should also have medals of St Nicholas and St George, and that'll be the end of the Soviet Union.'[153]

As the Soviets planned for the long term, the Germans did pretty much the opposite.

For the Luftwaffe, and the Germans in the East in general, and despite all the evidence to the contrary, there was a belief that just one more push, just one more victory, would be enough and they would win the war. The Soviets were beginning to not only understand this Nazi mentality but also how to use it to their advantage.

> The strategy of the Russians was to withdraw but never to stop fighting and thus always keep the Nazis busy ... They never allowed the Germans – including the Luftwaffe – time for a breathing spell, let alone a long rest. They forced upon the Nazis the 'war of permanency' ... a wound was opened over and over again, never allowed to close, and the life-blood of the body of the Luftwaffe dripped away, much more blood than it could afford to lose.[154]

This life-blood was not only aircraft rolling off the production lines, it was the pilots and crew to man them and here again the Nazis' short-termism was doing real damage to the Luftwaffe.

Back in 1939, Nazi Germany only had five official flight schools: three for bombers, and one each for naval aviation and fighters. The system was comprehensive and took a year to train a fighter pilot and twice as long for a multi-engine bomber aviator. The products of the schools would go on to become some of the finest military pilots the world has ever seen, men who in spite of their relatively small numbers would dominate the skies of the Second World War for a considerable time. The problem was that there were only a few of them. Jeschonnek's objection to Milch's fighter production plan might seem absurd given the manpower drains the Luftwaffe was subject to, but he spoke the literal truth: the Luftwaffe simply wasn't turning out enough pilots to crew more planes. In fact, in 1942 only 1,666 fighter pilots graduated from flight school and joined their units, though each arrived with a whopping 210 hours of flight time already racked up. This wasn't enough to replace the growing losses in the east, the North African desert and Mediterranean and against the British Isles. Either a huge surge was needed in the number of trainee pilots, or the teaching curriculum had to be reduced – preferably both.

Unfortunately for the Luftwaffe, training was not seen as a top priority and both Jeschonnek and Milch never got to grips with it. Its only champion at a senior level in the service was the tall, Prussian ex-cavalryman Hans-Georg von Seidel. The Luftwaffe's Quartermaster General since 1938, von Seidel was in many ways an unlikely cheerleader for training, but it was a cause he took up with real conviction, hectoring Jeschonnek about it whenever they met. The issue was that they barely ever met, working in buildings hundreds of miles apart and having a relationship that one subordinate politely described as 'antagonistic'. Given their positions, the two men should have been working hand in glove but instead they detested the very sight of each other. Von Seidel even requested a transfer on no fewer than five separate occasions to get away from his prickly boss, but each time it was refused. So when von Seidel asked Jeschonnek for more fuel for training, his reply was blunt: 'First we've got to beat Russia, then we can start training.' As for Milch, the supposed arch-organiser, when he was interrogated after the war and asked about training, his response was one definitely born with the benefit of hindsight: 'The Luftwaffe training programme, and with it the Luftwaffe itself, was throttled to death by the gasoline shortage.'

With limited front-line strength and no chance of huge reinforcements from the factories and flying schools of the Reich, Goering's Luftwaffe had few real options for 1942. Perhaps the two with the greatest possibilities were: firstly, an all-out bombing offensive on the Soviet Union's economic chokepoints to try and strangle at birth their growing industrial might; and secondly, a shift along the whole front to a defensive posture to jealously husband their resources, with a view to a massive concentration for the decisive summer campaign. Both options would also entail a ruthless stripping of strength from secondary theatres in the Mediterranean and the Channel to feed the east. The former was a stretch, given the total lack of a strategic bomber force in the Luftwaffe, even if the vast majority of the existing two-engine bomber fleet were massed together. So, on balance, it was probably the latter approach that would provide the biggest possibility of success – be boring, keep sorties and casualties low, maximise serviceability and build up spares, repair facilities and logistical support.

The option actually adopted by the Luftwaffe, as the crucial year of 1942 got going, was none of the above.

With a total and utter disregard for not only the long term but also the basic military principles of concentration of force and maintenance of the main aim, the Nazis' air force decided to scatter-gun and do a little bit of everything. The folly of this path would be laid bare over the skies of Stalingrad that winter and across the entire frontline the following year.

CHAPTER 15

Convoys, Crimea and Kharkov

While the north of the Eastern Front was a relative backwater overall, the far north held the Lend-Lease lifeline that was pumping desperately needed supplies and materiel into the body of the Soviet military. The Western Allies had very few possible routes to reach the Soviets, and by far the best available was by sea north of Great Britain, turning north-east before Iceland, through the Norwegian Sea and heading into the Arctic and the Barents Sea to reach harbour at Murmansk or even Archangel. It was a hazardous route at the best of times and one that was extremely vulnerable to an air and sea blockade that, if successful, could starve the Soviets of the equipment they needed to stay in the war.

With this in mind the Luftwaffe in the far north decided to try and sever the convoy route. There was, however, little in the way of 'grand strategy' about Luftflotte 5's offensive against the convoys in the late spring; it was more of a reaction to events as they unfolded – much as with most of the Luftwaffe's operations in the east in the first half of the year. The German commander, the congenial fifty-one-year-old Pomeranian Hans-Jürgen Stumpff, was a solid staff officer and well-liked among peers and subordinates, but a lightning rod of charisma and brilliant tactician he was not – after all there was a reason he was given Luftflotte 5 in the far-off north. He had already tried to attack shipping, but it had been small scale and piecemeal. In turn, the VVS strategy was to neutralise the Luftwaffe by attacking its air bases and keeping it grounded. The usual reconnaissance and tit-for-tat sorties rumbled on, the Luftwaffe maintaining a slight edge through the endeavours of its Experten, who wrought havoc among their opponents.

During April 1942 a specially camouflaged Me-109 appeared on the fascist side. This fighter, painted in stripes, always flew above the main formation of patrolling fighters. This German pilot and his wingman never took part in group combats. They only jumped pilots that were 'dreaming' and had strayed from the others. We started hunting him, but the fascist ace wasn't easy to catch.

Lieutenant Sergey Kurzenkov was writing about Rudolf 'Rudi' Müller, a Knight's Cross winner and, along with Heinrich Ehrler and Theodor Weissenberger, one of JG 5's leading Experten in the region. Facing Müller and his comrades was the VVS's own picture-postcard hero, Lieutenant Colonel Boris Safonov. Safonov was a celebrated pilot and newsreel favourite, tall, handsome, with a winning demeanour and self-deprecating smile. A Hero of the Soviet Union twice over, he flew Lend-Lease Kittyhawks and his personal score was already in double figures by the time of the 1942 Luftwaffe offensive.

With the coming of spring and the retreat of the Arctic ice, the convoys began in earnest. First up was PQ 12 in early March, but bad weather and poor coordination hampered Stumpff's plans and not a single ship was sunk.

What was needed by the Germans was a joint air and sea operation, with waves of bombers and torpedo planes, acting in concert with U-boats and even surface vessels if possible. The follow-on convoy – PQ 13 – didn't come up against that sort of assault, but this time the Germans did manage a slightly better fist of it, the ubiquitous Ju 88s sinking two ships, while U-boats sent another three to the bottom.

For the crewmen of the British Merchant Navy and their allies from a dozen other nations, these were perilous times. Their ships were transports, not designed to defend themselves with speed, evasive manoeuvres, or armament – often the tramp steamers they manned had nothing more deadly than a single old drum-fed Lewis gun bolted onto a handrail. As for the conditions, the pack-ice may have been retreating, but the weather was still extreme, with freezing air temperatures day and night and sea water so cold that it was a death sentence for any sailor unfortunate to be in it for anything more than a minute or two at most. In fact, conditions were so poor that PQ 14 didn't even get to battle its way through Luftwaffe attacks – the fog was so dense that the convoy was unable to avoid armadas of floating icebergs that damaged sixteen of the twenty-four transports, forcing them to turn back to Iceland for repairs and better weather. One unlucky ship was found by a lone U-boat and sunk, but it was the only casualty.

Understandably, the Soviets were furious. They needed masses of supplies and they needed them quickly. The British Admiralty responded with PQ 15, a large convoy that set sail in May. Stumpff ordered an all-out effort, but an attack on the 16th was intercepted by the VVS.

We intercepted a group of Germans, about twelve ju-88s and the same number of fighters. The Fritzies immediately turned away and we followed without attacking. Then they doubled back, but we weren't going to let them reach Murmansk, so they made another loop and again we followed. This manoeuvre was repeated two or three times. Eventually we radioed to Kutakhov [the much-decorated Pavel Stepanovich Kutakhov would become the commander-in-chief of Soviet Air Forces in 1969]: 'Come on, what are you waiting for? Attack!' We were impatient for battle, even though outnumbered, the Germans would never have attacked in such a situation. And so Kutakhov attacked and was the first to get shot down. But he managed to bail out and I saw his gangling figure dangling from a parachute. Naturally I was worried. The German pilots were assholes – those who say they were chivalrous knights are mistaken – they'd finish off parachutists with a few extra bursts. And sure enough, as Kutakhov descended the Germans began firing at him.[155]

Another major attack by the Ju 88s of KG 30 on the 17th also failed, with only three ships sunk in total, the vast majority of bombs exploding harmlessly in the sea.

Ten days later it was the turn of PQ 16 to face the expected German onslaught. The tension onboard the ships can only be imagined: would they get through unscathed; what was waiting for them? Their luck ran out south-east of Barents Island with the appearance overhead of no fewer than 101 Ju 88s. This was a major effort by the Luftwaffe and the pilots pressed home their attacks, determined to send the whole convoy to the bottom of the sea. Wave after wave flew in, bombs raining down, and five merchantmen took massive hits and sank. The anti-aircraft defence was fierce, throwing up walls of flak, even when one of their own specialist gunships – the *Empire Lawrence* – was itself hit and blew up. Finally the assault petered out and the remaining ships sailed on towards Murmansk. Stumpff smelt blood, and decided to continue his attacks, even as the convoy began its final run in to the harbour on 30 May 1942.

The day itself dawned cloudy and overcast. The men of PQ 16 felt that the worst was over and they could finally relax as they neared the port. Above them they could see an approaching flight of Soviet Northern Fleet fighters, coming to escort them in to safety. They didn't know it, but in the four Kittyhawks were some of the best pilots the Soviets had: Major Aleksey Kukharenko, Captain Pavel Orlov and Lieutenant Vladimir Pokrovskiy, with the lead taken by none other than Boris Safonov himself. Suddenly six Ju 88s appeared from the west and prepared to attack. Safonov spotted them and took his flight straight into the middle of them, breaking their formation apart and scattering them. All became chaos as the four Soviet flyers chased down the bombers, wing and nose guns blazing, even as the Junkers fired off every gun they had to defend themselves. No one saw where Safonov was, but Soviet ground controllers heard him shout on his radio, '*Dvukh trakhnul!*' – 'I smashed two!' – and then they heard him claim a third. Minutes later they heard him again: 'My engine is damaged, I have to ditch ...' That was his last message. Safonov was a hugely experienced pilot and would have known that ditching in the icy waters was a virtual death sentence. A search was launched immediately, but predictably revealed nothing; the Barents had taken him. Safonov's death was a bitter blow to the Soviet air force. He had flown 234 sorties, fought in thirty-four air combats and was credited with twenty personal and six shared kills – a huge tally for any Soviet pilot.[156] German records report the loss of two Ju 88s that day, not three, and there are unconfirmed reports that it wasn't engine failure but none other than Rudi Müller who ended Safonov's life that day, pouncing out of the cloud and ambushing the Soviet before he even knew what was going on. This seems very unlikely though and in all probability Safonov was not one of Müller's eventual ninety-four kills before he was himself shot up and forced to belly-land on the frozen Lake Bolschoje near Murmansk the following year. Captured by a Red Army ski patrol, Müller just disappeared from the official records. There were unconfirmed sightings of him in prison in Murmansk in 1947, but other reports said he was shot dead while trying to escape from a Soviet POW camp in the autumn of 1943. Whatever the truth, he never returned to his home in Frankfurt-am-Main.

Back with PQ 16, the failure of the 30 May attack had not put Stumpff off and he gave the green light to attack the convoy while it was moored up in Murmansk having its cargo unloaded. This new tactic caught the Soviets somewhat by surprise and ended up claiming two freighters, the *Subottnik* and *Empire Starlight*, but extremely heavy anti-aircraft fire held the Germans off from doing more damage. JG 5's Sergeant Hugo Dahmer said of it: 'The anti-aircraft fire at Murmansk was the worst I have ever seen. The port area literally boiled with muzzle flashes from the guns below. It was absolutely incredible to see how even a single German airplane managed to survive that barrage.'

That was the last attack on PQ 16. In all the Germans had sent 770 motor vehicles, 147 tanks and seventy-seven planes destined for the Soviets to the bottom. But 2,507 motor vehicles, 321 tanks and 124 aircraft had got through. Luftflotte 5 would need to do much, much more.

Stumpff was nothing but persistent, though, rightly understanding that the game wasn't up yet. Murmansk was actually quite a small port, with its workforce concentrated in the immediate town – destroy the town, went Stumpff's thinking, and there would be no one to unload the ships. Plus, from Murmansk, the offloaded materiel had only one route out: the Kirov railway line heading south – cut the line and the flow of supplies would stop. Stumpff decided to raze Murmansk to the ground. However, unlike so many city raids the Germans launched, Stumpff decreed that leaflets be dropped to warn the population of what was going to happen, giving them time to get away, although in reality there was little chance of the Soviet authorities allowing their workforce to just pack up and head off. Days later, on 18 June, the Luftwaffe dropped 5,000 incendiaries on the town's wooden buildings. The result was devastating. Ground winds fanned the flames, even in the extreme cold, and half the town's 1,600 houses were reduced to ashes. The Soviet Hurricane pilot Lieutenant Sergey Kurzenkov said of the attack, 'It was hard for us to try and fend off the continuously incoming bombers ... strong winds blew constantly, the fascists made great use of the drying heat and the strong gale ... in the centre of the town almost all the wooden houses burnt to the ground, but the fascists never succeeded in destroying the harbour.' His boss, Admiral Arseniy Grigoriyevich Golovko, commander of the Northern Fleet, wrote in his diary: 'Yesterday and the day before, Murmansk was subjected to repeated bombardment. A large fire destroyed everything that remained after the previous fire. The material stores in the port area could be saved. The port installations and the railway are intact, and the work in the port continues.'[157]

There were more than twenty follow-up raids, including on the Kirov railroad, and the VVS was reduced to just nine serviceable aircraft defending Murmansk, but still the supplies flowed. The German offensive had failed to destroy PQ 16 at sea, then failed to stop it unloading and then failed again in stopping the supplies being sent south – and Murmansk harbour was still operational.

The battle was finely balanced, though. If Luftflotte 5 could concentrate enough resources and coordinate with the Kriegsmarine properly then they still had a chance of cutting Moscow's northern supply link to the west. The test would be the next convoy – PQ 17. This would be by far the largest convoy to date, with thirty-five merchantmen and escorts. Stumpff concentrated 264 planes (190 of them bombers and torpedo planes) for his attack and liaised with his naval counterparts to launch a series of hammer blows against it. For once, the Germans got their timing right, hitting the convoy in waves from the air, from the sea, from the air and so on. 'We made a united diving attack through a cloud bank, came down below the clouds, firing like mad with our machine-guns, went farther and farther down, dropped our bombs, and pulled up into the sun.'[158] Fierce anti-aircraft fire took its toll too:

> Suddenly there was a terrible bang, and for a few seconds I could see nothing but splinters. When I could see again, I noticed that we were heading straight towards a destroyer. Our left engine was on fire, as was the hydraulic oil that had leaked into the cockpit. I was on fire myself at various parts of my body. The dashboard and all instruments in the cockpit were destroyed.[159]

Ship after ship was hit, with the Luftwaffe sinking eight and the U-boats nine by themselves, with a further seven shared between them. The convoy had been ordered to scatter and that allowed the German attacks to pick them off one by one – for the Allies it was a disaster. Several hundred thousand tons of shipping were lost in a single week and with it went 3,350 vehicles, 430 tanks, 210 aircraft and 100,000 tons of other supplies; this was in total roughly what the Soviets had lost at the disastrous Battle of Uman back in 1941. The eleven surviving ships delivered 986 vehicles, 164 tanks and eighty-seven aircraft – in terms of planes this was roughly five to six days' worth of losses for the VVS at the time.

The Germans were now undoubtedly on top. If they could continue the pressure they might choke off the Lend-Lease supply line completely. That opportunity came in October with PQ 18, but this time the British Royal Navy stole a march and sent an aircraft carrier as escort. With fighter cover the whole way, the Luftwaffe bombers flew into determined opposition that chopped them out of the sky. Losses were high and successes few; only thirteen of the forty ships were sunk despite the massed assaults. The survivors docked and unloaded. The equipment that got through from that single convoy was enough to equip an entire Soviet tank army.

The Luftwaffe response was to just give up. Having taken a knock back, the majority of the bomber units were sent to the Mediterranean to face the Anglo-Americans in a contest they could never win and the Arctic convoys were allowed to sail unmolested, handing mountains of materiel to the Soviets, including 3,052 aircraft in that first year alone and some 13,000 tanks overall.

Having frittered away precious aircraft, crews and potential recovery time in the far north, it was now the turn of the far south of the front to absorb more of the Luftwaffe's limited strength. The Crimea is a sort of semi-island in the Black Sea, only joined to the mainland by a thin isthmus of land to the north, with a sliver of sea between the Taman peninsula in the Caucasus to the east and the Crimea's own Kerch peninsula that stretched out towards it across the Sea of Azov. Barbarossa had taken the Wehrmacht onto and into the Crimea the previous autumn, but the Soviets still had a bridgehead at Kerch and the legendary fortress of Sevastopol in the south-west. Facing an enemy on two fronts, and fearful of a Soviet counter-offensive from Kerch, General Erich von Manstein's Eleventh Army was set on a plan – *Unternehmen Trappenjagd* (Operation Bustard Hunt – named as such on account of Von Manstein's indulgence in the sport) – to firstly throw the Soviets off the Kerch peninsula, destroy their 44th, 47th and 51st armies and then turn back on Sevastopol to finally take it. Hitler, too, was dead-set on the plan, believing it was the only way of safeguarding the Romanian oilfields at Ploesti from long-range bomber attacks by the VVS: 'In the era of air power, Russia can turn the Romanian oil fields into an expanse of smoking debris ... and the very life of the Axis depends on those fields.' Notwithstanding Hitler's fears of air attack, the VVS was actually fairly weak in the area, but it was supported by Black Sea Fleet air units.

The Fleet itself had played comparatively little part in the campaign so far, its senior commanders fearful of losing their capital ships to the Luftwaffe. There was no threat from the Kriegsmarine due to fuel shortages, as Grand Admiral Raeder pointed out to Hitler, stating that its supplies 'have been cut by fifty percent', leading to a 'very difficult oil situation', and that this was causing 'an intolerable restriction on the mobility of our vessels'. What diesel the Navy had was directed at the U-boat battles in the Atlantic, and not sent east to the Black Sea.

The VVS had put up stern resistance the previous autumn, as Von Manstein bitterly complained:

The Soviet Air Force dominated our airspace! Its fighters and fighter-bombers incessantly attacked any discernible targets ... Not only did the frontline infantry and batteries have to dig in, but it was also necessary to dig pits for every vehicle and horse behind the battle zone as protection against enemy aircraft. It got so bad that flak batteries no longer dared to fire in case they were immediately destroyed from the air.

The fighting further north had totally changed this situation, with more and more VVS units sent to the Ukraine and the Moscow front, leaving the Crimea command relatively hollowed out.

Given the limitations of the aerial opposition and the geography, Löhr's Luftflotte 4 should have been more than capable of providing Von Manstein with all the support he needed, but as Goering admitted, 'the Luftwaffe was no longer sufficient for the great tasks'. Berlin's answer was to compensate by bringing in reinforcements from the central front to bolster Löhr's forces. So, von Richthofen's superb Fliegerkorps VIII was reassigned from Luftflotte 2 to support Von Manstein directly with its eleven bomber, three Stuka and seven fighter Geschwader. The Soviets were caught off-guard, Major General Nikolay Semenovich Skripko, the burly deputy commander of the ADD who arrived in the sector in May, observing: 'The command of VVS-Crimean Front did not take into consideration that the numerical strength of Luftflotte 4 was by no means fixed; it could be considerably increased when the enemy prepared a large offensive operation, and that is exactly what happened at Kerch.'

The air offensive launched on 8 May followed the by-now traditional Luftwaffe pattern of trying to wipe out the VVS on the ground at the outset. Skripko again: 'After dealing heavy strikes against our airfields, the enemy's aviation, started blocking them – preventing our fighters from taking off and intercepting his bombers.' It was a huge effort, with the Germans launching 2,000 sorties on the first day alone.

The VVS did, somehow, manage to get aircraft into the skies but once aloft they came up against some of the finest Experten the Luftwaffe had to offer. The results were predictable. By the end of day one, JG 52 alone reported forty-seven aerial kills (seven of them to Graf) against the loss of a single Bf 109 to a forced landing – Graf's wingman, Alfred Grislawski, who survived. Two other Experten alongside Graf came to dominate the aerial battle that May: Graf's arch-opponent, the Austrian Gordon Gollob, and Captain Heinz 'Pritzl' Bär. Gollob, a humourless man, whose real name had been Gordon McGollob on account of his Scottish ancestry before the OKL had ordered him to change it, was locked in a race to reach the magical number of 100 kills with Bär, his subordinate in the 'Ace of Hearts' JG 77. Bär was the polar opposite of Gollob, a sensitive and charming man whom many comrades felt was a bit too highly strung for the bloody end of air fighting. Nevertheless, he was a superb pilot and on 16 May he was on ninety-three kills, with Gollob just four behind him. The two men were at a distinct advantage as the Crimean front was not a priority for Moscow, so the Soviet pilots mainly had to do battle in old I-16s and even I-153s. Undeterred, the VVS threw every plane, no matter how old or obsolete, at the Germans and this allowed Bär and Gollob to score almost at will despite the bravery of the VVS pilots. 'These guys have some nerves. Each day they see their friends go down in flames, and yet they're back in the air with the same enthusiasm the next day.'[160] Bär chalked up five in a single day on 19 May and went to 103. Gollob wrote in his diary that day: 'I have refrained from reporting four of my last victories. I don't want to reach number 100 so fast, because I fear my superiors will have me grounded after that.' There may well be some truth in this; Mölders and Galland among others had been known to fly and not officially record kills in order to avoid Berlin's prying eyes and desire to tie them to desks. But one can't help but feel this diary entry is a little bit self-serving.

Whatever the truth, the result was that the skies were effectively swept clear of Soviet aircraft and this allowed Fliegerkorps VIII to concentrate on flattening the Red Army, despite the grumblings of the Eleventh Army Landsers who were forever asking for more Luftwaffe support. Lieutenant Anatoliy Ivanov, an I-16 pilot: 'The sky was filled with German aircraft. The fascist aviation kept coming in over our territory, bombing and strafing the ground troops.' These attacks were not without loss, as KG 55 alone lost eight He 111s to ground fire and the VVS continued to provide their Red Army brethren with as much support as possible: 'Just as we were taking off we were involved in combat with ten or twenty enemy aircraft. That day we fought particularly fiercely to defend the retreating ground troops.'

The pressure was too much and the Soviets retreated. Kerch fell, the majority of Soviet ground forces were evacuated by sea to the Taman peninsula and the VVS, having lost 417 aircraft, abandoned its airfields and relocated further east. Now only Sevastopol held out.

The capture of Sevastopol, renowned as 'the strongest land and naval fortress in the world', was Von Manstein's masterpiece of modern siege warfare. He knew airpower would be invaluable and from the start, Stukas and bombers were in constant use on the battlefield. A Luftwaffe captain in a Stuka unit said of the air attacks on the massive Maksim Gor'kiy II fortress and its 1,000-strong garrison,

'They were bombed and bombed again; one explosion next to another ... The whole peninsula was on fire ... One can only stand amazed at such resilience ... That is how they defended Sevastopol all along the line ... The whole country had to literally ploughed over by bombs before they yielded ...' A German lieutenant colonel of infantry said of those same Stuka attacks, 'Approximately three hundred Stukas are launched in merciless, deafening attacks ... Never, ever – neither previously or later – did the men of Infantry Regiment 42 experience anything like this.'

The Soviets were of much the same opinion: 'Panic is spreading, particularly among the officers.'[161] Conditions in the fortress and city were dreadful. A captured Red Army lieutenant, Joseph Avokian, reported during interrogation that, 'He was captured at Sevastopol after 83 days of bombardment. He had fought in Odessa and Kiev. He reported that they ate their own comrades in Sevastopol and in the prison camps.'[162]

By 4 July the battle was over. Sevastopol had fallen and with it a struggle that cost the Soviets 260,000 men captured (around half that number were also killed), 2,506 guns and mortars, 300 tanks, almost 4,000 vehicles and well over 700 aircraft in just two months. These were appalling losses, although not on the scale of the encirclement battles of the previous summer and autumn. The other side of the coin was that the undoubtedly heroic resistance of the defenders had virtually bled the Eleventh Army dry. Von Manstein's men were, arguably, the Wehrmacht's only real strategic reserve in the east in 1942 and they had suffered 24,000 casualties (their Romanian allies had lost 4,000 men as well). So great had been the bloodletting that the Eleventh would soon be broken up and disbanded.

For the Luftwaffe, and for von Richthofen's Fliegerkorps VIII especially, the Crimean battles showed what well-led aviation could do in a properly co-ordinated, all-arms battle. His aircraft flew 23,751 sorties during the assault and dropped 20,528 tons of bombs on Sevastopol itself. The campaign was a master class by the two finest German commanders in the East in their respective services, as Von Manstein himself noted:

Von Richthofen was certainly the most outstanding Luftwaffe leader we had ... He made terrific demands on the units under his command, but always went up himself to supervise any important attack ... We always got on extremely well together, and I remember von Richthofen's achievements and those of his Air Corps with the utmost admiration and gratitude.

As for the Soviets, their view in an after-action report was clear: 'Enemy aviation operated with impunity.'

However, the STAVKA knew that the Crimean operation was not the main event that summer. The Wehrmacht was bound to launch a major offensive during its favourite campaigning season and so the question for Moscow was where? Having been wrong-footed the previous year by thinking the main blow would fall in the south, they opted this year to prepare for an attack by Model's Army Group Centre to go one better than Typhoon and try and capture the capital. To draw reserves away from that expected assault, Marshal Semyon Timoshenko proposed launching a spoiler offensive aimed at Kharkov in the south, even as Von Manstein was throwing the Red Army out of the Kerch peninsula. What the STAVKA didn't realise was that Timoshenko's ill-conceived thrust would run smack bang into the Wehrmacht's own preparations for Case Blue.

As a harbinger of his new offensive, Timoshenko ordered the VVS to steal a march on the Luftwaffe by aping German tactics and launching a surprise attack on the first morning of the offensive to catch the Germans on their airstrips. The Soviets had concentrated some 926 aircraft and now sent in waves of Pe-2s, Il-2s and Su-2s to crush Fliegerkorps IV on the ground. Tons of bombs were dropped and hundreds of rockets fired but the sum total of their efforts was a single Bf 109 damaged, while the attackers themselves lost five I-16 fighters to patrolling 109s and anti-aircraft fire. The Soviets were learning but still had a way to go yet.

The German response was swift and accurate. Clouds of Bf 109s took to the skies on free hunting missions, sweeping out of the sun to wreak havoc among the VVS regiments. As soon as they had gained local air superiority, their comrades in the ground-attack Staffeln were free to hit Timoshenko's armoured spearheads and mangle his 1,200 tanks. Yet again the Luftwaffe was acting as an extension of the Heer, as Kesselring told his subordinates the previous summer: 'I instructed my air force and flak generals to consider the wishes of the Army as my orders.'

On 15 May Franz Halder wrote in his diary 'the force of the attack appears to have been broken by the efforts of our Luftwaffe'. Not surprising given that Fliegerkorps IV's Stukas alone claimed fifty-four Soviet tanks destroyed in just two days. The Stukas weren't alone either; the Ju 88s of KG 51 were just as busy, flying multiple sorties to support several surrounded German units between Ternovaya and Varvarovka and allowing them to escape. One of those rescued soldiers later wrote to the Junkers crews: 'Your untiring energy amazed us, and your actions gave us courage to hold out.'[163]

The Soviets were now in trouble. Their offensive had been stopped and they were themselves in danger of becoming encircled as they were pushed back to the Donets and the noose tightened around them. Their only avenue of escape was the bridges over the river. The Luftwaffe was given the task of shutting that particular door, and on 20 May Stukas from StG 77 dive-bombed the bridges, destroying five and damaging four more.

The Soviets threw in the newly created 2 VA to try and stem the tide, but this just led to more losses. Sergeant Ivan Kazakov, the radio operator in Hero of the Soviet Union Major Yuriy Gorbko's Pe-2, recalls that, returning unescorted from a successful bombing mission, they were bounced by an entire Staffel from JG 52. 'I watched as the Germans first shot down the right wingman of our *zveno* [the zveno was the VVS adapted version of the Luftwaffe's Schwarm formation]. Then they dispatched the left wingman, and finally seven fighters were concentrated against our plane.' Gorbko's gunners kept the fighters off until they ran out of ammunition and then the circling Germans swooped in and set the Pe-2 alight. Satisfied the bomber was finished, the Germans headed off as Gorbko looked for somewhere to belly-land his stricken plane. With his eyes scanning the ground, he didn't spot a set of overhead railway wires which tore the aircraft apart. Somehow Kazakov survived uninjured, as did the other crewman, Alkhovatskiy. Gorbko was not so lucky, being stuck fast in the cockpit, waist-deep in the glutinous mud of a marsh. Kazakov and Alkhovatskiy struggled to pull their pilot free as flames began to take hold of the wreckage.

> We started to pull and he groaned in pain. It was impossible to pull him out of the cockpit. By now, the fire had reached the navigator's position and the ammunition started exploding. But we didn't care, the life of our commander was more important than anything else. Then the flames reached the cockpit. "Well that's it," Gorbko sighed. He took his documents from his pocket and handed them to Alkhovatskiy, then he gave him his Golden Star ... the man was alive but there was nothing we could do to help him. He looked at us with eyes full of determination and pain and before we could understand what he was up to he pulled his pistol and shot himself in the head.

The two men managed to pulled the body clear and got it away from the aircraft as it burnt out. 'We carried him to the shore of a small lake, cleaned his head of blood and mud, and started weeping together.'[164]

Eight days after StG 77's attack on the Donets bridges, it was all over. The Soviets had been encircled and destroyed. Their losses were, once again, horrific. Some 75,000 men had been killed and 239,000 surrendered to the Germans – although official Soviet reports only listed 171,000 casualties. In terms of materiel, more than 5,000 guns and mortars were lost, along with 775 tanks – and all this in just over two weeks. Fliegerkorps IV claimed 227 of those tanks and over sixty of the guns, plus 3,038 vehicles and almost thirty trains and engines. For the Luftwaffe it was a great success, although, as usual, there were conflicting reports on aircraft losses. Fliegerkorps IV said it destroyed 596 Soviet planes in the air and a further nineteen on the ground, whereas the VVS admitted the loss of 542 aircraft – given the norm of over-claiming, the Soviet number is probably the more accurate. The flip side was Luftwaffe losses, with the Germans reporting forty-nine and the STAVKA broadcasting to the Soviet people the far more handsome figure of 200 German aircraft destroyed!

CHAPTER 16

Friends, Romans and Case Blue

The summer campaign 1942

Given the scale of the casualties the previous year, the Wehrmacht could not hope to repeat its feat of attacking with three separate prongs in the summer of 1942. In fact, looking at the numbers, the General Staff were dubious they could attack with one. The only answer was to take the begging bowl out around their Axis allies. The result for the Ostheer was four Armies, two from Romania and one each from Italy and Hungary, as well as various smaller contingents from the likes of Croatia and Slovakia.

The Luftwaffe too could have done with all the help it could muster, but it could hardly have picked more unsuitable allies if it had tried.

An Italian once said, 'When you have a fine plate of pasta guaranteed for life, and a little music, you don't need anything more.' As a statement it is enchanting, but when it's coming from the Under-Secretary at the Italian Ministry of War, General Ubaldo Soddu, it is hardly a ringing endorsement for the state's capacity for military action. As the historian Williamson Murray put it, it was nothing to do with the bravery of the Italian people; rather 'it had to do with national military organisations that did not exist to fight'. Back in 1939, on the eve of the invasion of Poland, Adolf Hitler had confided in his oldest ally and asked it to be ready to support Nazi Germany in a European war. Mussolini and his Foreign Minister and son-in-law, Count Gian Galeazzo Ciano, drew up a shopping list of the raw materials and military equipment their country needed to even countenance a war. The list included 6 million tons of coal (four months' worth of German production), 2 million tons of steel, 1 million tons of timber, 150 batteries of heavy anti-aircraft guns and most important of all, 7 million tons of precious oil – Ciano said of the list, 'It's enough to kill a bull – if a bull could read it.' In truth,

Fascist Italy needed even more than was contained on the infamous list. Mussolini had provided General Franco and his Nationalist forces with massive military resources during the three years of the Spanish Civil War and Italian industry had not come close to replacing the losses. The Italian Air Force – the *Regia Aeronautica* – had lost more than 200 aircraft in the conflict and several hundred more after the fighting had finished when Il Duce made Franco a 'gift' of all the remaining planes in theatre. This was serious stuff for Italy. Her aviation sector, as with most of her armaments industry, was heavily outdated and relied on old-fashioned craft techniques rather than modern production-line methods. As an example of the consequences of this style of working, it took the Germans 4,500 working hours to produce a Bf 109, whereas each roughly equivalent Italian MC 200 fighter took a staggering 21,000 hours to roll off the line. In 1941, with the country at war against Greece, and the British in North Africa and the Mediterranean, Italian factories managed to turn out just 2,400 planes in the same time that Great Britain knocked out 20,094. The following year was little better, with the Italian total crawling up to 2,818, and it would actually drop by 100 the next year. Command and control was sclerotic: a national co-ordinating body for war production wasn't even established until February 1943, by which time Italy was more or less finished as a combatant nation anyway.

Nevertheless, when hectored by Hitler in the spring of 1942, Mussolini not only increased the Italian Army contingent on the Eastern Front from a Corps to an Army – the 8th (so-called *ARMIR*) – but also ratcheted up his air force contingent to fifty-five MC 200 fighters and twenty-two Caproni 311 light bombers. The MC 200s, nicknamed the *Saetta* or 'Thunderbolt', were nothing of the sort, being 80 mph slower than a Bf 109, with 100 miles less range and carrying an armament of just two 12.7 mm machine guns. They had been relatively ineffective during the Barbarossa campaign despite some success over Dnepropetrovsk in the Ukraine, where they had managed to shoot down six S-B2 bombers and two I-16 escort fighters during a single action. As it turned out, their performance during Case Blue would be described by their Luftwaffe colleagues as 'most disappointing'.[165]

The Luftwaffe was also supported down in the southern Soviet Union by four other national contingents from Romania, Hungary, Croatia and Slovakia.

The Royal Romanian Air Force, or Fortele Aeriene Regale ale Romaniei (FARR for short), was created back in 1913, participating in Romania's disastrous intervention in the First World War. Having lost the fighting but won the peace by virtue of picking the winning side, Romania was not banned from having an air force after the war. However its aviation sector made Fascist Italy's look positively dynamic, with only three manufacturers in the whole country: two in Bucharest and one in the city of Brasov. Between them they would produce just 1,333 planes throughout the entire war – roughly what Great Britain made in three weeks in 1941. When Barbarossa was launched the FARR could field about 450 fighters of mixed parentage: British-made Hurricanes, Polish PZL P11s, German-imported He 112s and home-grown IAR-80s (the IAR-80 was equivalent in performance terms to the VVS's I-16), sixty-seven JRS 79B bombers and assorted trainers, reconnaissance and liaison planes. Along with Alexander Löhr's Luftflotte 4, they had faced 1,775 Soviet aircraft, including 600 from the Black Sea Fleet. On the second day of the war the VVS had begun their bombing raids on the Romanian port city of Constanza and had shot down two Romanian Hurricanes and one He 112. The Romanians fought back two days later, shooting down ten DB-3 and SB bombers out of a force of thirty-two en route to hit Constanza and their own airfield at Mamaiya. Another twenty-seven bombers were added to this total over the next fortnight. This success was short-lived, with dozens of aircraft lost during the costly Romanian capture of Odessa, and by the spring of 1942 the FARR was creaking. Domestic production was miniscule and the only possible external provider of aircraft was Nazi Germany, which was, of course, struggling to fulfil its own needs. The FARR was willing, though, as the Luftwaffe's lead Fighter Liaison in Romania, Lieutenant Colonel Edouard 'Edu' Neumann, said of the Romanians, 'Our co-operation was good and comradely ... The Romanians – even in their outdated IAR-80 fighters – were a valuable help.'[166]

Co-operation was less effective, from a Luftwaffe point of view, with Romania's bitterest enemies, the Hungarians. The two countries had been at daggers drawn with each other over disputed territory and their intermingled border populations for decades. They had been on opposite sides in the First World War and while Budapest had the satisfaction of seeing its soldiers march triumphantly through the Romanian capital after its capture in December 1916, they had then to swallow the bitter pill of the 1920 Treaty of Trianon that, among other things, had forbidden them from either having an air force or an aviation industry. Eighteen years later the Magyar Prime Minister, Kalman Daranyi, publicly cast off the Trianon restrictions and soon enough the Magyar Kiralyi Honved Legiero – MKHL, or Royal Hungarian Air Force – was established, which had grown by 1941 to a force of over 300 aircraft, including German Ju 86k bombers,

Italian CR 32 fighters and some Hungarian-manufactured Weiss Manfred WM21A Solyom dual-purpose reconnaissance/light bombers. Barbarossa had seen Budapest reluctantly provide the Germans with the 1st Royal Hungarian Air Force Field Brigade with a four-squadron bomber regiment of eighteen aircraft, two fighter groups with another eighteen planes and four reconnaissance squadrons, all commanded by Lieutenant Colonel Bela Orosz. The brigade was not as successful as either Berlin or Budapest hoped, being withdrawn in September after losing fifty-six aircraft (most of its original establishment) while only claiming to have shot down thirty Soviets. Having said that, they weren't a total washout and pilots from the unit were even decorated by Löhr himself at their airfield at Sutyska for their part in supporting the Eleventh Army's capture of Nikolayev in August.[167] After time at home to rest and recuperate, the Hungarians were back at the front in November with a new commander – Lieutenant Colonel Kalman Csukas – this time proving themselves to be more effective, claiming sixty-three VVS kills for a loss of eleven. Hitler, however, was unimpressed. 'Aviation fuel is in short supply and I need pilots who attack and not ones who go on pleasure flights. What the Hungarians have achieved in the aviation field to date is paltry. If I am going to send anyone some aircraft, then rather the Croats who have proved they have an offensive spirit. So far we have only had fiascos with the Hungarians!'

So what of the Croats? The Nazi invasion of Yugoslavia had led to a total dismemberment of the state, with a parcelling out of territory reminiscent of the partitions of Poland. An independent Croatia had been created under the leader of the extreme nationalist Ustase movement, Dr Anté Pavelic. Pavelic, a lawyer and rabid anti-Semite, would head a government that became one of the most blood-soaked in modern history, murdering untold thousands of Serbs, Jews, Roma and political opponents. His deputy, Slavko Kvaternik, explained the Ustase's policy as 'forcing one third of Serbs to leave Croatia, one third to convert to Catholicism, and one third to be exterminated'. They even aped their Nazi protectors by establishing concentration camps, such as the infamous Jasenovac, where up to as many as 200,000 or more people were murdered. Pavelic's original sponsor had been Fascist Italy, but the self-styled *Poglavnik* (Croat version of Führer) was keen to secure Berlin as his new patron and so offered Hitler ground troops and a contingent from the Zrakoplovstvo NDH – the Croat Air Force. Under the command of the Croat Colonel Vladimir Kren, some 300 volunteer airmen were sent to Germany to train before being deployed in the East during Barbarossa flying Do 17s and

Bf 109s. They performed well enough to merit a mention in the regular OKW report: 'With regard to air warfare a Croat formation has distinguished itself by carrying out daring low-level attacks.' This brief flash was not to last, as the unit soon became plagued by desertions. On 9 May 1942 it was Lieutenant Nikola Vucina who deserted, taking his Bf 109 with him, and the following year a further three pilots flew their 109s over to the other side: captains Nikola Cvikic and Bogdan Vujicic and Lieutenant Albin Starc. At that point the order went out that Croats were now forbidden to fly operational sorties, and the unit was finally withdrawn.

The smallest allied contingent came from the mini-state of Slovakia and their aerial contribution had the same issues of dubious loyalty to the Nazi cause as the Croats. The Shturmovik pilot Alexander E. Shvarev remembered an incident during the Battle of Kursk when he and his squadron landed back at their field after a mission only to see a Bf 109 come in to land after them. Too dumbfounded to react they watched bewildered as the canopy opened and the pilot put his hands up and climbed out of the aircraft shouting, 'Brothers, I'm one of you!' The pilot was a Slovak from JG 52's Staffel 13 (*Slovakei*), operating from Maikop.[168]

As the VVS and the Luftwaffe gathered their strength for the upcoming summer offensive, the support given by their respective allies couldn't have been more different. The Luftwaffe was having small cohorts of allied aircraft foisted on them which more often than not proved a burden to liaise with and a drain on scarce aircraft production, with around 800 to 900 aircraft being exported to them – notwithstanding that most were second-hand models or older. The part they would play in Blue would be marginal at best. By contrast, the VVS, despite Stalin's public grumblings about delays to the northern convoys and doubts about the quality of some of the equipment – 'The English Hurricane was a piece of junk rather than a fighter'[169] – was receiving vital transfusions of aircraft, munitions and high-grade aviation fuel at exactly the time it needed them. It wasn't all plain sailing with the Allies though. Churchill may have made his famous quote about making a favourable reference to the Devil in the Commons, but the Vice-Chief of the Imperial General Staff, the pipe-smoking artilleryman Lieutenant General Sir Henry Pownall, expressed the wider held view among the British at least of the Communist Soviet Union: 'I avoid the expression "allies", for the Russians are a dirty lot of murdering thieves themselves and double-crossers of the deepest dye. It is good to see the two biggest cut-throats in Europe, Hitler and Stalin, going for each other.'[170]

The stage was now set for Hitler's main offensive in 1942. His goal was to advance to the Volga River and the Caspian Sea, cut off the Caucasus and capture the estimated 2 billion tons of oil under its soil and rock. This oil would provide the Wehrmacht with the fuel it would need to prosecute a long war. As an official Wehrmacht report set out: 'The supply of crude oil will be one of the weakest spots of our defence capacity during the next year ... The shortage in crude oil of all kinds has reached a level that restricts the operational freedom of the Heer, the Luftwaffe and the Kriegsmarine, and hampers war production.'

Hitler knew that Nazi Germany's main external source of petroleum, Romania, was under severe strain. Its oilfields were steadily declining in productivity as the black gold under its fertile soil ran out; output had already fallen from 8,701,000 tons in 1937 to 5,577,000 tons in 1941. That oil did not all belong to Germany either; the febrile Romanian war economy needed as much of it as it could get and under the terms of the Tripartite Pact, some even went to Fascist Italy. Romania's military dictator, Marshal Ion Antonescu, was wholeheartedly committed to the destruction of the Soviet Union and knew just how vital his country's oil exports were to the Wehrmacht and said as much to Hitler in a telegram: 'In the last five months we exported to Germany and Italy amounts greater than our monthly output of 125,000 tons of fuel oil, which exhausted our available reserves ... Romania would do everything possible to increase her deliveries to Germany.' However, even with those assurances ringing in his ears the Marshal still had to inform Ribbentrop, the Nazi Foreign Minister, that 'as for crude oil, Romania has contributed the maximum which it is in her power to contribute. She can give no more ... the only way out of the situation would be to seize territories rich in oil'. Antonescu was only repeating what Hitler's own war economists were saying. Still sitting in the War Economy and Armaments Office, Georg Thomas wrote to Hitler in the strongest terms on the matter:

It is crucial to seize quickly and exploit the Caucasus oil fields, at least the areas around Maikop and Grozny. In oil fields that have not been completely destroyed, it will take about a month to resume production, and another month for its transport. We will have to seize those areas by no later than the end of the operations second month ... If this proves unsuccessful we must expect the most serious repercussions.

Just how Thomas thought the Nazis could deliver functioning oil output and then ship it thousands of miles was something he did not elaborate on.

However, he didn't need to, Hitler had made his decision. The Ostheer's summer offensive in 1942 had its goal – capture the oil-rich Caucasus – as he told the senior officers of Army Group South at a conference at the beginning of June, 'If I do not get the oil of Maikop and Grozny then I must end this war.'

The Germans concentrated 1.3 million men (300,000 of them from Romania, Italy and Hungary), 1,900 panzers and Löhr's Luftflotte 4, comprising von Greim's Fliegerkorps IV and von Richthofen's Fliegerkorps VIII. Over 60 per cent of total Luftwaffe strength in the East was invested in these two corps: 1,610 aircraft out of 2,644 stretched across the whole front. The figure would have been higher but the frittering away of resources in the far north, the Crimea, Kerch and Sevastopol had cost the Luftwaffe almost 1,200 aircraft since the start of the year – although it should be pointed out that the VVS itself claimed it had shot down 3,012 Germans and destroyed 1,059 on the ground, while their comrades in the Red Army had reportedly bagged another 1,197.

Whatever the exact truth of the figures involved, three things were clear for the Luftwaffe as the Ostheer prepared to launch Blue: firstly, by reinforcing Luftflotte 4 they had managed to at least achieve parity in absolute numbers in the southern sector; secondly, they were still shooting down at least five Soviet aircraft for every one of theirs lost (and for the Jagdwaffe the figure rose to twenty) and that qualitative edge would enable them to achieve local superiority over the new battlefield. As Macky Steinhoff said, 'We had a profound feeling of superiority over the Russian airmen during those days.' The issue looming over them was the old one of sheer numbers. Once the Soviets realised that Blue was the German main effort they would, and could, draw huge reinforcements from other zones to challenge the Luftwaffe. Luftflotte 4 would then need to call upon its own reserves – but from where?

Last but definitely not least was the question of fabled German superiority. The fact was that the VVS were catching up and quickly. During Barbarossa the Luftwaffe had caught an ill-prepared VVS on the ground and hammered it, but now improved training, camouflage and dispersal techniques meant few Soviet aircraft were bounced on their fields; one Soviet front had lost 522 aircraft on the ground by the end of July 1941, but only thirty-four in the whole first six months of 1942.[171] Their planes were getting better too. Most of the old stock were now burnt-out wrecks littering the western Soviet Union and their place was being filled not only with British and American models but with modern Soviet-made aircraft too, like the excellent Yak-9 fighter, capable of speeds of 375 mph and packing a punch with a 20 mm cannon, two 12.7 mm machine guns and able to carry rockets and bombs to boot. The Yak would be produced in greater numbers than any other Soviet fighter and was just one of a growing stable of new models that allowed the Soviets to compete with the Luftwaffe. The men behind the controls were improving too, a fact that didn't go unnoticed by their German adversaries: 'From my own experience and numerous accounts by my pilots, I note that the Russian fighter pilots had learned a great deal. Our aerial victories were achieved in increasingly hard combats. The Russians have become better flyers, more aggressive, and more alert.' JG 54's Hannes Trautloft wrote this entry in his diary on the same day two of his pilots failed to return from a free hunting mission. The Soviets were improving by studying their enemy too. An official VVS report analysed the key tactics utilised by their Jagdwaffe opponents:

> Encountered by our fighters, the Germans as a rule evade turning combat. Instead they carry out surprise attacks against aircraft in the rear of our formations, diving from above or attacking from below ... .the following method was noted: One pair is flying in the opposite direction from the sun, obviously with the intention to reveal themselves, while another pair is flying higher, covered by the sun. If our fighters attempt to charge the pair that reveal themselves, they are attacked from the rear by the upper pair.

Another successful tactic was the same one used by Rudi Müller up in the far north around Murmansk – surprise. 'During dogfights with ordinary Messerschmitt pilots, all our pilots fought well, even the newcomers, and losses were very low. Most of our casualties occurred during return flights, when the newcomers relaxed and were jumped by the veteran hunters of the Messerschmitt units.'[172] The best pilots in the VVS were adapting as well.

> Surprise is the most important thing in battle. Some of our pilots were too eager to fire, they'd bang out a burst of tracer and the enemy, forewarned of an attack, would escape. But if there were no tracer bullets you could simply approach and kill. If you missed you could go even closer. That's how I saw it, and I asked my ground crew not to load tracer rounds into my machine-guns.[173]

The die was cast, and on 28 June the Germans launched Case Blue with an attack towards the city of Voronezh. Taken by surprise, the

Soviets were slow to react and soon the Landsers felt like it was the old days once again, with their panzers roaming forward, protected by an overhead umbrella of swastika-bearing aircraft that ranged far and wide, smashing Soviet formations and positions into smithereens. The Luftwaffe sergeant Hermann Buchner recalled: 'We dropped our bombs on our targets and then finished off by flying low-level attacks on any enemy positions we could see, concentrating on breaking up vehicle convoys and destroying as many vehicles as we could. As we pressed home our attacks, gradually everything lit up in very spectacular fashion, especially when we hit munitions dumps.' Their opponents in 2 VA hit back hard, but once again the Experten of the Jagdwaffe made their presence felt and the Soviets were still making some basic errors, which even some of their own pilots couldn't understand.

We warned the commanders of the new regiments about the German aces' regular visits, but they ignored what we told them. At approximately 1730 hrs they sent four Yak-1s into the air. These aircraft started patrolling above the airfield at slow speed, at 3,000 feet in what can only be described as a parade formation. At 1800 sharp six Messers appeared. One of them pulled off, made a manoeuvre and focused on the tail of the last Yak. In quick succession the German pilot shot down the first, the second, and the third Yak. The fourth only managed to avoid his attack by sheer luck. More Yaks were scrambled and another two were shot down.[174]

The Jagdwaffe pilots couldn't believe it all either: 'Sometimes half their aircraft were shot down, but the Ivans still kept coming!'[175]

'It is just like last summer. Hasn't Ivan learned anything?'[176]

The situation was noted by 2 VA's deputy commander, Fyodor Polynin: 'Our 4th and 24th Tank Corps are subject to constant pressure from the air. We have too few fighters available. I suffer huge losses in fighters and Shturmoviks.'

By now the Germans had responded to the rapidly increasing numbers of heavily armoured Shturmoviks by fitting 20 mm cannon gondolas to their Bf 109s. The effect of this massive increase of firepower was devastating. Three-quarters of all attacks using gondola guns resulted in a kill, despite the solid weight of armour plating fitted to the Soviet flying tank. As a Bf 109 pilot said, 'Any Russian pilot who is subjected to its fire is in deep trouble.'[177]

Shturmovik pilots began to describe themselves as '*lyotchik-smertnik*' – 'doomed to death'. The gondolas were far from ideal though, as attested to by one of the Luftwaffe's premier aerial killers, Günther Rall.

> The Il-2 posed great problems for us because of its strong armour protection. Against the Il-2s we were equipped with 20 mm cannon gondolas mounted under the wings, but when the fighter-to-fighter battles became tougher I had these arms removed. The ammunition feeding mechanism was troublesome and often simply broke off during the tight turns in fighter combat. Things grew even more difficult when the Russians started equipping their IL-2s with rear gunners. The IL-2's rear gunner was very dangerous. They often tricked us by pointing their machine-gun straight upward, giving us the impression that the gunner had been shot dead. Then when one of our greenhorns approached at close distance from behind, the gunner lifted his head, swung his machine-gun against the Messerschmitt and shot it down.[178]

Indeed, this latter modification would become a major headache for the Jagdwaffe as Shturmoviks multiplied in number across the front line. Those Il-2s without a rear gunner, though, were still vulnerable to the favourite German tactic of the attack from below and behind.

> Suddenly on leaving the target, I felt a terrible jolt from below and my aircraft went into an uncontrollable climb. I pushed the control stick forward, using both my hands and knees, and throttled down to zero. From 600 metres I got down to almost 200. I throttled up but the engine ceased, giving out a terrible smell of burning oil. I decided to land in a field. But I didn't know my airspeed and overshot, and landed a few metres away from a farmhouse. I was okay – not a scratch, no bones broken, just really shaky from the shock. It turned out that a German fighter had come in from below and opened fire. I didn't even see him.[179]

For now the Luftwaffe was in the ascendant. Von Richthofen wrote in his diary, 'Fliegerkorps IV hammered the Don bridges, destroying sections and inflicting terrible damage. Exploding, burning columns line the bridges, while three times as many line the roads.' Vasiliy Chuikov – later to gain fame for his defence of Stalingrad – bore witness to the German onslaught and couldn't help but admire their prowess:

> In modern warfare victory is impossible without combined action by all types of forces and without good administration. The Germans

had this kind of polished, co-ordinated action. In battle the different arms of their forces never hurried, did not push on ahead alone, but fought with the whole mass of men and technical backing. A few minutes before a general attack their aircraft would fly in, bomb and strafe the objective under assault, pinning the defending troops to the ground, and then infantry and tanks with supporting artillery and mortar fire would cut into our military formations almost with impunity.

The VVS, as usual, didn't shy from the fight and met the Experten head on. It cost them dearly. By the time Ivan D. Gaidenko was sent to command a squadron in the 20th Guards Fighter Regiment in August, the front-line units had taken a beating.

I took over a squadron, and do you know what sort of personnel it had? My deputy was a captain who'd received a ten year jail sentence for cowardice! But they sent him to the front instead. Meanwhile the other pilots were NCOs straight from academies in ankle boots, leg wrappings and thin little overcoats. I interviewed them and asked how many flying hours did they have? One of them said, 'I'm the most experienced with ten solo flights in I-16s. The rest have made four or five solo flights.' How could one send pilots like that into battle?

But if the VVS was bleeding, so were the Germans. At the same time as Gaidenko was interviewing his new charges, Luftflotte 4 was reporting back to Wilhelmstrasse that its operational strength had reduced to just 720 aircraft – less than half of what it had started the offensive with. It couldn't expect reinforcements from other, quieter sectors either; the Luftwaffe was stretched everywhere and could barely put another 500 planes into the air over the rest of the Eastern Front. The Experten were pushed harder and harder, spending more time in the air than on the ground, and attrition continued to take its toll. Above Army Group Centre, JG 51's Hans Strelow had been making a name for himself, firstly by shooting down seven Soviet aircraft in a single day and then by reaching a total of sixty-eight kills in such a short space of time he became the youngest ever holder of the Oak Leaves to his Knight's Cross, at the tender age of twenty. So successful was the young ace that his commander calculated that he was responsible for 10 per cent of all Soviet aircraft shot down over the central zone during the entire spring – one pilot! Returning from home leave, Strelow had thrown himself back into the fray, downing a Pe-2 in his first sortie before the rear gunner of his next target hit him with a long burst of fire. Forced to crash-land behind enemy lines, he saw Soviet infantry leap out of their nearby positions and sprint towards his wrecked plane. Fearful of his possible fate at their hands, the twenty-year-old Strelow pulled out his service pistol and blew his own brains out. He was JG 51's only combat loss for the entire month.

With no reinforcements in sight, the OKL felt a change of leadership might pep up the troops and Wolfram Freiherr von Richthofen was promoted to take command of Luftflotte 4. After working hand in glove with the brilliant von Manstein, von Richthofen now found himself increasingly tied to the highly orthodox and tactically unimaginative commander of Sixth Army, Friedrich Paulus. Paulus, a gifted staff officer, was out of his depth commanding the Wehrmacht's largest field formation (Sixth Army would eventually grow to over twenty divisions – von Manstein's Eleventh was only nine divisions at its height) and saw the Luftwaffe merely as an extension of his own conventional artillery. Von Richthofen was not happy with the fuel situation either, as his Staffeln were left thirsty while ordered to resupply the Heer's forward units: 'We fly in two hundred tons of fuel, but are ourselves operating on a reduced scale because of breakdowns in our supplies.' Nevertheless, Luftflotte 4's War Diary was clear: 'Sixth Army, General Paulus: Forward everywhere with support from all air units.'

Nazi high command was now convinced the Soviets were beaten. The OKL issued a report stating that:

The enemy appears in large numbers in the air on Sixth Army's front. Our fighters are able to score substantially. The commander of Luftflotte 4 reports a considerable drop in the quality of the Russian airmen. According to this report our fighter pilots encounter no serious opposition in air combat, it is only a matter of catching the enemy, and when this is done, our fighter pilots are able to shoot down large numbers of Russian aircraft. Obviously, the enemy still has large quantities of materiel at his disposal but is hampered by the low training qualities of the personnel.

At the Wolf's Lair, Hitler beamed with delight and made a fateful decision – it would be safe to split his southern forces. One half would push south and take the Caucasus, while Sixth Army would drive straight east to the River Volga and act as the offensive's hard northern shoulder. The Sixth would take with it all four allied armies as flank protection and it would reach the Volga at an industrial city strung out over miles of river bank and dominated by its factories, grain elevators and an ancient Tatar burial mound called the Mamayev Kurgan that towered several hundred feet over the city.

The city was an ancient one. Almost 500 years before the war, it had started its existence as a Tatar fortress and trading settlement. It had been captured by renegade Cossacks and the Russian Tsars alike, the latter claiming it and naming it Tsaritsyn. During the Civil War it had been besieged and swapped hands more than once between the Reds and Whites. It was then once more renamed in 1925, this time in honour of the man who, according to Soviet legend, saved it for the Bolsheviks. Its new name was Stalingrad.

CHAPTER 17

Stalingrad

Approaching the city from the open steppe, von Richthofen launched a series of air raids on it, designed to kill the inhabitants and flatten its major industrial centres. Starting on 23 August, over 2,000 sorties were flown, dropping hundreds of tons of bombs and killing an estimated 40,000 people. The fuel storage facility in the north of the city was attacked, with burning gasoline pouring out of the shattered tanks and down into the river, with the flames and smoke rising over 200 metres into the air. Stalingrad shook under the bombardment, its poorly trained anti-aircraft defences lacking the ammunition to do anything but act as a hindrance to Fliegerkorps VIII's attacks, while the VVS's defending 102nd Air Division was outnumbered in the air. The water works were hit next and then the residential south-west of the city, its wooden houses burning fiercely in the summer heat. The newer apartment blocks fared no better; their exterior whitewashed walls still stood, but the roofs and internal walls were blown away, leaving nothing but empty shells. Vasiliy Chuikov was now commanding the beleaguered 62nd Army, tasked with holding the city and the west bank of the mighty Volga. His supply lines ran right across the river and were under constant attack by the Luftwaffe, Stukas wreaking havoc among the tugs and ferries bringing over food, ammunition and reinforcements. Every move the craggy-faced general made was pounced on by the ever-watchful Luftwaffe and his troops were pounded from above with high explosive and cannon shells.

'What of our counter-attacks?'

Chuikov's broad-shouldered chief of staff Nikolai Krylov replied: 'They petered out. German aircraft have been over the city again since daybreak. They are pinning down our forces everywhere.'[180]

The German view of the same attacks was almost as incredulous as to the accuracy and the effect.

Our Stukas are coming. We fire off white flares so they are able to recognise our forward lines and drop their bombs on the enemy as close as possible to us. Everywhere white and yellowish-white flares rise to the sky. How can the planes possibly recognise where the German outposts are? They circle and then suddenly go into a dive. With a deafening howl of sirens they come diving down. Far in front of us, directly in front of us, and, my God, also behind us! Giant craters are made as fountains of earth darken the sky. Visibility is nil.[181]

Another German soldier described the scene: 'A mass of Stukas came over us, and after their attack, one could not believe that even a mouse was left alive.'[182]

But the Germans couldn't land a knock-out blow. Somehow, Chuikov's men kept on fighting and Paulus's only answer was the bludgeon. The Luftwaffe wasn't used to shape the battlefield properly; the Soviet artillery batteries on the eastern bank were left unmolested, the ferry points weren't destroyed and the trickle of hope from the east kept on flowing. For the German aircrew it was simply smash, smash, as the Stuka pilot Herbert Pabst recalled: 'We ploughed over the blazing fields of the Stalingrad battlefield all day long. It is incomprehensible to me how people can continue to live in that hell, but the Russians are firmly established in the wreckage, in ravines, cellars and in a chaos of twisted steel skeletons of factories.' In the air the VVS were inspired by the resistance of their Army brethren, as noted by the American reporter James Brown, who interviewed some of the flyers temporarily rested from the front.

Three airmen who had been active in the southwestern combat zone since late July arrived in Moscow, and I interviewed one of them. He carried the Lenin Order and the Order of the Red Banner. He received me at his room in the Hotel New Moscow. My first impression was that I had never previously seen someone so dead-tired and worn out. He told me that he had piloted a MiG-3 and that he had shot down fourteen German aircraft. He added that his comrades flew Shturmoviks.

His two compatriots entered the room. They appeared to be just as fagged out as he was. One of them seemed to be particularly high-strung. Having sat down for no more than a couple of minutes, he rose and started walking up and down the floor. He kept repeating that Stalingrad would hold out. 'We are going to drive the Germans back because that is what we have to do,' the nervy flyer said.[183]

They weren't the only ones who felt that Stalingrad was a turning point. Aron Shapiro, a Pe-2 pilot, remembers: 'It is remarkable but the main preoccupation of the bomber crews was not the possibility of getting shot down, but the shortage of aircraft. Everyone was burning with the desire to fly against the enemy.'

Soon Paulus's entire Army was tied down in the city, his front-line companies being ground into bloody rags by the kind of house-to-house fighting they weren't trained or equipped for and soon nicknamed the 'Rattenkrieg' – 'Rats' War'. Private Wilhelm Hoffman was assaulting the city's main grain elevator. 'If all the buildings of Stalingrad are defended like this then none of us will get back to Germany ... The soldiers are calling Stalingrad the mass grave of the Wehrmacht.'

Chuikov told his men, 'The loss of Stalingrad would destroy the combat spirit of our people. I swear not to abandon Stalingrad. We shall hold Stalingrad or die here!'

It wasn't just soldiers who were dying. As the fighting in the ruined city went on into October, and then November, the never-ending brutality of it all wore down the humanity of the men involved. German infantrymen, desperate for a drink of water, would promise a few scraps of food to scarecrow children to go and fill their water bottles at the river's edge. Soviet snipers, guessing what was happening, turned their sights on their own. One German soldier, Albrecht Schrimpf, saw it all at first hand: 'I think the war was very cruel, but which war is without cruelty? And it was especially cruel if the Russian soldiers were drunk when they attacked. One night we had to make a counter-attack to win back the position of another company and we found the company commander badly wounded and upon him was a drunken Russian soldier cutting off his face.'[184]

Stalingrad helped make monsters of men, but way back from the front in the occupied Ukraine there was no such excuse. What was happening there, as elsewhere in the occupied territories, was sheer mindless barbarism, as pointed out by the German Armaments Inspector for the region in a sarcastic report to his superiors in Berlin: 'If we shoot all the Jews, let the POWs die, subject large parts of the population of major cities to famine, and let parts of the population in the countryside succumb to starvation – then one must ask: who is going to uphold production for us?'

Luftflotte 4 was now split across Stalingrad and the Caucasus offensive, its main combat power increasingly concentrated on the city that Hitler was obsessing more and more about. The stated objective of Blue – the capture of the mineral wealth of the Caucasus – had been lost amidst the increasing muddle of the fighting and the Soviets knew it. Marshal Timoshenko had warned his peers on the Supreme Defence Council, 'If Germany succeeds in taking Moscow, that would be a grave disappointment for us, but it would not disrupt our grand strategy ... The only thing that matters is oil. As we remember, Germany kept harping on her urgent oil problems in her economic bargaining with us from 1939 to 1941, so we must do all we can ... to keep the German armies out of the Caucasus.'

Down in the Caucasus on the Manych River, on the very border between Europe and Asia, General Hermann Breith's 3rd Panzer Division knew it too as the sight of the Luftwaffe became an ever rarer occurrence. One of the 3rd's forward commanders, Lieutenant Tank (yes that was his real name!), led his Berliners in a night river assault across the Manych into Asia. Their nineteen boats beached on the far side and the men swarmed off and pushed outwards to form a tiny bridgehead. The Soviet response was immediate and violent. Counter-attacks were launched, supported by mortars and artillery, and soon Tank's men were running out of ammunition and were in danger of being overrun. As dawn came up at around 0600 hrs, Tank radioed the battalion and demanded support: 'Where is the Luftwaffe?' He expected his call to go unanswered, but from the sky appeared a handful of German planes that swept in, bombing and strafing the Soviets. Tank and his men were relieved, but it would be the last Luftwaffe intervention they would see for quite some time. It was little comfort to Tank and his panzer-grenadiers, but the VVS on hand were not of the highest quality – the majority of what the Soviets could bring to bear was further north fighting the life and death struggle with the Jagdwaffe over Stalingrad. Alexsandr Pokryshkin was one of the relatively few veteran flyers in the Caucasus and he led an attack against Tank's 3rd Panzer:

We headed for the Manych ... contrary to my instructions the young pilots stuck close to me, flying disorderly and uncertain in the formation. They all remained on the same flight level. When we were turning away from the Manych after our low-level attack, a group of four Messerschmitts charged us from behind. I gave my men the signal to attack and turned to meet the enemy. But instead of following me, my pilots closed up and headed for home at full speed. The Messerschmitts went after them without taking any notice of me.

Walter Tödt, flying with the Croatian Lieutenant Colonel Franjo Dzal, also noted the poor quality of their opposition.

> We spotted two MiGs below, and diving out of the sun managed to catch them by surprise. Dzal flew ahead of me and was the first to attack. As soon as the Russian whom I had singled out discovered the threat, he rolled over on his back and turned to avoid me. While Dzal's victim had already fallen in flames, my Russian simply dove into the ground. A victory without a single shot being fired!

Despite victories such as this, the fact was that the Luftwaffe couldn't be in two places at once, plus von Richthofen's losses weren't being made good quickly enough. The strain on the flight and ground crews was beginning to tell as well. 'The continuous dive-bombing missions wore down the flight crews. Stomach influenza and dysentery inflicted the men because of bad rations and unhealthy billeting conditions.'[185]

As the supply situation worsened, Luftwaffe foraging parties were sent out, returning with handfuls of watermelons, which only gave the men diarrhoea.

Even Hermann Graf, by now the highest scoring ace in the world, was near the end of his tether. 'I had to take a day's rest. I just couldn't take any more.' Graf had just lost two Katschmarek in quick succession – Johann Kalb had been shot down and captured, and Heinrich Füllgrabe had a mental breakdown and was grounded.

With Sixth Army and Luftflotte 4 haemorrhaging as the relentless struggle continued, the Soviets were patiently building up their strength for a powerful counter-attack. Ground forces were massed north and south of Stalingrad, aimed at overwhelming the vulnerable Romanians of their 3rd and 4th Armies. The VVS was heavily reinforced as well with no fewer than four of Novikov's new Air Armies: the Seventeenth (Southwest Front), Sixteenth (Don Front) and Eighth (Stalingrad Front). The Voronezh Front's Second Air Army was also earmarked for the counter-strike and Novikov commanded the whole fleet of 1,414 aircraft personally.

Soviet deception – the famed *maskirovka* – helped fool the Germans into believing that any counter-offensive would be a pretty small-scale affair and limited to an attempt to cut the railway line into the city from the west. Berlin's eye was also distracted to the Mediterranean, where the British Eighth Army under Bernard Montgomery had decisively crushed Erwin Rommel's German–Italian forces at El Alamein and Anglo-American forces had landed far to the west in French North Africa. An already stretched Luftwaffe was ordered to rush units south to try and head off the threat, at exactly the same moment the Soviets gathered themselves for their attack. Winter had arrived and with it snow, fog and freezing temperatures. When the Soviets launched Operation Uranus on the morning of 19 November the conditions were dreadful and the Luftwaffe couldn't get off the ground, let alone intervene. Von Richthofen wrote in his diary, 'Once again the Russians have made masterly use of the bad weather. Rain, snow, and freezing fog are making all Luftwaffe operations on the Don impossible.' The Romanians bravely resisted at first, but they were outgunned and outnumbered and soon enough the Soviet spearheads had batted them aside and were charging westwards. Ferdinand Heim's 48th Panzer Corps attempted to seal the breach but met disaster as the German 22nd Panzer Division and the 1st Romanian Panzer Division failed to join together and were washed away in the deluge. With Soviet tanks storming ahead, now was the time the Luftwaffe was desperately needed to pound the leading Red Army units into scrap, but the skies remained relatively clear as most of the Luftwaffe sat grounded: 'We were unable to carry out any air operations at all ... we couldn't even get a clear picture of the situation from the air.'

Hans-Ulrich Rudel and his men were some of the few Luftwaffe aircraft to get airborne:

The weather is bad; low lying clouds, a light fall of snow, the temperature probably 20 degrees below zero. We fly low. What troops are those coming towards us? ... Masses in brown uniforms – are they Russians? No. Romanians. Some of them are even throwing away their rifles in order to be able to run faster, a shocking sight ... The guns are abandoned, not destroyed. Their ammunition lies beside them. We have passed some distance beyond them before we sight the first Soviet troops.

They find all the Romanian positions in front of them deserted. We attack with bombs and gun-fire – but how much use is that when there is no resistance on the ground? ... Relentlessly I drop my bombs on the enemy and spray bursts of MG fire into these shoreless yellow-green waves of oncoming troops ... I haven't a bullet left, not even to protect myself against the contingency of a pursuit attack ... On the return flight we again observe the fleeing Romanians, it is a good thing for them that I have run out of ammunition to stop this cowardly rout.

Rudel could only report what he saw, but it is worth mentioning that not all the Romanian divisions ran away. Outnumbered and with hardly any anti-tank guns, let alone panzer support, many Romanian troops bravely held out until they were outflanked or overwhelmed, dying in their trenches in the snow. When the Soviet pincers met at Kalach on the Don River a few days later, the Sixth Army was officially cut off in Stalingrad.

In the ruins of Stalingrad, Chuikov wrote: 'All of us, from the private to the general, felt proud to be the sons of the Soviet people, felt the pride of the unconquered.'[7186]

What happened next has been the subject of intense controversy and scrutiny ever since. Hitler needed to decide if the Sixth Army was going to be ordered to break out or to stay put. The key factor in that decision was the issue of resupply. Could the Luftwaffe keep Paulus and his men supplied via an airlift or not. Kholm and Demyansk had been relatively successful air transport operations, but Stalingrad would be of a wholly greater scale. Together, Demyansk and Kholm had held about 100,000 men – the force trapped in Stalingrad was almost three times as large.

Since the events themselves, blame for the tragic error of the airlift has overwhelmingly been laid at Goering's door. Von Manstein wrote, 'I am unsure whether Goering's frivolous assurances to Hitler were due to a false appreciation of existing capabilities, or to a desperate need for admiration. Whatever the cause, Goering was responsible.' This statement is not borne out by the facts. As the Soviet pincers were closing, Hitler was in Berchtesgaden, ostensibly having a few days' leave, and with Goering in Carinhall chairing a major conference on Germany's perennial oil problem, the Nazi dictator turned to the one man who should have been able to give him expert advice on Luftwaffe capabilities – Hans Jeschonnek. Jeschonnek arrived at the Berghof, Hitler's mountain retreat, and was ushered into conference with his Führer immediately. Jeschonnek knew that Hitler had cancelled the planned attack at Velikiye Luki and assigned its would-be commander, von Manstein, to head a new 'Army Group Don'. This Army Group had one mission: relieve Sixth Army in Stalingrad and restore the Ostheer's southern front. Both men almost certainly thought that Paulus's encirclement would last a few weeks at most and with that in mind when Hitler asked the Luftwaffe chief of staff if Sixth Army could be supplied by air, Jeschonnek, ever the devotee of his leader, replied, '*Ja, mein Führer*.' From then on those involved were trapped. Jeschonnek, whose knowledge of air transport was limited at best, should have deferred to his own staff and said he would report back – he didn't. Goering, who knew even less about air transport than Jeschonnek, should have intervened and stopped the merry-go-round – he didn't. Paulus should have dismissed as nonsense any plan to supply his huge force by air – he didn't either. By the time the groundswell of opinion from the commanders on the scene – Morzik, Von Richthofen, Pickert, Hube, Strecker, Jaenecke, Seydlitz-Kurbach and Heitz – made it clear that there was no chance at all of the Luftwaffe being able to successfully complete the operation, the decision had been made.

It is clear that the decision to institute an airlift was a collective one at the most senior levels of command in Nazi Germany and while it is without doubt that Goering must shoulder a portion of the blame for it, Jeschonnek must at least share that burden. He knew his East Prussian air transport chief Fritz Morzik well and he also knew Morzik's own view on launching such any airlift operation: 'Every possible effort must have been made to obviate the necessity for one.' As it was, muddle and happenstance as much as crass stupidity by senior commanders who should have known better would seal the fate of Sixth Army and determine the near-destruction of the Luftwaffe's transport arm.

The orders for the airlift went out and as in previous emergencies, the result was the virtual closing down of much of the Luftwaffe's training programme as aircraft and instructors were sent east. Hundreds of Ju 52s were gathered on forward airfields and joined by a motley collection of He 111s, Ju 86s and even Fw 200 Condors and the dreaded He 177s. The latter were included despite the deaths of seventeen crewmen in mechanical accidents in them that same spring. None of this large armada were high capacity transports designed for the easy loading and unloading of significant tonnages. The now legendary figure of 300 tons of supplies required per day for Sixth Army to survive would have to be shuttled in to just one main airfield at Pitomnik, with inadequate facilities and amateurish organisation. Approaching aircraft would have to run a gauntlet of massed anti-aircraft fire and sustained VVS attack and as the Red Army pushed the main German line further and further west, the transports had to fly far longer routes with the resulting loss of lift capacity to fuel usage. The Soviets were also determined to try and halt the airlift at source, launching raids on the main airfields like Salsk.

We approached Salsk at dawn, the airfield was swarming with planes ... We flew back and reported the situation. Our commanders immediately scrambled two regiments of Shturmoviks ... I flew in at 800 metres while a huge column of Shturmoviks followed me at 4–600 metres ... I led the Shturmoviks to the target and they attacked with bombs and RS missiles. At the second pass they opened up with machine-guns. That was it. The partisans told us later we'd destroyed over 60 German planes and burnt a storage dump containing fuel and ammo.[187]

Bad weather also severely hampered the operation, closing Pitomnik for days at a time. With no steady flow of ammunition, food and fuel, Sixth Army lost ground and casualties skyrocketed and soon enough Soviet artillery was able to bring Pitomnik into range. Now, the risks to crews and aircraft rose sharply and wrecked planes littered the ground. Daily deliveries were well below what was required. Only on 7, 19 and 20 December were the tonnages flown in even close: 282 tons, 289 tons and 291 tons respectively. On most days it was a third of that. Between 25 November and 11 January the daily average was actually around 105 tons. Clutching at straws, the Luftwaffe drafted in Milch, hoping he could deliver some sort of miracle. His organisational brilliance did indeed make a difference and more supplies got through, but it was too little, too late. When Pitomnik fell to the encircling Red Army, the airlift had to switch to the tiny and totally unsuitable Gumrak field, nearer the city centre. Gumrak's handling capacity was a fraction of Pitomnik's and only a trickle of flights were successfully made. Soon even that sliver of hope was lost as Gumrak itself fell and the Luftwaffe was reduced to flying over the Pocket, air-dropping supplies out of the side doors of aircraft and hoping that at least some of them would be picked up from the snow by the surviving members of Sixth Army. When the newly promoted Field Marshal Paulus defied Hitler and finally surrendered rather than commit suicide, it was all over. The last flight of the failed airlift was by Lieutenant Herbert Kuntz of KG 100 on 3 February 1943. His commander, Hansgeorg Bätcher, told him: 'Have a look to see whether fighting still continues anywhere or whether escaping parties can be seen, then drop your load.' Kuntz's He 111 was packed with bread, chocolate, bandages and ammunition, and as he flew towards the city not a single anti-aircraft gun fired at him. The VVS were nowhere to be seen either; it was as though the Soviets wanted Kuntz and his crew to bear witness to their final victory. The crew, Hans Annen the observer, radio operator Walter Krebs and Paske the engineer, all scanned the ground looking for signs of fighting but saw nothing. They dropped down to 300 feet, then 250, where suddenly they thought they saw something through the ground fog, and the order was given: 'Load away!' The supplies drifted down on their parachutes; maybe they were found by the last starving and emaciated holdouts, but probably not. Kuntz signalled his base, 'No more sign of fighting in Stalingrad.'[188]

Over the next couple of weeks various Luftwaffe flights reported seeing groups of soldiers out on the steppe heading west through the snow. Sometimes they managed to drop some supplies to them. In the end none of them got through to the new German lines to the west. The land swallowed them up.

Case Blue had failed spectacularly and Hitler's gamble had ended in disaster. The Caucasus was hurriedly abandoned as the Germans fled back to Rostov in disorderly retreat and the Ostheer's entire southern wing teetered on the brink of calamity. The German Sixth Army was gone, along with swathes of the Fourth Panzer and Second Armies and all four allied armies were expunged off the order of battle.

For the Luftwaffe it was equally bad. Over 500 aircraft were lost in the airlift – fully one-third of Nazi Germany's entire transport fleet, plus large numbers of converted bombers. More than 1,000 air crew had perished, many of them irreplaceable instructors from the flight schools. Multi-engine training would never recover and neither would the Luftwaffe's air transport arm. That winter, as the town of Velikiye Luki further north was besieged, its 7,000-strong garrison was forced to rely on air resupply. With no airstrip in the Pocket and only a handful of transport aircraft now available, Heinz-Joachim Schmidt, the commodore of Luftflotte 6's KG 4, fitted his Stukas with bomb containers full of food and ammunition and dropped them to the desperate defenders. It was never going to be enough and when the breakout was eventually ordered, most of the surviving defenders were killed on the steppe. In the end only some 150 reached the German lines. By 1955 another eleven had been repatriated from Soviet POW camps. The captured garrison commander, Lieutenant Colonel Eduard Freiherr von Sass, was publicly hanged by the Soviets along with six of his men in the town's main square in January 1946 for supposed 'war crimes'. It was little more than an act of state revenge.

In the end the only bright spark for all the Luftwaffe's effort was the fact it had managed to evacuate about 42,000 wounded, sick and hand-picked specialists from Stalingrad before the end and given that only 5,000 of the 90,000 men who finally surrendered ever made it home, they were definitely the lucky ones.

One man who did not survive was Ernst Speer. The Armament Minister's brother was serving with Sixth Army and was caught up in Stalingrad. He contracted jaundice and was hospitalised, but remained in the Pocket as the fighting raged. His brother Albert later proclaimed he had tried to save Ernst by having him flown out, but by the time he got it organised in January it was too late as Ernst's unit was splintered and he couldn't be found. In the end he was listed as missing believed killed, along with tens of thousands of others.

> My brother was in Stalingrad and personally I tried to bring him out by plane. The man in charge of all the air forces around Stalingrad promised me to do his utmost to find him, but he couldn't be found. Goering's assurance that he could supply the besieged city from the air was just one of those things which happened quite often in Hitler's surroundings. People were afraid of telling the absolute truth and they wanted to please him, and Goering saw Hitler in a desolate, depressive mood so he made his promise possibly without asking his generals beforehand.

The OKH deputy chief of staff, Walter Warlimont, wrote scathingly of Hitler at the time:

> He has realised that his deadly game is moving to its appointed end, that Soviet Russia is not going to be overthrown at the second attempt and that now the war on two fronts which he has unleashed by his wanton, arbitrary actions, will grind the Reich to powder... he can no longer bear to have around him the generals who have too often been witnesses to his faults, his errors, his illusions and his day-dreams.

Despite these sentiments, Walter Warlimont did not join the ranks of the anti-Hitler resistance; instead he slavishly served his Führer until the very end.

For the Luftwaffe's allied contingents, Blue had also been a costly failure. The Italians had lost ten aircraft shot down while claiming forty-seven VVS kills, but the majority of the men wanted nothing more than to go home. Desertion was rearing its head among the Croats and Slovaks again and the Romanians were increasingly looking to protect their own air space and little else. For the Hungarians much of their aerial contribution had been lost during the Soviet offensive against their 2nd Army in January. Most of their aircraft were based at Ilovskoye and when they refused to start due to the extreme cold they were blown up to avoid them falling into Soviet hands. As the Red Army neared the airfield, dozens of aircrew and ground personnel were killed defending it, including their highly decorated commander, Lieutenant Colonel Kalman Csukas. Csukas wasn't the only high-profile Magyar casualty. Istvan Horthy, fighter pilot and eldest son of Hungary's dictator, Admiral Miklos Horthy, was killed in an air accident at Ilovskoye back in the late summer. Only the Finns were still holding their own. During 1942 they had shot down 458 Soviet aircraft (355 in the air and 103 by anti-aircraft fire) versus a loss to themselves of thirty-four.

1942 was a momentous year for the Luftwaffe in the east. Its pilots continued to be showered with medals as they scoured the skies of the VVS. Some 105 Knight's Crosses were awarded to pilots of the Jagdwaffe that year, ninety of them going to pilots in the east (eighty-eight to Bf 109 flyers and two to BF 110 aviators). The Oak Leaves went to thirty-two fighter pilots – twenty-seven of whom were based in the east, and the ten men awarded the Swords were all in Russia. Luftwaffe scores went ever higher; Hermann Graf became the first ever pilot in history to reach the magical number of 200 kills, JG 51 reached its 4,000 victory mark in November, swiftly followed by JG 52 in December. But the blood price had been huge, even among the Experten. Thirty-three Knight's Cross winners died in action in 1942, twenty-six in the east, with twelve of the fifteen posthumous Knight's Cross awards going to eastern pilots. Casualties among the officer ranks were even worse, with dozens of lieutenants and captains lost. One such loss was Lieutenant Max-Hellmuth Ostermann, a Knight's Cross holder with Oak Leaves and Swords and with 102 victories to his credit when he was shot down and killed back in August over Lake Ilmen. His commander, Hannes Trautloft, wrote in his diary, 'We often, and sometimes, light minded, speak about an "irreplaceable loss", where perhaps some less strong word could be used. But in this case "irreplaceable" felt too little. Of course, we carried on the fight even after the death of Ostermann. But no other pilot of my Geschwader embodied the nature of a fighter pilot so purely as Ostermann.' As the officer ranks were culled, more and more Staffeln were filled with NCO pilots. Forty-five of the Eastern Front Knight's Crosses went to NCOs, including six to men of *Unteroffizier* rank. The Luftwaffe refused to just promote anyone though, their unofficial motto being, 'Better no officer than a bad officer.'

On the other side of the line, the VVS was getting better and better, even as the Jagdwaffe was losing its leadership cadre, and everyone knew it. The Luftwaffe's own Lieutenant General Walter Schwabedissen wrote:

As early as the beginning of 1942 Russian ground attack aviation had, for the most part, recovered from the defeat of 1941. During the course of the winter operations it proved to be even superior to the Luftwaffe on several occasions. From then on the Germans observed the gradual strengthening of Russian ground attack aviation despite the personnel and material losses suffered ... offensive operations were properly coordinated, and produced a considerable effect on the Germans, especially on their morale.[189]

The War Diary of JG 54 commented on a VVS attack on its base at Gorodets, 'In spite of all hostilities one must admit that the "comrades" pressed home their attack with great courage.'

If the Germans knew it, so too did the VVS. 'Although the Germans had some weak pilots, most were experienced warriors ... after Rzhev we were at the same level with the Germans ... they were much more careful then.'[190]

PART FIVE

1943

As 1943 dawned, the much vaunted Thousand Year Reich suddenly looked decidedly frail. The Anglo-Americans were in the process of throwing the Axis out of North Africa and Mussolini's hold on power in Italy was precarious. Berlin's other Axis allies in Eastern Europe were shell-shocked at losing so much of their military power in the Soviet Union on the Don River and Tito's Communist partisans were setting occupied Yugoslavia alight. The OKW nervously looked across the English Channel at the build-up of forces in the south of the country – would the liberation of France begin in 1943? Above all of this loomed Stalingrad. Nazi Germany simply couldn't afford another defeat of that magnitude.

The debate raged as to what to do in this critical year. Von Manstein led the calls to go over to the strategic defensive in the east. He argued that the Germans should adopt a mobile, flexible defence, trade space for time and let the Soviets attack them and then counter-punch, draining them of their strength while husbanding their own. Adolf Hitler, on the other hand, was still obsessed with the Cannae concept – one huge victory that would finally finish off the Soviet bear. It was an illusion, but as the proverbial drowning man grasps at straws, so too did Hitler and his eye would alight on a city called Kursk in south central Russia.

For the Luftwaffe in the east, 1943 would be dominated by two offensives, 1,000 miles and more apart: Hitler's last major throw of the dice at Kursk to try and regain the initiative in the Soviet Union, and back home in the skies over the Reich, where the RAF's bomber offensive would be joined by the might of the United States and more and more German aerial combat power was drawn home and away from the Eastern Front.

CHAPTER 18

Another Battle at Kharkov

The STAVKA followed up its remarkable victory at Stalingrad by launching a powerful armoured thrust in the south aimed at liberating Kharkov and shattering the Ostheer's southern wing for good. General Markian Popov's armour-heavy group was sent headlong forwards and soon German-held Kharkov was threatened with encirclement. Inside the city were Paul Hausser's II SS Panzer Corps and in a chilling repetition of his earlier disastrous decision, Hitler ordered that retreat from the city was unthinkable and that it must be held to the last man and the last bullet. For once his order fell on deaf ears – or rather ears that were prepared to ignore their far-off leader. With Hausser's connivance, Von Manstein pulled the Waffen-SS corps out of the city, letting it fall to the Soviets. Then, in a brilliant move, the two generals turned the tables on Popov and smashed his corps into so much scrap metal. The Soviet offensive was annihilated, 615 tanks were destroyed and Kharkov and Belgorod retaken. At a stroke the south was stabilised and safe – for now.

The Kharkov counter-stroke was a classic operation of manoeuvre and timing and once again von Manstein and von Richthofen were to be found working hand in glove to deliver stunning results, just as they had in the Crimea and at Sevastopol the previous summer. It would be, however, the last time these two men – the best their respective service arms had to offer – would work together. With the Anglo-Americans preparing to leap across the Mediterranean to Sicily, von Richthofen was dispatched south-west to try and perform a miracle and fend off the expected Allied assault. In Italy he would find another world of aerial warfare, one where the Luftwaffe was not only outnumbered but also outclassed, outgunned, out-everythinged! By the end of the year the Italian peninsula had been more or less swept clean of the German air force and Von Richthofen was a leader with no one to lead. Diagnosed in 1944 with a brain tumour, he retired on health grounds in November and never served again. He was captured in May 1945 by the Americans, who would have tried him for war crimes had his death not been imminent. Wolfram von Richthofen passed away on the 12 July 1945 in the Luftwaffe hospital at Bad Ischl in Austria.

As in the previous year (and the year before that), Adolf Hitler's plan for 1943 in the east was to launch a single major offensive that would cripple the Red Army and pave the way for final victory – as a strategic concept it was hardly breaking new ground. The Nazi dictator's forces were limited and they faced a Soviet foe that was getting stronger week by week as the Soviets' relocated factories were now in full swing and Lend-Lease supplies were pouring into the country from the Anglo-Americans. Yet again, the big question for both sides was where would the blow fall? Hitler discounted the north as being of no strategic value and Moscow was out as her defences were far too strong. A thrust back across the southern steppe towards the Volga and the Caucasus was beyond German military means and in any case would only be a rerun of the previous year's disaster. Pouring over the maps at his daily conferences, Hitler thought he'd found his answer – Kursk.

The Red Army's winter offensive had created a large bulge in the line straddling the northern flank of Army Group South and the southern end of Army Group Centre. A powerful armoured assault from both north and south could meet in the middle and cut off a host of Soviet Armies. Having put hundreds of thousands of Soviets into the bag, the Ostheer could then exploit east and tip the balance back into Nazi Germany's favour – it would be 1941 all over again.

Except it wasn't.

The Soviet armed forces of 1943 were not the Purge-ravaged herds the Wehrmacht had faced back then. The Red Army was on its way to becoming an extremely professional, mechanised behemoth, capable of multiple, simultaneous large-scale offensives that were now way beyond Germany's abilities. Worst of all for the Nazis, thanks to British Ultra decryptions and a highly placed Communist spy at Hitler's headquarters – codenamed 'Werther' – the STAVKA knew exactly where the attack would come and it was determined to be ready.

For the Luftwaffe, multi-engine training had been drastically reduced by the losses to the transport arm and the instructor crews during the attempted relief of Stalingrad and the fighter schools were having to send pilots to the front with average flight hours of just 160 hours – it had been 210 back in 1942. Against the Anglo-Americans in particular, this was proving fatal. The USAAF and RAF outnumbered their opponents and their new pilots arrived with 360 and 400 hours of flying time respectively.[191] The VVS academies weren't at that level yet, but they were improving, as JG 54's Hans Ekkehard-Bob admitted. 'It was also obvious that that the Russians had improved their tactics. We were no longer able to catch them by surprise. Those days were past and gone.' These new tactics were mainly modelled on the German Rotte, Kette and Schwarm formations. The Soviet versions were the '*pary*' and the '*zveno*'. The 'flocking' method was also developed by the Soviets, with aircraft flying in seemingly random patterns to avoid getting jumped by surprise. This type of flying put huge stress on aero engines, but as Soviet engines were only designed to last around eighty hours before they were replaced anyway, it didn't matter that much.

The VVS now outnumbered the Luftwaffe by five to one and the concentration of the best pilots in the best machines in the new Guards regiments was having a real impact, especially on the longevity of newly arrived pilots in the German Staffeln. The Reich's training schools couldn't turn them out quickly enough as a full quarter of graduates didn't survive beyond their first four missions. The old days of front-line Staffeln breaking replacements in gradually, with time on quiet sectors before they were sent into action, had gone. Now, the shortfall was at such a level that even instructors were being sent back to the front to help make up the numbers. Those instructors, the majority of them aces themselves, rejoined their Experten comrades and continued to take a heavy toll of their Soviet enemies, and the eastern fighter groups' tallies kept on rising; JG 54 reached the 4,000 kill mark in February, while JGs 51 and 52 were nearing 6,000 each.

As the fighting continued unabated up and down the length of the Eastern Front, back in Berlin the OKW began to mass its forces for its Kursk offensive, codenamed *Zitadelle* – Citadel. On the ground, the northern pincer would be formed by Walter Model's Ninth Army, while Erich von Manstein would lead the southern pincer composed of Hermann Hoth's Fourth Panzer Army and Werner Kempf's Army Detachment Kempf. Von Manstein favoured a swift attack, pretty much right after the Kharkov victory, but Hitler turned him down flat, opting instead to heavily reinforce all three assault formations and wait for better weather. Men, panzers and guns poured into the designated assembly areas until the Germans had managed to concentrate three-quarters of a million men, almost 10,000 guns and mortars, and the vast majority of their armoured might – close on 3,000 panzers and assault guns, including the new generation models of Tigers, Panthers and the gigantic Elephants. In terms of sheer combat power this was not far off what Barbarossa had begun with – barring the lack of infantry – and this time it would all be concentrated on a few hundred square miles rather than tens of thousands. However, while Hitler's self-imposed delay was understandable, it was also potentially fatal. Pre-warned, the STAVKA began a build-up of its own and it had a far deeper well from which to draw.

The roads and railheads into the salient were jammed day and night. Well over a million Red Army soldiers moved into the bulge and began to dig. Supported by 300,000 civilian labourers, they built six huge concentric belts of defences, constructed to a depth of well over 180 miles (nearly 300 kilometres). The Voronezh and Central Fronts, for example, dug 2,600 and 3,100 miles of trenches respectively (4,200 and 5,000 kilometres). Nests of machine-guns and anti-tank batteries were connected by multiple trench lines interspersed with strongpoints and barbed wire. Over 25,000 artillery and mortar pieces were massed almost wheel to wheel, the barrels set on pre-set firing zones to cover some of the densest minefields ever laid. Convoys of trucks brought those mines forward over 1,200 miles (2,000 kilometres) of newly built roads and 686 new bridges, to where waiting engineers and infantrymen unloaded them and dug them into position. Soviet records state they laid 503,663 anti-tank mines, interlaced with 439,348 anti-personnel ones, sown in dry gullies, stream banks, road-side ditches and around the anti-armour belts to discourage German mine-clearing parties. The Soviets also moved in over 5,000 of their own tanks to meet the expected '*Panzerkeils*' (the Panzerwaffe's wedge assault formation) head on. All of this from a force of which Erhard Milch had said: 'Russia will no longer have any army. The Russians are finished.'

With such a relatively compact battlefield, air superiority would be hugely important to either side.

The VVS prepared for the battle much as its comrades in the Red Army did, with a huge build-up in front-line and reserve forces, massive logistics and strength in depth. Novikov moved in the First, Second, Third, Fifteenth and Sixteenth Air Armies (about a third of the VVS's total frontline strength) and stockpiled supplies of fuel and ammunition as well as ample reserves of replacement aircraft so that the regiments could conduct an extended campaign without slackening in the intensity of their effort. The fighter units were primarily equipped with the new Yakovlev Yak-9 and Lavochkin La-5 aircraft, which gave the Soviet pilots near parity with the Luftwaffe in terms of quality, and very large numbers of Ilyushin Il-2 Shturmoviks and Pe-2 Peshkas were brought forward as well to provide a ground-attack capability, although this wasn't to every VVS pilot's pleasure: 'The hardest plane to escort was the Shturmovik. They flew so slowly, but if we fighters flew at their speed we'd be sitting ducks. That's why we normally flew above the group, either in circles or in loops.'[192] The Shturmovik was indeed a formidable adversary, nicknamed the 'Iron Gustav' or 'Cement Coffin' by the Jagdwaffe pilots, who realised early on just how hard they could be to shoot down, encased as they were in thick protective armour plating and bullet-resistant glass. As it was, the Experten had to come up with new tactics to destroy them and one of the first to do so was, unsurprisingly, Werner Mölders. Back in 1941 he had taken a new pilot, Herbert Kaiser, on a 'teaching' mission against a formation of Shturmoviks to show him the ropes.

He positioned himself off to one side of, and some distance away from, the last Il-2 in a formation of six. He then turned in quickly and opened fire at the enemy's cockpit from an angle of some thirty degrees. The Il-2 immediately burst into flames and crashed. 'Do you see how it's done?' Mölders' voice came over the radio. 'Right, now you take the next one.' I carried out the same manoeuvre and, sure enough, the next Il-2 went down on fire. 'And again!' It was like being on a training flight. Another short burst and the third Il-2 was ablaze. The whole lesson had lasted no more than 12 minutes!

The VVS had reacted by altering the aircraft's design and adding in a rear gunner – although to save on weight that same gunner was provided with only a fraction of the armour plating surrounding the pilot!

Nevertheless, the new design didn't save them all, as was attested by the greatest air ace of all time, Erich 'Bubi' Hartmann:

Well you can't believe it, but the Shturmovik, which was their main ground-attack aircraft, flew like American B-17s in formation and didn't attempt to make any evasive manoeuvres. And all they had was one peashooter in the back of each plane. Also, some of the pilots were women. Their peashooter was no threat unless they had a very lucky hit on you. I didn't open fire until the aircraft filled my whole windscreen. If I did this, I would get one every time.

Other Experten had their own ways of dealing with the ubiquitous Shturmovik, one swearing that the best way was to hit the flight leader, who was often the only experienced pilot and the only one briefed on the target, and then the others would usually scatter for home.

Notwithstanding, they were considered so important that Stalin himself intervened in their production, sending a note to the factory managers responsible for their manufacture when he thought they weren't making enough progress: 'They are as essential to the Red Army as air and bread ... I demand more machines. This is my final warning!' A 'final warning' from the Soviet dictator was not to be taken lightly by any Soviet citizen who wanted to stay alive and the production lines started rolling in earnest.

Facing the Soviets would be the newly created Luftflotte 6 in the north under the command of the promoted Ritter von Greim and Otto Dessloch's Luftflotte 4 in the south. As was usual for the Ostheer's summer offensives, Staffeln were stripped from other sectors to beef up these two lead formations. Outnumbered by three to one, the forces deployed still comprised about two-thirds of the entire eastern Luftwaffe, and the airfields surrounding the salient were crammed full of waiting aircraft.

To conserve vital aviation fuel for Citadel, air operations over much of the rest of the Eastern Front in the run-up to the offensive were reduced to a bare minimum, but inexplicably the OKL decided now was the time to launch a belated foray into the arena of strategic bombing. Several missions were launched against a variety of targets: the giant tank factory at Gorky, the synthetic rubber processing works at Yaroslavl and the rail marshalling yards at Yelets. Opinions differed on the results, although Albert Speer was unconvinced. 'Our air force claimed to have bombed a synthetic rubber plant in Russia and that it would be out of action for a year or longer, but our experts looked into it and said it would be repaired in a few weeks.'[193] It would seem an odd time to mount such attacks to say the least, especially as the shortage of aviation fuel was becoming very worrisome with Soviet partisans launching no fewer than 1,098 separate attacks against the railway lines bringing it up from the German rear. The resupply figures made grim reading for the Luftwaffe commanders; von Greim's new Luftflotte used 8,634 tons of B-4 blue fuel in June (low octane fuel for bombers and general purpose flying) and only received 5,722 tons. High octane fuel for the fighters was even worse. Consumption in June was 1,079 tons of C-3 green fuel and only 411 tons reached them – all at a time when they were trying to build up reserves for the coming offensive. The Luftwaffe were ready to play their part as usual, but given the supply situation they could only keep up a high operational tempo for a few days at most, would it be enough to support Von Manstein and Model to break through the Soviet defences and head into open country and a great victory? For once even the Nazi supremo seemed ill at ease. The famed panzer general Heinz Guderian challenged him face to face:

'My Führer, why do you want to attack in the East at all this year?'
Hitler: 'You are quite right. Whenever I think of this attack my stomach turns over.'
Guderian: 'In that case your reaction to the problem is the correct one. Leave it alone.'

At that point the obsequious Field Marshal Wilhelm Keitel, Head of the OKW, butted in, trying to explain to the bristling panzer general the political importance of the offensive.

Guderian's response was blunt. 'How many people do you think even know where Kursk is? It's a matter of profound indifference to the world whether we capture Kursk or not.'

But it was too late for the Germans. As the 48th Panzer Corps' Friedrich von Mellenthin observed, 'Germany is in the position of having caught a wolf by its ears and can't afford to let it go.'

On the night of 3 July, as darkness finally fell on the hills of Butovo at the southern end of the Kursk salient, a small clearing party of ten engineers from the Germany Army's élite Grossdeutschland Division crawled gingerly forward into the no man's land between their forward trenches and those of the Soviets defending the slopes. Their commander, Lieutenant Baletshofer, knew they only had a few hours before the summer sun came up. If they hadn't done their job and cleared a path through the mines by then, they would be lying exposed right in front of the Soviet guns without a shred of cover. The tiny unit worked like men possessed, feeling for the buried mines with bayonets and then carefully digging them up and moving them out of the way before going on to the next one. In just five hours they lifted 2,700 mines by hand. That's one mine per man per minute. Minutes before dawn broke Baletshofer and his men retraced their own steps and fell exhausted into the slit trenches, every man lathered in sweat – the job was done.

As Baletshofer and his men grabbed some much needed sleep, Captain Leyk, the commander of the Grossdeutschland's 3rd Panzer Grenadier Battalion, was sitting in his foxhole waiting for H-Hour as a sudden rain squall came in and soaked everyone right through. His regimental commander, Colonel Karl Lorenz, had been clear in his orders to the veteran Leyk – 'take the hills and don't stop for anything'. By 1445 the rain had finally stopped and Leyk looked upwards, scanning the western sky. 'On the dot.' His eyes had picked out the unmistakable gull-winged outline of a flight of Stukas. As they approached, high over Butovo, they banked, dived and the wailing began. With Bf 109s covering them, the German dive-bombers began crashing their bombs into the Soviet first line of defence. Then another Staffel came in, and another, then a fourth and a fifth and in no time at all 2,500 bombs had been dropped on a strip of ground just two miles long and 500 yards deep. At 1500 the Stukas finished and the German artillery took over. After a further ten minutes of fire Leyk leapt up from his trench and led his battalion forward. The German grenadiers ran headlong across the minefield and up the enemy-held slope through the lanes cleared by Baletshofer and his men. The shell-shocked defenders tried to resist and called in their own artillery and mortar fire. Bitter, hand-to-hand fighting raged in the Soviet trenches, but the Grossdeutschland men weren't to be denied and by 1645 the first Soviet trench line had been taken. The cost was appalling. Nearly a third of the lead assault company lay dead on the hillside, along with Captain Leyk. Leyk's successor, Captain Bolk, was still alive but last a leg to a mine Baletshofer's team had missed.[194]

Now the Butovo heights had been gained, the stage was set for the main assault to begin on the morning of the 5th.

CHAPTER 19

Kursk

As the clock ticked down to H-hour, the VVS attempted its most audacious assault of the war so far. Its intent was to begin the Kursk battle with a knockout blow against the Luftwaffe. Determined to go one better than their failed pre-emptive strike before Timoshenko's disastrous Kharkov offensive the previous year, the Soviets hatched a plan to bomb Luftflotte 4's airfields on the morning of 5 July as they lay packed with waiting German aircraft. The attack would comprise 500 aircraft of the 1st, 4th and 16th VAs and would be timed to hit before any Germans were in the air, barring a few pre-dawn flights.

What the Soviet planners didn't know was that the timing could be even better than they thought. Unbeknown to them Luftflotte 4 had a plan of its own. Dessloch had decided not to attack the VVS on the ground as per previous offensives, as he considered that the Soviet supply of replacement machines was now so great that all it would achieve would be a few days' grace at best before the pilots were handed new aircraft. No – what he planned was to limit his assault to a massed strike against the forward Red Army positons so that Hoth's panzer spearheads could break through. To achieve this aerial armada, Dessloch's staff had sent out orders for the slower ground-attack and bomber Staffeln to take off first, reach cruising altitude and then circle while their shorter-range escort fighters took off and climbed to join them. This all made sense to the Germans. However, the unintended consequence could be that the Soviets would appear directly over the German air bases when none of their fighters were in the air. The skies would be full with slow ground-attack aircraft and bombers, easy prey for the new Soviet fighters – it could be a massacre and deal the Luftwaffe a crippling blow.

The fact that it wasn't was due to one thing – Freya. Freya was the Luftwaffe's early warning radar system and it had been deployed to cover Fliegerkorps VIII; at sixty miles out – the limit of its range – Freya detected the approaching Soviets, spitting out their height, direction and approximate numbers. Back at the corps' forward headquarters at Mikoyanovka the corps chief of staff, Major General Hans Seidemann, was just finishing dressing when his orderly officer burst in and reported the approaching Soviets. Seidemann, a Lipetsk graduate himself and an old hand on the Eastern Front, knew immediately what the Soviets had planned. Quick as a flash, he ordered his staff to contact the Jagdwaffe and get their fighters in the air as fast as possible. On the corps' sixteen separate air strips, all was chaos. Pilots ran from their tents and out to their waiting aircraft, all of them parked far apart from each other and with makeshift anti-splinter cover. Ground crew were frantically pulling off camouflage nets and helping the pilots get into their cockpits and taxi for take-off. In all some 140 Bf 109s from JG 52 and JG 3 were ordered up and in minutes the first of them were climbing as fast as their screaming engines would allow them. The VVS pilots were blissfully unaware of all the activity below and around them, their eyes scanning the ground for any sign of their intended targets. Coming out of the dawn sun, the hastily scrambled German fighters pounced on the Soviets, guns and cannons hammering. The Soviet bombers and their escorts were flying between 6,000 and 10,000 feet, exactly where the German machines had the most advantage in terms of speed and performance over their Soviet counterparts and 'it developed into the largest and fiercest air battle of all time'. The VVS were ravaged as the German Experten wreaked havoc. In less than an hour, 120 Soviet planes were shot down and the rest were scattered and heading for home and safety.

Not everything went the Germans' way. The VVS technician and mechanic Viktor M. Sinaisky was at Kursk and on the first day of the battle he was at his base when guards brought in a downed Stuka pilot, 'a huge German pilot, about two metres tall, a blond and handsome guy'. The Soviets tried to get him to talk, eventually threatening him with a pistol, and at that point the German said, 'In 20 minutes there will be 500 planes heading for Kursk, it will be a famous air raid. Over 200 bombers will fly over, the rest will fly in from north and south.' The Soviets scrambled immediately. 'We watched our regiment and the 88th Regiment taking off and climbing … then our 41st Regiment also took off and a slaughter started. We saw German bombers falling one by one. Soon their formation dispersed and they started turning back, no thoughts about Kursk!'[195]

In the air the battles raged all day. Loss statistics are disputed but it would seem that at least 200 Soviet machines were downed and at most perhaps as many as twice that number. Most sources agree that Luftwaffe losses stood at twenty-six.[196]

Whatever the actual figure for the VVS, it was clear that the Soviet air force had suffered a major blow. With the decimated fighter regiments temporarily out of action the Luftwaffe again switched to its role as airborne tactical artillery.

In the south, that meant supporting Paul Hausser's II SS Panzer Corps as it slammed into Lieutenant General Ivan Chistyakov's Sixth Guards Army, which was acting as cover for General Mikhail Katukov's First Tank Army. Chistyakov was a general who liked the good things in life and his field headquarters was situated in a house with a well-tended garden and a small apple orchard. As Hausser's Waffen-SS men advanced on that first morning, he was enjoying a second breakfast at a picnic table out in the garden. The forty-two year-old Katukov and his military council member, Lieutenant General Nikolai Popel, drove up to find out for themselves what was going on at the front. Popel, a stocky man with a bristling moustache who had fought the Germans back in the summer of 1941 at Brody, looked on in amazement as the two generals were ushered into the garden by an immaculately turned-out aide. There they found Chistyakov, happily tucking in to a table laden with food and drink. 'On the table were cold mutton, scrambled eggs, a carafe with chilled vodka, to judge by the condensation on the glass, and finely sliced white bread – Chistyakov was doing well.'

Smiling, Chistyakov asked them to join him, only to be rudely interrupted by German artillery fire that made them all scatter.

The Sixth Guards Army commander raced into his HQ demanding to know what was going on.

A wounded artillery commander staggered in and reported: 'My regiment has been in action for only an hour comrade General, and already one-third of our guns have been eliminated. The German aircraft are dropping vast numbers of small bombs which have colossal high-fragmentation effect. The Stukas are dominating the air space. They are just doing what they like up there, we are helpless.'

'And where are our aircraft?' countered Chistyakov. 'Where are our three Air Armies, and the long-range bomber divisions with their two and a half thousand machines which headquarters moved to the Kursk salient? Why was the Luftwaffe not smashed on its fields this morning as planned?'[197]

Why indeed? The day belonged to the Luftwaffe. The small bombs the Soviet artilleryman was referring to were a new and deadly innovation.

The SD-1 and SD-2s were bomb-shaped containers crammed full with, respectively, 180 x 2 kg or 360 x 1 kg mini-bombs – a forerunner of modern submunitions. Dropped on concentrations of troops and equipment out in the open, they were devastating. The Sixth Guards reeled back in confusion and were then hit by Germany's greatest Stuka Experte – the Silesian Hans-Ulrich Rudel.[198] The twenty-seven-year-old Rudel was both a teetotaller and a non-smoker and as a child seemed an unlikely candidate to become the most highly decorated man in Nazi Germany. A very delicate boy, his older sister said of him: 'Uli will never be any good in life, he is even afraid of going into the cellar by himself.' Indeed, his mother had to physically hold his hand to calm him during thunderstorms until he was a teenager. Graduating as a pilot, he became a master of dive-bombing and it was in the famous Ju 87 Stuka that he would rise to fame. Kursk would be a showcase for Rudel's talents in ground attack, the appearance of him and his men never failing to raise morale among the Landsers. 'To our delight, our Stukas arrived and, sirens screaming, hurled themselves at the Russians despite tremendous anti-aircraft fire. I recognised the insignia of one of our most successful flyers, *Oberst* Rudel – I think he was an *Oberst* at the time anyway.'[199]

For Kursk, Rudel had had 37 mm cannons fitted beneath his Stuka's wings so he could swoop in and shoot up Soviet tanks in their thinly armoured weak spots in the rear and on their top decks. His command used both their cannon and the new SD fragmentation bombs to blow away the Soviet 151st and 155th Guards Rifle Regiments near Berezov and by 1100 on 8 July almost fifty panzers had broken through and were heading for the main Belgorod–Kursk highway.[200]

The Soviets were staring disaster in the face. The panzers had to be stopped. Hausser's men were now threatening the rear of Katukov's First Tank Army. If they cut its supply lines and drove on they could win the battle. General Nikolai Vatutin, the extremely able commander-in-chief of the Voronezh Front, acted immediately. He ordered sixty T-34s and accompanying rifle battalions from the II Guards Tank Corps near Gostishchevo to cut into Hausser's flank at the Belgorod–Oboyan highway. As the Russians rolled forward towards the unsuspecting SS tankers, the only eyes that saw them were those of the Haitian-born Nazi Party member and ground-attack pilot Captain Bruno Meyer and his flight of three brand new Henschel Hs 129 tank busters, each armed with a 30 mm cannon. Officially on a reconnaissance mission, Meyer didn't hesitate when he spotted the Soviets coming out of a wood line beneath him. He radioed the situation in and led his flight into the attack. Back at his base near

Mikoyanovka, his sixty-eight-aircraft-strong Geschwader took to the air and raced to support him. In Staffel-strength waves the Henschels swept in, cannons hammering at the T-34s' rear engine compartments, setting them alight one after the other. The supporting Soviet infantry debussed and applied their usual tactic of firing every weapon they had at the slow-moving ground-attack planes. The Henschels had been conceived as the German answer to the Shturmovik and its designers had mimicked to some extent the armour-plating that made the Il-2 such a tough nut to crack and these steel shields kept Meyer and his Geschwader safe as they relentlessly hammered the Soviet tanks. There was no VVS air cover for the counter-attack either and this allowed Major Alfred Druschel's Focke-Wulf Fw 190 escorts to abandon their top cover role and sweep in to strafe the Soviet infantry and give the Henschels a clear run in. With no German ground forces involved, this was the first time in military history that such a large armoured formation was opposed solely from the air.

The results were staggering.

In a single hour, fifty of the sixty T-34s were destroyed and the Soviet counter-attack was annihilated. Hausser's flank was saved. Model signalled, 'For the first time in military history the Luftwaffe has succeeded, without support by ground troops, in annihilating a tank brigade which had broken through.'[201]

In the north, with Model's Ninth Army, it was tougher going. The experienced Bf 109 pilot Norbert Hannig was flying escort for a Stuka attack to support the withdrawal of a group of mechanised infantry who had got cut off in a railway station on the Orel–Tula line. There were no VVS planes around so Hannig observed the ground action closely, watching as the relieving troops smashed through the Soviets, supported by the Stukas dropping their 50 kg underwing bombs. 'We saw our infantry leap from their armoured half-tracks and storm the station building. Moments later they reappeared, shepherding the survivors, several of whom were carefully carrying a makeshift stretcher fashioned out of tent halves; presumably a wounded comrade.' Only later, during a rare spell of home leave back in Silesia, did Hannig realise that the man on the stretcher was in fact his elder brother Kurt, the trapped unit's commander, who had been killed by a shell splinter the previous night.[202]

The ground battle was fast becoming a gigantic slogging match, with German gains measured in metres against dogged Soviet defence.

The future Soviet premier, Nikita Khrushchev, was at Kursk and went to see Katukov when his First Tank Army was under real pressure. 'The next 2–3 days will be terrible. Either we hold out or the

Germans take Kursk. They are staking everything on this one card. For them it is a matter of life or death. We must see to it that they break their necks.'

Despite the fuel shortages, the Luftwaffe continued to mount as many sorties as it could, especially those of its Experten. The JG 3 pilot Lieutenant Joachim Kirschner was one such ace. He made a remarkable nine kills in one day at Kursk. No such luck accompanied Knight's Cross winner and 93-kill Experte Edmund 'Paule' Rossmann and his wingman, Lieutenant Seyler. Rossmann had already made a name for himself on the Eastern Front as one of JG 52's top pilots. 'We made repeated low-level attacks against the Soviet tanks. Loaded with armour-piercing rounds, our 20 mm cannon actually had quite an effect against some of the more "soft-skinned" Russian tanks. In total I managed to destroy fourteen tanks with my Messerschmitt 109.'[203]

Accounts of what happened that fateful day to Rossmann and his fellow pilot differ, with one stating that Seyler was shot down whereupon Rossmann landed to try and pick him up. The Soviets quickly arrived and in the ensuing gun battle Seyler was shot and killed and Rossmann was injured and captured. However, the VVS technician Viktor Sinaisky tells a different story. 'In 1943 I got a chance to study the Me-109 when two German pilots got lost and landed on our side of the front line. One of the pilots shot himself when we tried to take him prisoner, but the second, *Oberfeldwebel* Edmund Rossmann surrendered and cooperated with us while we learned how to service the planes.'[204]

Whatever the truth of the matter, another Experte had been lost from the Luftwaffe in the east. Rossmann would finally be released from Soviet captivity in October 1949.

For the VVS, Kursk was proving a sobering affair.

In the Battle of Kursk we lost few pilots but many planes, after three days we only had ten planes left. Vladimir 'Volodya' Bagirov, son of the First Secretary of the Communist Party of Azerbaijan, was killed. He rammed a Messer above the airfield. Commissar Moses S. Tokarev was also killed in the battle. He was leading the last eight La-5s escorting Shturmoviks, and was shot down by a pair of German fighters attacking out of the sun and from above and behind.[205]

The heavy casualties took their effect on the already-stretched nerves of the pilots.

Some of us did experience fear. I had a guy called Yumkin as my deputy squadron commander, we were on a flight and I spotted a group of enemy planes, while the rest of us attacked Yumkin disengaged. When this happened a second time I asked him 'Are you fucking scared?' Yumkin explained he was OK in formation but the moment he heard the word 'German' something happened in him and he became so scared he couldn't control himself. I told him 'We'll fly together in a pair. If you quit I'll chase and execute you.' I said this but I would never have done it. I flew several times with him and he began performing well.[206]

At Hitler's headquarters a worried Führer poured over the situation reports, increasingly exasperated at the lack of a decisive breakthrough. Then news came in from the Mediterranean – the Anglo-Americans had landed in Sicily. It soon became clear that the Italian Army on the island was a busted reed as thousands of its troops either surrendered or simply threw down their arms and melted away and Hitler now feared a general collapse on the new Italian front.

Back with Citadel, Model's northern attack had stalled in the face of dogged resistance. Only in the south were the Germans still making ground and on 12 July the largest tank battle in history took place at the tiny hamlet of Prokhorovka, between Hausser's II SS Panzer Corps and Rotmistrov's 5th Guards Tank Army. Well over 1,000 tanks and assault guns were involved in the melee and hundreds were destroyed or damaged. Neither side could claim a decisive victory after the clash but the battle did stall the SS men. Meanwhile, the 6th Panzer Division had somehow forced their way over the Donets River and opened the door to the Soviet rear. However, a Staffel of He 111s which hadn't been told of the successful assault bombed the German bridgehead just as the forty-five-year-old divisional commander, General Walter von Hünersdorff, was conducting an Orders Group with his unit commanders. Major Bieberstein, the commanding officer of the 114th Panzer Grenadier Regiment, and Captain Oekel, the commander of Bieberstein's 1st Battalion, were both killed. Twelve other officers were wounded, including Hünersdorff himself, and the 6th Panzers' drive faltered.[207]

The STAVKA could see the German advance was waning and launched an offensive to the north at Orel against Army Group Centre's Second Panzer Army. The Soviets poured in eighty-two infantry divisions, fourteen tank corps, twelve artillery divisions and some additional independent tank brigades. The Germans were hopelessly outmatched. Von Greim was forced to throw in every aircraft he could put into the sky, launching round-the-clock strikes in a desperate attempt to halt the Soviets. For Model's northern pincer it was a body-blow. His men had only managed to penetrate a maximum of seven or so miles (12 km) into the Soviet lines anyway, but now he had to withdraw forces and redeploy them to the north to avoid a major Soviet breakthrough.

Von Manstein, whose southern pincer had advanced twenty-two miles (35 km) into the Soviet lines, still believed victory was possible and told Hitler so in no uncertain terms. The dictator countered that he needed troops from Citadel to stop Italy falling.

Von Manstein was flabbergasted.

Sicily was not where the decisive battle would be fought – it would be in the East and Kursk could still be won if the Ostheer held its nerve. Anyway, there was no way divisions could be pulled out of the offensive and arrive in the Mediterranean in any shape to fight for weeks to come. The protests fell on deaf ears and Von Manstein's advice was overruled. Hitler cancelled his great offensive on 13 July, just eight days after it had started.

Citadel was the first German offensive in the east that failed to break through the Soviet defences and was a total disaster for the Ostheer. Over 50,000 men and hundreds of panzers and assault guns were lost. The panzer divisions themselves – Germany's famed Panzerwaffe, the very cream of the army, which had been carefully built up over the preceding months – were bled white for no discernible gain. As for the Luftwaffe, Kursk was its last hurrah in the east. Somehow, with limited supplies and logistics, it had managed to maintain local superiority over the battlefield, flying thousands of sorties, dropping thousands of tons of ordnance and savaging its VVS opponents in the air. It would not do so again.

CHAPTER 20

The Flakwaffe and the Strategic Bombing of the Reich

The biggest reason the Luftwaffe would now spiral down to ultimate defeat in the east was simple: the heavy bomber, specifically, the huge armadas of four-engine behemoths that the RAF and USAAF could field to pound the Third Reich to dust.

The British had launched their first air raids against Nazi Germany back in 1940 at the height of the Battle of Britain. Those attacks, ordered to 'avenge' a mistaken bomb drop on London by a flight of He 111s, had so enraged Hitler that he had ordered a complete change of strategy which had given Hugh Dowding's RAF Fighter Command the breathing space it needed to recover and turn the tide.

The trickle of raids carried out by Wellingtons and other two-engine medium bombers had been shrugged off by the Nazis – their payload capacity and accuracy was low and German defences were easily able to cope.

However, Great Britain had made a strategic decision to mount an offensive air campaign against the Nazi homeland and devoted a full third of her war economy to that end and as 1942 dawned the RAF had the capacity to begin a sustained assault. The man in charge of that assault – Arthur 'Bomber' Harris – was an advocate of area bombing, in effect the deliberate destruction of enemy cities to annihilate industry and break the population's will to resist. The Germans were about to be repaid in spades for the Blitz, the 'Baby Blitz', Coventry and every other attack of the previous two years. Jeschonnek loudly proclaimed his joy at the offensive: 'Every four-engine bomber the Western Allies build makes me happy, for we will bring these ... down just as we brought down the two-engine ones, and the destruction of a four-engine bomber constitutes a much greater loss to the enemy.' And indeed the losses were high. The RAF lost 3,486 aircraft in the

1942 campaign but Jeschonnek was clearly seeing the Allied effort through the spyglass of Germany's own issues with raw materials and resources. In actual fact they were just getting going. The figures speak for themselves; in three years the Luftwaffe had dropped 67,000 tons of bombs on the British Isles. The RAF surpassed this figure in just nine months. Nazi Germany wasn't the only target either. Key installations in occupied Europe were also prioritised and hit, including the busy rail marshalling yards at Rouen-Sotteville in France. Ominously for the Nazis that attack, in August of 1942, was carried out by General Ira Eaker's newly arrived USAAF. Led by Eaker himself, eighteen B-17 Flying Fortresses took off from their base at RAF Polebrook in Northamptonshire, bombed the yards in broad daylight and returned home safely without suffering a single loss.

On the ground, the German population were not nearly as sanguine as Jeschonnek. The panzer officer Hans von Luck was transiting through Berlin in March, en route from his division fighting in the Soviet Union to take up a new post on Erwin Rommel's staff in the deserts of North Africa. 'I drove into Berlin. How the city had changed since I was last there. The people seemed cowed and dispirited. Air raid shelters of all sorts were to be seen everywhere, at night all the houses and streets had to be blacked out. Berlin seemed like a ghost town.'[208]

Outside the capital, other German cities were suffering horrendously. Cologne was hit in May in the first 'Thousand Bomber' raid. A German Red Cross nurse in the city described what she saw.

I came out of the air raid shelter and Cologne was a wall of flames. Those who had been killed by high explosive bombs were propped up, their skin was a grey, pallid colour and their hair stood off their heads like wire nails. Of those who had died from incendiaries you could only find bits of bone which were gathered up in washtubs. Soldiers on leave from the front came to see us and we had to tell them their wife was dead, their children were dead, their parents were dead.[209]

Hitler grew increasingly alarmed, paranoid as he was about a rerun of the mass civil unrest that had heralded the end of Imperial Germany's war back in 1918.

Worse was to come for the Nazis as the RAF's night raids on German cities were matched during the daytime by USAAF attacks on key industries. The Schweinfurt raids, aimed at eliminating German ball-bearing production, sent shock waves through the upper echelons of the Nazi hierarchy, with Speer himself admitting, 'I often thought that bombing one of the bottlenecks of our armaments industry would be much more effective than the bombing of cities, and one of the aims I always considered was bombing the ball-bearing industry, and so when Schweinfurt was attacked it was like a nightmare coming true for me.'[210]

The Nazi response to the Anglo-American bombing offensives was two-pronged and both prongs would skewer the Luftwaffe and decisively hand the advantage in the East to the VVS.

Before the war the Germans were regarded, along with the Swedes funnily enough, as Europe's leading experts in anti-aircraft artillery. They were at the forefront of radar-directed gun aiming and the co-ordinated use of searchlights acting in concert with centrally controlled belts of guns of all different calibres. Indeed, the Germans invested a very significant amount of Luftwaffe resource in their flak arm. The 677,000-strong Luftwaffe of 1939 ballooned into the 1940 Luftwaffe of 1.159 million, of which no fewer than 571,000 personnel were in the flak force.[211] The decision was now taken to hugely expand this 'mini-army', a decision which would starve the Luftwaffe, and the Army incidentally, of desperately needed resources and prove ultimately fruitless as Germany's flak defences singularly failed to even dent the Allied bomber offensive.

The call went out for more volunteers from among the Reich's many state organisations, specifically the Hitler Youth, their female equivalent the Bund Deutscher Mädel (League of German Girls), the Labour Service and also among those too old for direct military service. The POW camps were trawled too and thousands of captured Soviets desperate to avoid the starvation and brutality of their existence put their hands up and became 'volunteer helpers' – '*Hilfswillige*' or Hiwis for short. By 1944 there were over 200,000 fifteen and sixteen-year-old youngsters enrolled, known as *Luftwaffenhelfer* and 100,000 Hiwis as well, plus ethnic Germans from outside the Reich's borders, the so-called *Volksdeutsche* – mainly from the ancient German settler communities in the Balkans and south-east Europe.

One such volunteer was the Transylvanian Saxon Sigmund Heinz Landau. 'On reporting to the air force barracks at Ploesti I was supplied with a Luftwaffe uniform without any insignia, attached to a battery and trained like everyone else ... Morale and comradeship were excellent. At the age of twenty I was the youngest member of the outfit, most of whom were between 25–30.'[212]

So all-pervasive, and rather surreal, was this recruitment approach that one battery commander habitually began to address his personnel as follows: 'Ladies and gentlemen, fellow workers, schoolboys and *tovarischi* [Russian for 'comrades').'[213]

This 'other army' would end up manning over 3,000 batteries by 1944, equipped with a huge array of weapons: 26,369 light, 4,945 medium and 14,231 heavy anti-aircraft guns. Of the latter some 10,224 were the superb 88 mm, which the army were crying out for as a tank killer par excellence, but instead 75 per cent of Germany's entire stock of 88s went instead to the Reich flak batteries. The results from this major diversion of resources and manpower were dubious at best. Advanced though some aspects of German gunnery were, they never managed to perfect a good proximity fuse, which meant the shells had to actually hit the enemy bomber rather than just burst nearby and rely on fragmentation to do its lethal work. This scientific gap massively degraded the Flakwaffe's effectiveness.

It was less finding a needle in a haystack, and more trying to hit one.

Each cubic mile of air space is made up of 5.5 million cubic yards and a single 88 mm shell had a killing zone of just a few thousand cubic yards for one-fiftieth of a second as it exploded. No wonder it took an estimated 16,000 shells on average to bring down a single high-flying bomber – not that the Nazi hierarchy were overly keen to share this information with the public. Hitler and his entourage remained fixated on guns, despite the lack of tangible results. For them the anti-aircraft artillery was as much about the 'visibility' of the defence as it was about shooting down enemy planes. The German population, though, were perhaps more cynical about the effectiveness of their flak protectors – a joke doing the rounds at the time was that a German soldier was condemned to death but given a choice as to the manner of his execution. He opted to die by anti-aircraft fire, so a tower was constructed and he was tied to the top, then three flak batteries blasted away at him for three weeks, but didn't hit him. So they stopped and went to cut him down, only to find he'd starved to death in the meantime!

With scarce raw materials and manpower diverted away from aircraft production and into the manufacture of guns, by the end of the year 90 per cent of Nazi Germany's aviation industry was back to only working a single shift, even as aircraft production among the Allies accelerated to unprecedented levels: 34,845 for the Soviets and a staggering 86,000 in the United States – one plane rolled off their production lines every half an hour – against a German sector that made just 10,898 fighters and less than half that number of bombers that year.[214]

Wilhelmstrasse's other prong – and the one that would directly lead to the defeat of the Luftwaffe in the east – was the draining away of its frontline strength back to defend the Reich. The Experten, the very core of the eastern Jagdwaffe who had somehow held the balance against the VVS, were sent west in large numbers, where they were thrown up against the dreaded '*Viermots*' (Luftwaffe nickname for the four-engine Allied bombers) and their escorts in an unequal battle they were doomed to lose. First to go in 1943 was JG 3 Udet; among its ranks were the likes of Lieutenant Joachim Kirschner, he of the nine kills in a single day at Kursk. He would reach a final tally of 188 kills before being shot down himself by an American Thunderbolt over occupied Croatia in December. Bailing out, he landed safely, only to be captured by Tito's Communist partisans, who promptly shot him.

JG 3 was followed by elements from JG 27 and then JG 51 Mölders. JG 52 was now the only complete fighter Geschwader on the Eastern Front. The situation with night fighters was just as bad, with only one *Nachtgeschwader* (NJG 6), with two single Gruppen (NJG 100 and 200), in the east compared to the five NGJs deployed in the west.

Facing the Anglo-Americans proved a rude shock for many Luftwaffe pilots who were used to easier times in the Soviet Union, as one pilot remarked to another:

'In Russia the flying is...'
'Easier! I tell you! We did some flying in Russia, that was fine, but here in the West it's just suicide.'[215]

He wasn't wrong. The Luftwaffe claimed to have destroyed 1,392 Soviet aircraft at Kursk, against a couple of hundred of their own, but over in the west the Luftwaffe was decimated, losing over 1,000 aircraft in the summer (335 single-engine fighters in July alone) as Sicily fell and the bombing of the Reich stepped up.

Their allies in the Italian Regia Aeronautica were a spent force too. By September the Italians had fewer than 800 operational aircraft in total and most of them stayed rooted to the ground, their pilots understandably none too keen to take off and face the overwhelming superiority of the Anglo-Americans.

At this moment of crisis, the Luftwaffe high command chose to implode.

After the Stalingrad debacle, Goering had increasingly retreated into his own world of hunting, feasting and art theft on a grand scale. Hitler's deputy would visit Paris for more of his infamous 'shopping trips', or simply hide out at Carinhall, his ultra-luxurious country mansion-cum-hunting-estate-cum-private zoo, north-east of Berlin in the Schorfheide forest. Set between the waters of the Grossdöllner See and Wuckersee, Carinhall was a mix of styles, half cosy hunting lodge with deep sofas and intimate fireplaces, half grand house with enormous rooms, halls, a sauna, a bowling alley and galleries crammed with looted art works. Goering even had a huge 321-foot-long model railway set complete with tunnels, bridges and miniature planes built in the attic for him to play with!

Named in honour of his Swedish first wife Carin, it was constructed in stages after her death from a heart attack in 1931. At vast expense, Goering engaged the architect Werner March, who was the designer of the Olympic Stadium in Berlin, to build it for him and once finished, Goering threw lavish parties there, more than once appearing to his guests wearing his favourite purple toga with outrageous gold jewellery. One such party was the wedding banquet for his second wife, Emmy Sonnemann. Goering's smaller hunting lodge at Rominten (now Krasnolesye in Russia) in East Prussia was afterwards named 'Emmyhall' in her honour. Just to make sure he always had somewhere to lay his weary head, the kleptomaniac Reichsmarshall also had an official state residence on Leipziger Platz in Berlin, an alpine house on the Obersalzberg near Hitler's own villa, three other hunting cabins (at Roeth, Pait and Darss), a house in Wenningstadt on the island of Sylt and the two castles at Veldenstein and Mauterndorf he had inherited from his late godfather. Gluttony and drug addiction meant the Reichsmarshall was unable to control his ballooning weight and he seemed to totally lose interest in the very air force he had worked so hard to create. His occasional forays into Luftwaffe business were bordering on the farcical. After admitting to his staff that he didn't know how to turn a radio on, he went on to discuss his view of one of the most important pieces of technology in air warfare – radar: 'I have frequently taken a look inside such sets. It does not look all that imposing, just some wires and a few other bits and pieces. The whole apparatus is remarkably primitive.'

Then, when asked by Milch if he would press Hitler for a change of heart in the employment of women in the aviation industry, he suggested that perhaps women could do their work at home so they could still watch their children at the same time.

Not that Milch was much better. After Hamburg was burned to ashes by the RAF, an outraged Hitler insisted the Luftwaffe strike back and bomb Britain in revenge, declaring, 'Terror can only be broken with terror,' but instead of standing up to the dictator and his nonsensical idea, Milch fawningly agreed with him. 'Our entire armaments effort ... is dependent on whether we can clear our own skies by carrying out raids at such a level that the British will call off their own attacks.'

The result was yet another pointless frittering away of the Luftwaffe's limited strength in a bombing offensive against Great Britain that achieved nothing militarily whatsoever. As for Jeschonnek, the Prussian's self-confidence was visibly draining away. Increasingly under attack by Hitler and other senior Nazis because of the inability of the Luftwaffe to stop the Anglo-American bombing raids, he began to crack. It all came to a head on the night of 17 August, when RAF Bomber Command hit the rocket research facility at Peenemünde on the shores of the Baltic where the V-1 and V-2 rockets were being designed. Taken in by a feint made towards Berlin by twenty Mosquitoes, he ordered the Berlin anti-aircraft defences to open fire, directly threatening the 148 German night fighters flying above the city at the time. At 8 a.m. the next morning he received a phone call informing him of the Peenemünde raid and the near-destruction of the vital facility. He walked outside to his shed, wrote a number of notes stating that he could no longer work with Goering and pledging his loyalty to Hitler, and then blew his brains out with his service pistol. When his funeral was held, Goering attended on Hitler's behalf, even though one of Jeschonnek's notes had asked that the Reichsmarshall not go. The Luftwaffe was now in the worst of all worlds. Goering was no longer even attempting to perform his duties but would under no circumstances allow anyone else to exercise authority for him. Jeschonnek was dead, replaced by Günther Korten. Keller's successor as head of Luftflotte 1, Korten was a solid officer but out of his depth as chief of staff. Milch could have been a possible candidate to stop the rot had Goering not decided he had gotten too big for his breeches and needed to be taken down a peg or two. The result was stagnation.

The Luftwaffe wasn't the only part of Germany's war effort that was suffering from paralysis – indecision reigned in the senior Nazi ranks. Goebbels wrote in his diary:

We are doing too much on the military and too little on the political side of the war. At this moment, when our military successes are none too great, it would be a good thing if we knew how to make better use of the political instrument. We were so great and resourceful in that way at the time of our struggle for power; why shouldn't we achieve mastery in this art now?

Back on the Eastern Front, the autumn saw casualties mount among the dwindling ranks of Luftwaffe pilots. Norbert Hannig, on his way back to his fighter Gruppe from some home leave in September, met his old chief mechanic, Sergeant Rommer, who filled him in on the latest news from back at the Staffel: 'Eckert's been killed in a crash, Paul Bienecke was shot down, bailed out and is in hospital, the boss was shot down behind enemy lines, he parachuted and is missing, Xaver Müller was brought down by light flak, exploded and killed ... They're waiting for you. You're going to be needed out there.' The loss of the accordion-playing Xaver Müller was especially hard for Hannig to take, given he had been Müller's wingman for some time and had made his first kill under his tutelage. Hannig recounted how Müller had just shot down a LaGG-3 when he radioed Hannig:

'Now it's your turn, I'll cover you.' I slammed my throttle forward, captured him in my sights and at a range of 150 metres opened fire. My guns hammered ... Pieces flew off the LaGG as it shuddered under the impact ... 'Abschuss!' I yelled. But a kill could only be confirmed if an enemy machine exploded in mid-air, was seen to crash into the ground, or if the pilot bailed out...

'He's still flying, have another go at him,' so I pushed the throttle forward and winged over towards the tell-tale trail of smoke. The LaGG grew rapidly larger in my Revi gunsight as I mentally checked off the range ... 100 m, 80 m, 50 m ... fire! This time it was Xaver who shouted 'Abschuss!'

When Hannig had arrived back in March as a newly qualified pilot he had been number twenty-six on his Staffel roster. Now, five months later, twelve of those men had been killed or reported missing, seven others had been posted elsewhere and only seven of the originals were left.[216]

As for the VVS, their pilots were gaining in experience all the time.

We used to fly in three-plane formations, while German flights consisted of four fighters in pairs. When engaging the enemy our three-plane flights immediately lost formation, as at the very first turn to the left for example the left wingman had to decrease speed, something totally unacceptable in battle. It meant every Russian pilot ended up fighting independently while the Germans remained in pairs. We immediately realised the advantages of the German system and adopted it ourselves.[217]

The Germans themselves could see the change: 'By this time the Russians were also flying in twos and fours, adopting not only our combat formations of Rotten and Schwärme, but also many of our tactics. They had become much more dangerous as opponents.'[218]

The arrogance and swagger that were once the sure-fire sign of every Jagdwaffe pilot were fast disappearing and being replaced by wariness.

The now-veteran fighter pilot Ivan D. Gaidenko said:

> German pilots were very good and well trained, and their planes were of high quality. But we managed to shoot them down, so they must have had their shortcomings. They didn't fight like us though. We'd engage the enemy outnumbered six-to-one if ordered to, but the Germans never fought in such situations, if they were outnumbered they simply quit ... They would also dodge an engagement if we had altitude superiority.

Gaidenko's comments ring true, but when the Jagdwaffe did have the advantage they were still more than capable of making it count. In November, as Kiev was surrounded and about to be liberated by the Red Army, a single flight of four Fw 190s were left on an abandoned airfield to try and provide the defending German troops with some sort of cover. Overhead a pretty much continuous stream of Shturmoviks flew in to bombard the German ground troops. Flying low and slow as they were, the Shturmoviks were sitting ducks for the 190s and their pilots – Norbert Hannig, Reinhold 'Lerge' Hoffmann, Alfred 'Fred' Gross and the buck-toothed Emil 'Bully' Lang. Working in pairs, the four pilots went up again and again, knocking down Il-2s almost at will. Lang shot down an incredible eighteen on 4 November – the world record for the highest number of aircraft shot down by a fighter pilot in a single day and never bettered since. That same day Hoffmann downed two, and Gross three, but the Germans still lost the city. Even now, as 1944 was fast approaching, the Jagdwaffe pilots still treated it all like a game, with Lang and Hoffmann desperate to keep on going up to reach the score of 100 and fifty respectively.

There was some mutual respect too. After a German bombing raid on the Volkhov River, the Jagdwaffe fighter escort stayed in the area to hunt Soviets. During an ensuing dogfight, one of the opposing Yaks was thought to be flown by a French pilot due to its unusual red, white and blue rudder markings and standing out as it did, all the Bf 109s latched onto it, including the renowned Austrian Experte Walter 'Nowy' Nowotny. Like all the others, he tried to shoot the Yak down and failed. After some incredible aerobatics Nowotny came on the radio and said: 'To all pilots, let him go home, he's earned it.'[219]

Only thirty-four Knight's Crosses were won by the eastern Luftwaffe in 1943, less than half of the number that were won in 1942. Correspondingly only seven Oak Leaves and two Swords were awarded as well. Partly this reflected the increasing skill of the VVS, but mostly it was a simple numbers game. The Luftwaffe in the east was dwindling fast. By the end of the year there were just 2,000 German aircraft at the front and a good proportion of these were old, obsolete models well past their sell-by dates. The bomber arm in particular was a shadow of its former self and more and more the Luftwaffe was becoming a short-range defensive weapon, desperate only to try and stop the Viermots from reducing all of Germany to rubble and hold the Soviets at bay in the east.

Meanwhile the VVS, despite its eye-watering losses, now stood at 8,800 frontline aircraft plus reserves and it was growing.

As defeat loomed, even the vaunted fighter arm began to see the writing on the wall, as one pilot acknowledged: 'We can't win the war unless a miracle happens. Only a few complete idiots still believe we can. It is only a question of a few months before we come to grief. In the spring we shall be fighting on four fronts and then, of course, we haven't got a hope. We've lost this war.'[220]

PART SIX

1944

This was the year when the Luftwaffe's chickens all came home to roost at once. Aircraft production finally began to really take off, but there was little fuel for the armadas of new planes and the pilots being turned out by the flight schools were now barely trained cannon fodder. The Mediterranean was more or less given up to the Anglo-Americans and in France Hugo Sperrle's Luftflotte 3 was a paper tiger. In the skies over the Reich the British and Americans were beginning to target the Luftwaffe's industrial lifeblood: its aircraft factories and the vital synthetic fuel production facilities that kept the Nazi war machine on the road and in the air – literally. The Nazi air force was given no choice but to go up again and again to try and halt the rain of death and destruction from above, only to be ground into dust by the overwhelming power of the two heavy bomber fleets and their deadly escorts which could now accompany their charges all the way to Berlin and back. As the Luftwaffe's graveyards in the homeland filled up, the eastern Luftwaffe was not only starved of replacements but was forced to send more and more of its remaining Experten back home in a vain attempt to stem the tide. They would fail.

CHAPTER 21

Cherkassy, Kamenets-Podolskiy and the North

At the beginning of 1940 the Luftwaffe could muster 1,369 fighters and 1,758 bombers to begin the invasion of France and the Low Countries.

At the beginning of Barbarossa a year later, she could field almost as many – around 2,600 aircraft all told.

At the beginning of 1944 the Luftwaffe was fighting the Anglo-Americans in Italy, the English Channel and in the skies over the homeland. This meant that in the East – her most crucial theatre – she could muster just 1,561 fighters and 1,604 bombers to oppose the VVS, roughly what she had when she started the invasion well over two years previously. The difference was that now the Germans were facing a Soviet air force that outnumbered them everywhere by at least five or six to one and whose quality was getting closer to theirs by the day.

You ask me 'Did we beat the Germans with sheer numbers of with skill?' Both! There is a school of thought that maintains we didn't need an Air Force of big numbers, only high quality. Those who argue this don't know what they're talking about. Numerical superiority with all the other factors ... decides the victory ... for a regular pilot, numerical superiority means you are outnumbered in every dogfight. Even if you're a good pilot, try surviving a battle of 6 against 12 ... if you send 1,000 planes against your enemy's 100 you must win. That's exactly what happened in the second half of the war. Our panes became as good as the Germans' and the experience and training of our pilots as high, so as soon as we gained numerical superiority our victory was assured.[221]

That growing confidence was reflected in the burgeoning Soviet awards system – in some ways mirroring the decorations so beloved of their Luftwaffe enemies.

As an aside, curiously for a nation that traditionally revels in individual dash and élan, the Italian Regia Aeronautica made a conscious decision to try and stop the emergence of aces by decreeing that a pilot could only claim a kill if he was the only one who had fired at an enemy plane and the claim could be verified independently by another source. If the enemy had been fired at by several opponents (which happened a lot in air combat), then it was credited to the unit and not the individual.

The VVS did not look to duplicate this approach, instead instituting a mass system of decorations to celebrate achievement. The lowest Soviet award was the Order of the Red Star and almost 3 million of them would be given out – a bit of the 'prizes for all' culture perhaps; then next up the ladder came the Order of the Red Banner (another 600,000 awarded) and then the Order of Lenin (only 41,000 this time). The Soviet version of the Knight's Cross was the coveted Hero of the Soviet Union, of which 2,420 of the 11,000 presented went to the VVS. The Hero award wasn't a medal as such but an honorary title, with the winner also getting the Order of Lenin and Golden Star Medal as visible signs of their achievement. You could earn the Hero title multiple times and of the 104 appointed twice, more than half (sixty-five) went to VVS flyers. Aleksandr Romanenko was one such man; appointed as a Hero of the Soviet Union in early 1942, he was shot down and captured that autumn. He escaped and joined a partisan unit before getting back to his own lines and rejoining his squadron. However, found guilty by the State of 'allowing himself to be captured', he was stripped of the award and his score of sixteen kills was officially reduced to nil. Allowed to carry on flying, he chalked up another twenty-four victories and was re-awarded his Hero title before finally being killed in combat over Kiev in December 1943. Only three men received the Hero title three times and two of those were from the VVS.

This prevalence of pilots among the very highest awards was mirrored in the Luftwaffe. About 7,500 men won the Knight's Cross during the war, with less than a quarter (1,730) going to the Luftwaffe and less than a third of those went to fighter pilots – roughly 1 in every 100 Jagdwaffe flyers earned it. However for higher awards it was the other way around: of 860 Oak Leaves awards, 192 went to the Luftwaffe, forty-one out of 154 Swords and an incredible twelve out of twenty-seven Diamonds.[222]

The VVS was now building up its own core of Soviet 'Experten', men like Romanenko and others like Hero of the Soviet Union Lev Lvovich Shestakov, the VVS's highest scoring ace in the Spanish Civil War against Franco's Nationalists and the German Condor Legion. Shestakov went on to lead his squadron against the Romanians at Odessa, causing so many casualties among the FARR pilots that Bucharest withdrew much of the remainder to avoid further bloodshed. Shestakov went on to fly at Stalingrad and eventually reached sixty-five solo and shared kills. His fellow VVS ace Vladimir Lavrinenkov wrote a book after the war about Shestakov called *His Call Code – Sokol 1* (*Sokol* is Russian for 'falcon'). According to Lavrinenkov's book, Shestakov fought a private war with a well-known Stuka ace – a 'Kurt Renner', who was awarded 'the Golden Knight's Cross'. No such pilot existed; 'Renner' may well have been Rudel and it may have been against Rudel that Shestakov met his maker. In the spring of 1944, Rudel was caught in a dogfight with a Soviet fighter and was desperately trying to escape him, diving into a valley and hugging the deck, at times less than fifty feet above the ground, constantly performing brutal evasive manoeuvres and leap-frogging over trees, as his rear gunner, Ernst Gadermann, desperately tried to either shoot the chasing fighter down or at least force it to disengage. However, Gadermann's gun jammed, so the Germans were essentially defenceless, but after one particularly vicious turn Gadermann shouted to Rudel that the Soviet fighter had crashed into the ground. Rudel wrote:

> Was he shot down by Gadermann, or did he go down because of the backwash from my engine during these tight turns? It doesn't matter. My headphones suddenly exploded in confused screams from the Russian radio; the Russians had observed what happened and something special seems to have happened ... From the Russian radio-messages, we discover that this was a very famous Soviet fighter pilot, more than once appointed as Hero of the Soviet Union. I should give him credit: he was a good pilot.

Unlike their Luftwaffe opponents, Soviet flyers didn't only get gongs and promotions; the Kremlin also saw fit to hand out kill bonuses in cold, hard cash. Alexander F. Khaila, a Soviet fighter pilot, remembers his railway worker father earning an excellent wage for the time of 160 roubles a month, but by the time young Alex became a pilot he could earn 440 roubles as a sergeant, or 750 as an officer (hence why Timoshenko's order in 1940 that all Air Force academy graduates were to be gazetted as sergeants from then on and not lieutenants as

[handwritten annotation: 4~6 times monthly pay]

before was so massively unpopular with the pilots themselves). On top
of this substantial salary, a pilot would bag himself 2,000 roubles for
shooting down an enemy bomber, 1,500 for a reconnaissance plane or
1,000 for a fighter. Khaila's fellow fighter pilot Vitaly Klimenko said
of the bonuses:

> If you were looking for an individual victory you had to catch the
> last in a bomber group, they were easy targets as they were normally
> young, dumb and inexperienced pilots. This meant I could count on
> a 2,000 rouble bonus. We would usually pool our money and if it
> was quiet at the front we would send a runner to bring us vodka.
> I remember that half a litre of good vodka was 7–800 roubles.

It wasn't just in the air that the Soviets were now enjoying a marked
advantage. The Ostheer lost 1.2 million men in the Soviet Union
between the launch of Citadel and the end of spring 1944 as battlefield
attrition burnt out the line divisions. To try and fill the yawning gaps,
reinforcements were sent east from occupied France, the men arriving
at the front with their pockets and haversacks stuffed full of cheeses
and hams to find themselves in a nightmare world facing the might
of the Red Army. Units were even taken away from the hard-pressed
Italian front and over a quarter of a million men were sent to the
Ostheer from the training schools. Rear area and support services were
combed out for men who could be reassigned to combat units and
several hundred thousand wounded were sent back to their regiments
at the front, signed off as 'fit for duty'. Yet even after all these measures
the Ostheer was still 300,000 men short of the establishment the OKW
estimated it needed to hold the line.

The Luftwaffe played its part too, more of its vital ground and
support staff being sent to the discredited Luftwaffe Field Divisions,
which had already absorbed over 200,000 personnel the previous year.
Almost half those men were now dead or missing, their inexperience
and lack of training leading to them often being senselessly slaughtered
by better trained and equipped Soviet formations. Desperate as ever
not to admit failure, Goering refused to back down on the concept
though, insisting instead that more of the Luftwaffe's highly specialised
and expert 'black men' be transferred out to act as infantry. This
would never be allowed in the VVS, the USAAF or by the British. One
Polish ace who served with the British RAF always kissed the hands
of his chief mechanic after every sortie he made: 'These are the hands
which keep me alive.'[223]

The Soviets thought the same.

Relations between pilots and ground crew were the best one could ever have. The pilots knew their lives depended on us. After the war my pilot Boris sent everyone his photo – except for me! He lived in Tula so I called him and asked him why I didn't get a photo, and he said 'Viktor, I didn't have any good photo paper and had to use whatever I had, but I couldn't send such a photo to a person on whom my life depended during the war.'[224]

By now both air forces were flying the best machines their respective countries could offer and for the first time they were fairly evenly matched. The ubiquitous Bf 109 was slowly being replaced in German frontline Staffeln by the 'Butcher Bird' – the bullfrog-fronted Focke-Wulf Fw 190. More robust than the Messerschmitt and better armed, it was an excellent aircraft and popular with its pilots, as noted by two of them who excitedly discussed it at length to the benefit of their British interrogators:

'The Focke-Wulf is said to be really good.'
'Apparently it is quite marvellous.'
'It's said to take off better, although it's heavier, but is considerably faster.'
'Very much faster!'
'It has a radial engine.'
'Apparently it's an absolutely marvellous thing!'[225]

Lieutenant Heinz Lange of JG 51 had an equally high opinion of the new aircraft: 'The Fw-190 was easier to handle and stronger in air combat. It could sustain more battle damage than the Messerschmitt. I regard the aircraft as a major improvement … maybe the Messerschmitt was better in turning combat, but against Il-2s the Fw-190 was superb because of its superior armament.'[226]

Not that it was universally accepted among the Experten. Erich 'Bubi' Hartmann swore by the Bf 109 and earned the sobriquet the Soviets gave him, 'Black Devil of the Ukraine', by flying a painted Messerschmitt christened *Karaya One*. He would eventually record no fewer than 352 kills, all of them in a Messerschmitt.

For the VVS it was the new generation of MiGs, LaGGs and Yaks they admired: 'The MiG fighter would land very easily, you could almost take your hand off the stick. What can I say about the Yaks, the cockpit was quite comfortable, with a good view and good glass. The scariest fighter was the I-16, the rest were peanuts ... The Messer was a good fighter, the Focke-Wulf was also good but it was less manoeuvrable than a Messer.'[227]

With the Allied advance up the spine of Italy bogged down in heavy defensive fighting, the Wehrmacht took the opportunity to begin building up its forces in the West. Berlin knew that 1944 would be the year the Anglo-Americans would finally establish the much anticipated 'Second Front' in Europe by landing on the coast of occupied France. The questions were 'where' and 'when'. As men and materiel were pulled out of the Soviet Union and sent west to recuperate and refit, the German General Staff made a silent prayer that the Eastern Front would stay quiet. Those prayers were never likely to be answered.

The Soviet armed forces were now extremely impressive organisations. Lend-Lease supplies fed them, clothed them and carried them and in leaders such as Zhukov, Koniev and Rokossovsky they had some of the stand-out commanders of the war. For them, now was not the time to take their foot off the Ostheer's neck, and they began by breaking the siege of Leningrad after the longest encirclement in modern military history.

Army Group North had long been the neglected orphan of the Eastern Front and when the Red Army launched its offensive in early January it was brushed aside. On 27 January, fifteen days after Operation Iskra (Russian for 'spark') kicked off, it was all over – Leningrad was free after 872 days under the barrels of German guns. The Luftwaffe had barely played a role in German resistance; they simply couldn't compete with the 1,500 aircraft the VVS and Baltic Fleets put into the skies.

With their German allies in retreat, the end was in sight for the Finns. The Finnish air force had been the most successful of all the non-German contingents fighting the Soviets, but had been hampered from the start by a lack of political will from Helsinki to really take the fight to the Soviets and by their perennial shortage of modern equipment.

Captain Jorma 'Joppe' Karhunen, a 30-kill officer flying with LeLv 24, had been in the fight since the beginning. 'The Brewster 239 was good against the older Russian fighters, the I-153 Chaika and the I-16, so 1941–42 was the best time for us. In 1943 it was significantly more difficult when the Russians began to use their newer fighters against us ... Later, with the Yaks, Hurricanes, Tomahawks, LaGG-3 and MiGs, it became a fight to the death.'[228]

Nazi Germany never managed to get even close to the incredible feats of Lend-Lease in supporting their own allies and the Finns were a perfect example of this failure, being sent just 162 Me 109G-2s and thirty G-6s by the autumn of 1944, plus maybe 100 or so Ju 88s and Do 17s.

The Soviets planned to follow up the relief of Leningrad with a major offensive against the Finns to knock them out of the war. They massed 260,000 men and more than 1,500 aircraft to break Helsinki's defensive Mannerheim Line and threaten the Finnish capital itself. The weakened Luftwaffe could only afford to send forty-six aircraft from Estonia under the command of Lieutenant Colonel Kurt Kuhlmey to lend a hand. It wasn't nearly enough to make a significant difference and once the Mannerheim Line was breached the Finns sued for peace to avoid total defeat and occupation.

With their northern flank secure and Army Group North falling back, the Soviets began a general advance into the Baltic States, hoping to reach the borders of German East Prussia itself. Despite trumpeting that they were acting to 'liberate' their Estonian, Latvian and Lithuanian brethren, the VVS didn't hesitate to bomb civilian targets, with the Estonian capital, Tallinn (then called Reval), shuddering under the impact of high explosives and incendiaries. Eight-year-old Marja Talvi and her family were asleep in their suburban house about eight kilometres from the city centre when the bombs started to fall. 'The pine trees saved us from the bombs and fire because it was forbidden to cut them down.'[229]

The Balts had no illusions as to what awaited them under another Soviet occupation and that went double for those who had volunteered to fight alongside the Germans against Moscow. One such volunteer from Latvia, Mintauts Blosfelds, was caught in a VVS air raid as he and his Waffen-SS unit retreated west on a road packed with refugees.

> The moment we heard the swishing sound in the air we dropped down beside the wagons and the bombs exploded with ear-splitting reports around us. I felt a powerful blow on my right side which threw me under my wagon ... My nose was bleeding and I had a large cut on my forearm, my ears were ringing and I felt dizzy. My friend [Peteris] Lazdans had fared worse. Bomb fragments had hit him in the buttocks, his trousers had been ripped apart and were filled with blood.

Several other Balts were pilots in the Luftwaffe – most attached to JG 54 Grünherz, as the 'northern' fighter group. Artur Gärtner, a German

JG 54 pilot, remembered them as 'splendid comrades who took part in operations with a lot of zeal and eagerness'. Others remembered their reactions when they realised their homelands would fall to the advancing Red Army, with one of their number resorting to flying over his parents' deserted farmhouse near Cesis in northern Latvia and blowing it to pieces in repeated strafing attacks rather than letting the Soviets have it!

The Latvians weren't the only 'non-Germans' in JG 54. Alongside them were a handful of Scandinavians – mainly Danes, like Captain Ejnar Thorup, who was shot down and killed south of Chudovo. 'During an operational flight *Hauptmann* Thorup was fired on from the ground. His engine began to smoke and he attempted to make an emergency landing behind his own lines. As he did so his aircraft broke up and Thorup was thrown from the aircraft together with his seat, and was recovered dead.'[230]

Norbert Hannig, another JG 54 man at the time, also remembered the unequal nature of the struggle. 'The Russians usually outnumbered us by at least 8–1, often it was much more. Casualty figures began to rise, ours as well as theirs.'

The Soviet flyers were also copying Jagdwaffe free hunting tactics as well. 'Such missions are the best, you're free to fly anywhere. Your job was to catch lousy pilots and shoot them ... it was much easier in all respects.'[231]

Farther south, it was the Soviets' turn to use fast, powerful, manoeuvre warfare to encircle their enemies and look to annihilate them. In this endeavour they were hugely helped by Adolf Hitler's increasing micro-management of the battlefield and his dogged adherence to the 'hold to the last man and last bullet' theory of defence.

First up was the Cherkassy Pocket (more accurately called the Korsun Pocket) down in the Ukraine, where 56,000 Germans, Scandinavians and Belgian Walloons were surrounded out on the snow-covered steppe. The Luftwaffe had no option but to instigate another airlift to supply them, albeit on a far smaller scale than at Stalingrad. Flying from the excellent all-weather facilities at Uman, the Germans succeeded in bringing out 2,825 wounded and sick men, and taking in 2,062 tons of supplies in a fortnight, often in dreadful conditions and under heavy anti-aircraft fire. Not only did the Luftwaffe keep the beleaguered troops supplied, they also kept the relieving armoured spearheads going, dropping jerry cans of fuel out of the side doors of Ju 52s and into snow-drifts, from where grateful tankers retrieved them to fill up their thirsty panzers.

The Luftwaffe did just enough to make the difference and when more than 30,000 of the trapped men managed to swim the freezing waters of the Gniloy Tikich to safety, the Pocket was dissolved.

Almost as soon as one pocket was gone, another was created, this time at Kamenets-Podolskiy when the 200,000-strong First Panzer Army was trapped by a Zhukov offensive. The Army commander, the vastly experienced Hans-Valentin Hube, was determined not to suffer the fate of Paulus's Sixth Army and under the direction of his superior, von Manstein, he began a masterful 'wandering pocket' operation to lead his men back to the German lines in the west. The airlift required this time was far larger than at Cherkassy and it was no surprise when the vastly experienced Fritz Morzik was put in charge of the operation. Working hand in glove with Otto Dessloch's Luftflotte 4, the Germans demonstrated just how much they had learned since the Stalingrad debacle. Now, as the Pocket moved west, so-called 'pocket parties' of four men, each equipped with radio beacons, emergency flight path flares and signal flares, would reconnoitre possible landing strips and dropping zones and lay them out ready to receive supplies. Those flights mainly came in at night to avoid the attention of VVS fighters – how things had changed from earlier on in the war! Morzik was ruthless about what was taken in to cut down on any wastage. That meant absolute priority was for fuel and ammunition. Food was not on the list, the men being told to live off the land and eat their horses. The Pocket kept moving and discipline didn't break down, despite the dreadful conditions in the Army that one officer recorded in his dairy at the time:

> The men have tied their soles to their uppers with string, for marching is half the victory. Food is less than meagre, and a handful of snow is the only refreshment. Worst of all is the situation for the wounded. Vehicles are available only for the most serious cases, everyone else, even those with leg wounds, have to march ... Many give up ... and die, alone, by the side of a muddy road or choose the grim lot of captivity.[232]

By the end of the first week of April the First Panzer had escaped the Soviets and the Germans could take stock of the recent fighting up and down the front.

For the Jagdwaffe, losses were running at an average of 250 aircraft a month since the start of the year; this was heavy but not catastrophic. The bomber arm, though, was in a different position, having shrunk considerably as far greater emphasis was placed on fighters. Alexander

Werth, the famous Russian-born British journalist and writer, was in the Ukraine in March 1944, talking to a VVS colonel whose view was illuminating:

> The German air force is much weaker now than it used to be. Very occasionally they send fifty bombers over, but usually they don't use more than twenty. There's no doubt that all this bombing of Germany has made a lot of difference to German equipment, both on land and in the air. Our soldiers realise the importance of the Allied bombings; the British and Americans, they call them '*nashi*' that is 'our people' ... A lot of German fighters now have to operate in the west and we can do a lot of strafing of German troops, sometimes without much air opposition.

CHAPTER 22

'Target – Fuel and Aviation'

Anglo-American bombing was indeed making a huge difference to the battle between the VVS and the Luftwaffe, although the overall picture was complicated to say the least.

Speer, now in charge of a vast army of 14 million industrial workers, had performed economic miracles and his reforms were beginning to reap real dividends. With Italy switching sides the previous year, Germany's commitment to continually supply its erstwhile ally with thousands of tons of oil, coal, steel and other raw materials had ceased. The German seizure of the country had even yielded a welcome bonus of depots and rail yards full of gasoline and war materiel that was quickly shipped north over the Alps. Speer had augmented this windfall by ruthlessly running down existing stockpiles and concentrating scarce resources on the best performing factories. He had only just begun to scratch the surface as to what might have been possible had the Nazis inaugurated anything like the sort of economic programme that Great Britain or the United States had implemented. Much of the German armaments sector was still operating in something of a cottage-industry type manner, with only four factories employing more than 10,000 workers and the largest having 14,000. By contrast the British had more than a dozen factories with a workforce over 10,000 and two had an incredible 25,000 staff each. Nevertheless, Speer's programme saw the manufacture of just about every weapon of war growing dramatically in 1944, not least aircraft, to which a full 41 per cent of Germany's total armaments capacity was dedicated (panzer production got a paltry 6 per cent by comparison). In January that year 1,258 fighter planes came off the production lines and by September the monthly figure would be at its highest ever during the war at 3,031.[233] The Germans would end up rolling out 40,600 aircraft in 1944 – the only year of the conflict when they outstripped the Soviets (only by just over 300 it must be said) – including 26,236 fighters. That figure, impressive as it was, could have been even higher if the Germans had ever fully resolved their attitude to the appropriate balance between quantity and quality in production terms. They had scoffed for years at the craft-like nature of Italian manufacturing and its inability to produce volume when set against manufacturing precision and yet they were almost as guilty. Those aircraft coming out of the factory gates at Messerschmitt, Junkers and Focke-Wulf still had the finest upholstered crew seats of any aircraft in the world. Valuable hours had been spent machining down bulkheads and non-vital fittings for no real reason and even minor non-load-bearing parts were finished to close tolerances that spoke far more of engineering obsession than practical manufacturing.

As it was, two-thirds of the 1944 production armada went to face the Anglo-Americans. The eastern Luftwaffe would have to make do with what it was given. Having said that, at a loss rate of around 250 per month and a replenishment rate of just over twice that number, the Germans had a reasonable chance of at least keeping their numbers stable in the east and holding the VVS at bay, as long as aircraft could continue to be produced, the supply of new pilots kept up and they had the fuel to get into the air. All three would prove to be a problem for the Luftwaffe in 1944.

The advent of 1944 brought increased co-ordination to the Anglo-American bombing attacks, as well as a growing sophistication in its implementation. Improvements to bomb aiming technology, steadily increasing bomber numbers and hard-earned experience from 1942 and 1943 led to a new phase of the offensive. The RAF still favoured night raids on German cities and this was now combined with more attacks on targets in France in preparation for Operation Overlord and repeat raids on the sites hit by the Americans during the day. As for the Americans, they continued with their daylight strategy and looked to launch more all-out assaults on specific sectors of German industry that were vital to the Nazis' war effort. Goebbels said of it, 'The situation grows daily more intolerable, and we have no means of defending ourselves against this catastrophe.'

Hitler's propaganda chief wasn't exaggerating. By the end of March the major industrial city of Cologne was a virtual ghost town. Its pre-war population of 800,000 had shrunk to just 20,000 holdouts, somehow carrying on amid the rubble. Workers who had moved out of the cities to avoid the bombs now had hours of daily commuting to reach their offices, factories and workshops and return home, all the while listening fearfully for the wail for the air-raid sirens that would send them once again scrambling to safety underground.

The Allied planners now drew up a new list of priority targets and sitting atop it was the German aircraft industry. During the aptly-named 'Big Week' from 20 to 25 February, the US Eighth and Fifteenth Air Forces (1,028 B-17 Flying Fortresses and B-24 Liberators plus 832 fighter escorts) planned to cripple Nazi Germany's entire aircraft production capability. A total of twenty-six factories were targeted, among them the Messerschmitt factories at Wiener Neustadt, Regensburg, Brunswick and Gotha (these latter two made Bf 110s); the giant complex in Leipzig (32 per cent of all Bf 109s were made there); the Junkers site at Bernburg (Ju 52s, 88s and 188s); the Fw 190 plants at Tutow and Oscherlesleben; and the He 111 facility in Rostock on the north German coast. In a single week 10,000 tons of American bombs deluged the sites, causing widespread destruction. Over 500 Bf 109s, sitting in the finishing yards and ready to be shipped to the Jagdwaffe, were reduced to mangled wreckage, Junkers production was temporarily slashed by half and no more Bf 110s were built for several weeks. Speer was ill at the time (he would actually be away from full duties until June) but the system he had put in place sprang into action and in less than two months all the affected facilities were back up and running at full capacity – apart from Regensburg which had suffered massive damage and would take longer to repair. The price paid by the Americans for this temporary disruption to production was high. They lost 300 aircraft and hundreds of young crewmen, a hefty percentage of the 4,145 aircraft the US Eighth Air Force would lose in total during the war over Europe. The Americans were in good company; RAF Bomber Command would lose 8,325 aircraft, and over 55,000 men – almost 50 per cent of its entire establishment.[234]

However, costly though it was, the 'Big Week' assault sent shock waves through the OKL and the Nazi high command. More fighter units, desperately needed on the Eastern Front, were sent back west to strengthen the defences of the homeland and yet more resources were pumped into the already-dubious anti-aircraft umbrella.

At this critical juncture in the Luftwaffe's fight for survival, enter stage left a fifty-two-year-old Pennsylvanian called Carl 'Tooey' Spaatz. Born of immigrant Dutch stock, this married father of three daughters would now deliver the death blow to the Luftwaffe in the east and condemn it to a rapid ruin at the hands of the VVS. He had been the first commander of the US Eighth Air Force on its establishment in Great Britain and he now commanded both the Eighth and the Fifteenth Air Forces in a huge concentration of destructive aerial power. An advocate of the mass bombing of German economic targets rather than the carpet bombing of residential areas, in the early spring he presented his boss, Dwight D. Eisenhower, with a paper he simply called the 'Oil Plan'. Spaatz's biographer, David R. Mets, said of both the plan and Spaatz himself: 'It is hard to think of another commander in the USAAF who had enough influence with General Eisenhower to hold off, as well as Spaatz did, the diversions proposed by Leigh-Mallory.* Neither is it easy to think of any other who had both the perception to identify oil targets as decisive and the strength to conserve a part of the U.S. strategic air striking power for them.' (*Mets was referring to RAF Air Marshal Trafford Leigh-Mallory's counter-proposals to focus all the Allied bombing effort on targets in occupied France in the run up to Overlord. Leigh-Mallory was the nominated air commander for D-Day.)

In essence, the Oil Plan was simple. It stated that there was a fairly high likelihood that a heavy and sustained assault on the Nazi oil sector, specifically its synthetic fuel production and storage facilities, could significantly degrade the Wehrmacht's ability to wage war. However, Spaatz himself was quick to point out that the plan was no magic wand: 'The chimera of one air operation that will end the war ... does not exist.'

As it turned out, Spaatz was only partially right. He had correctly identified not just any weak spot in the Nazi war economy, but THE weak spot.

Germany was blessed with huge coal deposits and all manner of other raw materials, in large measure everything a modern industrialised economy needed – all except for one crucial element, oil. Germany barely had enough black gold under its own landmass to fill a bath. As such the German economy was heavily dependent on oil imports, especially from the rich fields around Ploesti in Romania. Successive German governments had realised just how vulnerable this left their economy and so had invested heavily in synthetic fuel production – mainly the hydrogenation process that transformed lignite coal into gasoline.

The Nazis had also attempted to build up reserves in the late 1930s in preparation for the impending war and the Soviet Union had, of course, sent Germany 900,000 tons of oil under the terms of the Nazi-Soviet Non-Aggression Pact. Even so, blitzkrieg and Barbarossa had guzzled away at the Third Reich's resources so much that Hitler felt he had no option in 1942 but to launch his major summer offensive on the Eastern Front with the stated goal of securing the bounty of the Caucasus oil lakes. As it was, German synthetic oil production that year stood at 4,600,000 tons against a total consumption over 50 per cent higher at 7,300,000 tons. The shortfall was made up from very limited domestic drilling and the output from Ploesti's wells.

The following year saw an overall improvement in the Wehrmacht's fuel position. Home production from natural wells (mainly in Austria of all places) and synthetics rose to a smidgeon under 7 million tons and the Italian capitulation made a positive impact as existing stocks were captured by German forces in the rapid occupation of the peninsula and the requirement for the Reich to export scarce supplies to their erstwhile ally ceased overnight. Faced with this unexpected windfall, Berlin prudently began to build up some limited reserves.

This then was the picture for petroleum in general, but of course aviation-grade fuel is at the top end of that spectrum. To produce the performance required in aero engines, particularly high-performance fighter engines, there needed to be a high octane content in the fuel and, preferably, high-energy additives such as tetraethyl and ethylene dibromide. Those additives were only manufactured in four factories that the Germans could access: three in Germany itself and one in Italy. Output was so low that the Jagdwaffe was forced to use sub-optimal 100-octane C4, or even lower grade 87-octane B4 fuel while the Anglo-Americans had 130-octane and consequently a significant edge in performance in the air. The only upside for the Luftwaffe was that the VVS didn't have the critical additives either; instead the Soviet pilots compensated by running their engines at maximum power for pretty much all the time they were in the air. Their engines swiftly wore out under the strain but by that time replacements were so plentiful it really didn't matter to them. For the Germans, total aviation fuel production tonnage was always too low: 20,000 tons a month in 1939 and still only 50,000 tons by 1941. With the adoption of the Milch Programme in 1942, much more aviation fuel was required to fill the tanks of the increased number of aircraft rolling off the lines and it was increasingly prioritised, so the bounty of 1943 was especially useful regarding aviation fuel and major efforts were made to build up reserves. By the end of 1943 the Nazis had stockpiled 33,786 tons. Production was also steadily growing, with the January figure standing at 159,000 tons, climbing to 181,000 tons in March – the highest it would ever attain – and allowing OKW to amass a back-up of 119,738 tons by the end of April. Prophetically, at that very moment Wilhelm

Keitel's own staff at OKW prepared a short report which they sent to Speer on his sickbed, stating that in their opinion an Anglo-American attack on the synthetic fuel sector could very well lead to a rapid Nazi defeat and the loss of the war. This chimed with another report spread among his bedside papers – this time from the OKL staff themselves – confirming that the entire oil industry now lay within 'the zone threatened by air attack' and stating that it was extraordinary that it hadn't been attacked in force already.

The unknown staff officer who authored the report was not to remain puzzled for long.

On Friday 12 May, on the anniversary of the German assault into France over the Meuse at Sedan some four years earlier, 935 US Eighth Air Force B-17 and B-24 bombers took off from their bases across southern and eastern England with their bomb bays full of high-explosive and incendiaries. They climbed into the clear sky and formed up into their defensive box formations and headed towards twenty synthetic oil plants scattered across central Europe. Foremost among them were the facilities at Zwickau and Merseburg-Leuna but the targets also included the factories at Bruex, Bohle, Zeitz, Chemnitz and Lützkendorf. Together these twenty sites formed the bulk of Nazi synthetic oil manufacture – some 374,000 tons per month, including all aviation fuel production. German air defences scrambled to intercept and soon the skies were filled with aircraft as the American escorts battled to keep the Jagdwaffe away from the precious bombers and the German pilots pressed home their attacks with abandon. Both sides took heavy casualties; forty-six Viermot bombers were brought down along with twelve of their fighter escorts and Luftwaffe losses were equally high at twenty-eight pilots killed and another twenty-six injured. As the Americans headed back west and the smoke on the ground cleared, it was obvious that some damage had been done but not enough from an Allied point of view. Daily production at Zwickau was reduced by 18 per cent for example, but furious repair work was soon underway to rectify the shortfall. The bombers would need to be sent over again.

While on the ground the authorities felt they may have got off fairly lightly, in the rarefied atmosphere of Hitler's headquarters the alarm bells were frantically ringing. Although still ill, Speer felt he had no option but to warn Hitler of the danger: 'The enemy has struck us at one of our weakest points. If they persist at this time, we will soon no longer have any fuel production worth mentioning. Our one hope is that the other side has an air force general staff as scatterbrained as ours!'

Unfortunately for the Nazis, the Allies' air generals were of a wholly higher calibre than their own. Plus they had the benefit of the Ultra decryptions, which was a huge advantage. On 16 May Bletchley Park forwarded a top-level message it had decoded that ordered the immediate heavy reinforcing of flak batteries around synthetic fuel plants, even to the point of taking them away from aircraft production factories. A further message from the 21st was directed at all Wehrmacht units: 'Consumption of mineral oil in every form ... be substantially reduced ... in view of effects of Allied action in Romania and on German hydrogenation plants; extensive failures in mineral oil production and a considerable reduction in the June allocation of fuel oil etc. were to be expected.'

The Anglo-American response was to press on and raid after raid was launched. Both sides now knew how important this battle was and threw aircraft into the sky. In two days of attacks at the end of May another eighty-four US bombers were shot down, while the Jagdwaffe lost sixty-two pilots and aircrew as they desperately resorted to sending up every aircraft they had, including Bf 110-equipped night fighter units in a desperate attempt to smash the bomber streams. Excellent though the twin-engine 110s were at hunting the RAF's Lancasters in the dark over the Reich, they were no match for the American daylight escort fighters, who blew them out of the sky, massacring their irreplaceable specialist crews.

By now oil production was severely degraded, as confirmed by another Ultra intercept from 6 June.

> As a result of renewed interference with production of aircraft fuel by Allied action, most essential requirements for training and carrying out production plans can scarcely be covered by quantities of aircraft fuel available ... To assume defence of Reich and to prevent gradual collapse of ... German Luftwaffe in east it has been necessary to break into OKW reserves ... most extreme economy measures and strict supervision of consumption, especially for transport, personal and communications flights.

6 June was, of course, D-Day and the launch of Overlord gave the Germans a two-week breather while the bombers pounded targets in France to support the invasion. With their job then done, they turned back to Germany's creaking oil industry with a vengeance. More and more attacks went in and it became a race for the Germans to try and repair the damage faster than the Allies were causing it – and it was a race the Allies were winning. At the end of July over

90 per cent of German oil production facilities had been hit and output had collapsed. By September not a single oil production facility was in full operation and production fell that month to just 12,000 tons. The situation deteriorated quickly: in April the Luftwaffe had 180,000 tons of aviation fuel to hand; by D-Day this had plummeted down to 50,000 tons and hit an all-time low of 10,000 tons in August.[235] OKW was still holding its main strategic reserve of nearly 120,000 tons, but this was only now equivalent to five weeks' supply at current rates.

An exasperated Speer, now back at work after his lengthy convalescence, continually appealed directly to Hitler for more and more fighters to protect the plants as they were systematically reduced to a pile of blackened rubble and twisted metal, but the Nazi dictator's gaze was fixed firmly on the invasion front in France and that is where he chose to send much of the Luftwaffe's remaining strength. The result was inevitable. The Luftwaffe in the east was ordered to use any stocks it had, to cut back on training and non-essential flying and to conserve every drop they could.

Back in the East, the Soviets retook the Crimea and crushed the 235,000-strong German Seventeenth Army and its Romanian allies in a lightning offensive. The Seventeenth's commanding general, Erwin Jaenecke, had loudly proclaimed, 'At Sevastopol stands the Seventeenth Army, and at Sevastopol, the Soviets will bleed to death.' Days later he was pleading with Hitler to allow the evacuation of his men by sea from the fortress port. Paul Deichmann's under-strength Fliegerkorps II was brutally swept aside in the south, losing its only remaining airstrip on the Kherson peninsula in the evening of 9 May when the last thirteen Jagdwaffe fighters in the region flew out to relative safety further west. Even so, Deichmann refused to leave the Army in the lurch and sent his Ju 52 transports in during the night of the 10th to bring out over 1,000 badly wounded men. With the naval evacuation finally sanctioned, the ships desperately needed air cover but Deichmann simply didn't have the fighters to do the job. The result was tragedy. On the morning of the 10th two transports, the *Teja* and the *Totila*, appeared off Khersones and proceeded to take on board around 9,000 men before heading back to the Romanian port of Constanza. In less than an hour they were attacked by a twenty-strong formation of Soviet aircraft, somehow fending them off and steaming as fast as they could towards safety. They were never going to make it. A second attack by another twenty-one aircraft came in at about 9.30 a.m. and the *Totila* was hit by three bombs. The ship, with 3,000 Germans and 2,000 Romanians on board, sank very fast. The *Teja* and her escort ships couldn't stop to help the survivors, overloaded as they were and fearful of the next air attack. That very attack appeared overhead about four hours later in the middle of the afternoon. This time it was eleven Lend-Lease A-20 Havoc bombers (designated DB-7s by the VVS) that swept in and hit the *Teja* with multiple bomb strikes. Explosions rocked the ship and it sank quickly, the three escorts only able to pluck some 400 survivors out of the water. Around 8,000 men were lost in total that day.[236]

CHAPTER 23

D-Day: The Eastern Jagdwaffe Drains West

On the eve of Overlord, the bloated and glutinous Hugo Sperrle had a meagre 815 aircraft at his disposal in the west in Luftflotte 3 and only around 600 of those were operational, the rest lying idle mainly for want of spare parts. They would face a combined Anglo-American force of more than 5,000 planes. That didn't stop their pompous and vain-glorious commander from issuing the following ridiculous order of the day the morning of the invasion to his command:

> Men of Luftflotte 3! The enemy has launched the long-anticipated invasion. Long have we waited for this moment, long have we prepared ourselves, both inwardly and on the field of battle, by untiring, unending toil. Our task now is to defeat the enemy. I know that each one of you, true to his oath to the colours, will carry out his duties. Great things will be asked of you and you will show the bravest fighting valour.

Above the landing beaches, Sperrle's soaring rhetoric was not matched by Lieutenant Wolfgang Fischer of JG 2 who, along with eleven other Fw 190 pilots, was poised to launch an attack on Gold Beach early that first morning. Slipping through the clouds and somehow avoiding the Anglo-American fighter cover, Fischer saw the huge sweep of the Seine bay filled with endless Allied shipping. All he could muster was, 'Poor Germany.'

Fischer and his comrades managed to return safely to base, which was a feat in itself, as the Allied aerial armada filled the sky, riddling everything with a swastika on it with holes.

Goering's response was to send every single aircraft he could lay his hands on to be slaughtered over Normandy. 'I will not leave a single fighter ... every single aircraft which is airworthy will be sent forward ... come hell or high water.' True to his word, the orders went out and 300 aircraft were pulled away from the Eastern Front and sent to France in the first four days after the invasion. Arriving on their newly assigned French airstrips, the eastern Jagdwaffe pilots were sent up to face the Anglo-American onslaught as fast as they arrived. They comprised the core of the Luftwaffe in the east, the very Experten who had for almost three years kept the VVS in check despite being outnumbered at every turn. It was these men who were memorably described by the historian Christer Bergstrom: 'Almost three years of war had developed a core of veterans within the Luftwaffe units – men who were absolute masters in aerial combat, virtual flying war machines.'

In the east these men achieved victories that almost defied description. 'As we stuck to the bombers a Russian fighter suddenly latched onto my tail but Steinbatz shot it down at the last moment. Shortly afterward I managed to bag a MiG-1. By this time we were flying at about 1,500 feet altitude, pretty far into the Russian rear area. I knocked down my second enemy at 1058 hrs, number three went down at 1102, and number four at 1107.'[237]

They were the mainstay of the Jagdwaffe in the east and now they were being sacrificed in the giant mincing machine in the west. Vastly outnumbered, the Luftwaffe lost 600 aircraft and hundreds of pilots over France in just two weeks, among them Karl-Heinz Weber, score of 136; Eugen-Ludwig Zweigart with sixty-nine victories; Herbert Huppertz with a score of sixty-eight; Siegfried Simsch, fifty-four kills; Friedrich Wachowiak with a score of eighty-six; August Mors, with a score of sixty; Karl Kempf, sixty-five kills; and Emil 'Bully' Lang. Lang, the seventeen-in-a-day hero of Kiev back in the previous November, was shot down and killed by American Thunderbolts near St Truiden with his score standing at 173. The famous Experte Johannes 'Macky' Steinhoff said that air combat in the East was little more than a harmless game in comparison to the West.[238]

So severe was the attrition in pilots that the Nazis were even prepared to abandon some of their most cherished racial bigotries and allow turncoat Russians to fly for them. Up until now the edict from Hitler had been clear: 'under no circumstances can we allow the sub-humans to bear arms for the German cause' and this despite the almost 100 VVS pilots who had defected to the Germans, bringing their aircraft with them. This 'Russian legion' even had an ex-Soviet senior officer to lead it: Colonel Viktor Ivanovich Maltsev, the ex-VVS commander in Siberia and head of the Civil Air Fleet. Maltsev had been arrested, tortured and then released during Stalin's Purges back in the late 1930s and when war came he took the opportunity to defect from a regime he hated. Left kicking his heels in the care of his German minder, Lieutenant Colonel Walter Holters, for over three years, Maltsev was now finally allowed to broadcast an appeal on the radio to his fellow Russians:

> Millions of honest Russian people have been tortured to death. The peasant class is ruined and has been transformed into a herd of desperately poor and hungry slaves reduced to silence ... I have broken with the Soviet power, I am taking up arms again and, together with hundreds of thousands of other Russian volunteers, am going into mortal combat against the Soviets.

Two VVS pilots who would go into that 'mortal combat' with him were Captain Semyon Trofimovich Bytchkov and Senior Lieutenant Bronislav Romanovich Antilevsky (both decorated Heroes of the Soviet Union). Bytchkov had been sentenced by a military tribunal to five years in a labour camp for a crash in 1942 before having his sentence lifted and going on to shoot down no fewer than seventeen German aircraft. In December 1943 he was downed by anti-aircraft fire and captured unconscious in his cockpit. After recovering in a German hospital, Bytchkov was sent to a camp in Suwalki for imprisoned Soviet pilots. Interviewed for propaganda purposes at the time, he said, 'Not only did nobody torment or torture us, as we had been warned, it was quite the opposite – we encountered warm-hearted and comradely behaviour from both German officers and soldiers, including respect for our rank and decorations.'[239]

Agreeing to collaborate with the Germans, Bytchkov co-founded the 1st Aircraft Regiment of the Committee of Liberation Movement of the People of Russia under the auspices of Vlasov's Russian Liberation Army (*Russkaya osvoboditel'naya armiya* – the ROA) and became the ROA's chief of night-time bombing.

CHAPTER 24

Operation Bagration: The Death of Army Group Centre

With large numbers of eastern Experten transferred west, the VVS's growing strength became even more pronounced and the stage was now set for it to finally wrest the initiative away from the Luftwaffe and keep it for the rest of the war. By now the Germans had the planes they needed – aircraft production was at an all-time high and the aircraft yards back in Germany were filling up – but there were neither the trained pilots nor the fuel to get them in the air. Goering was being made to eat his own words from earlier in the war: 'The building of our aircraft should not depend in any way on the fuel programme. I would rather have a mass of aircraft standing around unable to fly owing to a lack of petrol than not have any at all.' Well now he had exactly that.[240]

The STAVKA was now preparing to launch their most ambitious offensive yet. Codenamed 'Bagration' after a Georgian Tsarist marshal who had become a hero during the Napoleonic Wars, it was the Soviets' first ever major summer offensive and was tasked with nothing less than the total and utter annihilation of the Ostheer's Army Group Centre. This time it was the Germans who had to plan to be attacked in the summer campaigning season and for the first time in three years they would be without their most talented field commander, Erich von Manstein. The conqueror of the Crimea and Sevastopol, the magician of Kharkov, had been retired by his master. On 30 March Hitler had summoned Von Manstein to Berchtesgaden, awarded him the Swords to his Knight's Cross and then told him, 'I have decided to part company with you and to appoint someone else to the Army Group. The time for operating is over. What I need now is men who stand firm.' Von Manstein would never hold a command again.

Now more in charge of the Ostheer than ever, Hitler placed his bet and just as the STAVKA had gotten theirs wrong in 1942, so Hitler did the same in 1944, believing the blow would fall further south on Army Group North Ukraine. In preparation the dictator had concentrated forty-five divisions (thirty-five German and ten allied Hungarian) along a 219-mile long front and the majority of the Ostheer's panzer and panzer grenadier divisions – eighteen in total. Ernst Busch's Army Group Centre, by contrast, had to defend a 488-mile front with only thirty-eight divisions and a smattering of panzers.

The Luftwaffe in the east was just as skewed. Luftflotte 4 in the south had 845 aircraft, including 390 ground attack planes, 160 single-engine fighters and forty-five twin-engine fighters. While Ritter von Greim's Luftflotte 6 covering Army Group Centre had almost as many planes in total, 775, only 100 were ground attack and another 100 single-engine fighters, the bulk of its strength being 370 bombers (mainly outdated He 111s) unsuited to defending against an enemy ground offensive. Worse was to come when fifty of Luftflotte 6's fighter contingent were ordered to Normandy just before Bagration was launched on the 22nd.

As for the VVS, never before had the Soviets managed to mass such an overwhelming force to face their nemesis. The figures were staggering: twenty-one fighter divisions, fourteen strike divisions, eight divisions of bombers, another sixteen of heavy bombers and six more of night bombers, plus 179 reconnaissance aircraft. All in all, almost six thousand aircraft.[241]

The VVS commander, General Konstantin Verschinin, left nothing to chance and carried out extensive reconnaissance of the front lines, drawing too on the substantial intelligence available from the very large numbers of partisans operating in the region. All the information gathered pointed to the same thing: the Germans were almost totally immobile, their infantry units were weak and they were relying very heavily on their artillery to make up for these glaring deficiencies and act in a direct fire role if attacked. The Army Group only had two divisions as a true reserve, the understrength 20th Panzer and a horse-drawn infantry formation. The gun lines, which should have been lying in hard cover behind the defensive fortifications, were instead positioned on forward slopes or in strongpoints in order to be effective against any enemy tank assaults. The 1,000-plus Shturmovik pilots were briefed accordingly: hammer the German guns into the dirt.

The Kremlin picked 22 June as launch day for Bagration – a conscious decision to avenge the horror of Barbarossa three years earlier. Even before the massed weight of the Soviet artillery began to plough up the German defences, the sky above Busch's Army Group was thick with wave after wave of the VVS. As ordered, the Shturmovik 'Cement Boxes' swept in at low altitude, blithely flying through the German ground fire and lashing the enemy gun lines with rockets, bombs and cannon fire. Nearby ammunition stores exploded, bunkers and slit trenches were caved in and the guns themselves were turned into misshapen lumps of metal. The effects were devastating. Dozens of guns were knocked out in the first hours, their crews lying dead or wounded in their shattered gun-pits. The Shturmoviks were causing chaos, but as ever their fighter escorts disliked their job:

> We were sent to escort Shturmoviks, which flew as low as 1,000– 1,200 metres. I couldn't fly that low, I would have been shot down. I would fly higher, but the camouflaged Shturmoviks were not easy to see against the snow or forest, so we'd often lose them. Sometimes the Messers would find them before us, and then we'd hear over the radio; 'Hats! Hats! Cover us!' ['Hats' was the slang name the Shturmovik pilots used for their fighter top cover.][242]

As the Red Army rushed forward, Busch tried to react, moving his few mobile formations to try and meet the Soviet spearheads, only for the VVS to sweep in again, this time hitting command and control centres, logistics points and traffic junctions, as they set road convoy after road convoy alight. The Soviet aerial onslaught was so powerful that Wilhelmstrasse rushed reinforcements to Luftflotte 6 as fast as it could. A hundred fighters arrived from the Italian front (pretty much every fighter left defending the peninsula), dozens from other sectors on the Eastern Front and the fifty only just sent to France turned round and flew back to their old bases. So bad was the situation that the OKL even made the extraordinary decision to send forty fighters already with the Normandy front out to von Greim's beleaguered formation. The new arrivals found themselves sent straight up to face VVS fighters that outnumbered them five or six to one in every dogfight and with so many of the eastern Luftwaffe's Experten fighting for their lives over Normandy, for once the Soviets found themselves making bloody inroads into their Jagdwaffe opponents. As a report from one of the Luftwaffe's own flak divisions stated acerbically, 'One can only comment on the measures undertaken to meet the Russian offensive, "half measures" and "too late".'[243]

The German fighter pilots didn't give up though, rising every morning to meet their enemy, but it was not enough. The immobility of the Army Group and Hitler's ridiculous 'Fortress' policy condemned tens of thousands of German soldiers to remain in indefensible cities such as Minsk and be surrounded, cut off, killed or marched into captivity.

Finally, in mid-July, the stunned Germans managed to launch a counter-attack with Werner Friebe's veteran 8th Panzer Division. The 8th was a powerful, experienced formation and while its intervention couldn't hope to throw the Red Army back, it might be enough to buy the retreating Germans the time they desperately needed to form a new line and save them from disaster. Faced with chaos behind the front and the absolute urgency of the situation, Friebe took the fateful decision to move his division into its jumping-off positions during daylight. It was a calculated risk and one the East Prussian general would never have taken in France, faced by the Anglo-American air forces, but he knew the VVS and they weren't in the same league – were they? First to appear were the Soviet reconnaissance planes, who lost no time in reporting roads packed with long columns of panzers, assault guns, half-tracks full of panzer grenadiers and endless supply lorries and fuel bowsers. Next came the dreaded Shturmoviks – wave after wave of them. '8th Panzer Division was caught on the move by Russian aircraft. Long columns of panzers and lorries went up in flames, and all hopes of a counter-attack disappeared.'[244]

The total collapse of Army Group Centre followed swiftly and as the Germans were tumbled backwards towards the pre-war Polish border, the Luftwaffe lost all its forward air bases with their spares, equipment and facilities. Operations were severely disrupted, damaged aircraft were set alight and abandoned and escaping fighters took off to fly west with members of the ground crew crammed into their cockpits to save them from Soviet gulags.

In five weeks it was all over. Army Group Centre had been wiped off the Wehrmacht's Order of Battle. Twenty-eight of its thirty-eight divisions had ceased to exist and over 350,000 men had been killed, wounded or were missing, along with thirty-one generals (including lieutenant generals Robert Pistorius and Rudolf Peschel of the 4th and 6th Luftwaffe Field Divisions respectively, who were both killed). Casualties were even higher than at Stalingrad. The Soviets took 85,000 prisoners and paraded them triumphantly through Moscow's Red Square and the surrounding streets. After they were herded past the crowds of Muscovites, the Square and adjoining roads were washed down with giant hoses – symbolically cleansing them of taint from the despised 'Fritzies'.

The eastern Luftwaffe too was shattered. Despite a rush of reinforcements and new shipments from the factories back in the

Reich, the Luftwaffe's total strength in the east dropped from 2,085 aircraft in early June to 1,760 by the end of July.[245] Fighter strength was, of course, far lower.

For the Soviets, and for the VVS in particular, it had been a stunning success. They had advanced 435 miles, at a pace that almost matched the Nazi blitzkrieg back in 1941, and had achieved an ascendancy over their hated enemy they would never relinquish. Within the STAVKA it was acknowledged that the performance of the VVS and the weakness of the Luftwaffe were two of the keys to Bagration's success.[246]

CHAPTER 25

No Pilots, No Jets and No Allies

With brand-new fighters rolling off the production lines in the Reich in ever greater numbers, the Jagdwaffe's priority was to have the pilots to fly them. Yet training, hit hard by a lack of instructors since the Stalingrad calamity in 1942 and more recently by fuel shortages, was in freefall.

Norbert Hannig did a stint at Jagdgruppe Ost's (the Jagdwaffe's eastern command structure) training school at Liegnitz in Lower Silesia in 1944.

> There was no formal training involved in becoming an instructor. It was just something you got on with and did ... Each of the instructors was in charge of three trainees ... The pupils fell into two categories. They were either green youngsters straight from training schools, or experienced operational pilots from other types of units, mostly disbanded former bomber crew, now converting onto fighters.

Hannig and his fellow instructors did their best to pass on their experience to the new pilots but so huge was the pressure placed on the Luftwaffe by Anglo-American bombing raids that Hannig and his pupils were organised into *Einsatzstaffeln*, i.e. replacement operational squadrons, to be used against incoming bombers if the need arose. During their first such sortie, Hannig and eleven other Fw 190s went up against almost 300 B-17s and their P-51 Mustang escorts. One 190 returned undamaged, two landed damaged, five made emergency or crash landings with wounded or dying pilots, the other four were shot down. All four pilots had bailed out, of which the Germans claimed two were shot and killed by the Mustangs as they floated down in their parachutes.[247]

The Jagdwaffe was now two completely different forces split 50–50; one was made up of experienced veterans like Hannig and the Experten, while the other was composed of novices who were little more than cannon fodder, arriving at their Staffeln and disappearing so quickly that hardly anyone bothered to learn their names anymore. They had been given little or no training in modern fighters – indeed it wasn't uncommon for a new pilot never to have flown a fully armed fighter before he stepped into one for his first combat mission. He would have hardly done any take-offs and landings in formation and would never have fired the MK108 and MG151 cannons and machine guns fitted to his aircraft. In fact his entire training would have lasted barely two months and he would have had a few hours of flying time at best. Most of them were dead before their tenth operational sortie.[248]

Comments from the veterans betrayed their bitterness at it all.

'All we have now is young pilots with no experience.'
'What sort of training have the newcomers had? It's pitiful and appalling.'[249]

Johannes 'Macky' Steinhoff said: 'We were assigned young pilots who were timid, inexperienced and scared … it was hard enough leading and keeping together a large combat formation of experienced pilots, with youngsters it was hopeless.'[250]

The Experten and their wingmen were still shooting down an average of at least ten to twelve Soviets for every one of them getting hit, but their ranks weren't being replenished by new pilots who were surviving, gaining experience and learning their deadly trade. The numbers spoke for themselves – of the 107 Jagdwaffe Experten who each scored over 100 kills, only eight joined their Staffeln after mid-1942.

By this time, Goering had disappeared into a land of delusion and paranoia that was only inhabited by other senior Nazis. He hardly ever appeared at the interminable daily military conferences held at Rastenburg that Hitler used to try and lead a war that was happening hundreds of miles away to the east, west and south. But like a spoilt child, the Reichsmarshall still refused to hand over the reins to anyone else who, even now, might have made a difference. As a senior officer with the OKL remarked, 'Goering seems to have run the Luftwaffe with much the same methods as those used by the Queen of Hearts in Alice in Wonderland, and with much the same effectiveness … For him the Luftwaffe was just another toy.'

His possible successor, Erhard Milch, had by now been, in the words of Bruno Loerzer, 'organised out' of the service already.

Goering had long wanted to rid himself of a subordinate he saw as being a potential threat: 'Milch is always working against me ... What does Milch think he's doing anyway? Six months ago he told me not to worry ... What kind of a pig-sty is this? Things have become worse than they were under Udet! Where is the increased production? There is none, except for fighters!'

Goering's opportunity came gift-wrapped during the Me 262 debacle.

German scientists had been working on jet propulsion for years and even when all development programmes had been effectively cancelled back in 1942 to focus on existing models, Willy Messerschmitt had disobeyed Wilhelmstrasse's orders and had continued to work on a design that later on became the famous Me 262. When Adolf Galland flew a prototype for the very first time in May 1943, it took his breath away: 'For the first time I was flying by jet propulsion! No engine vibrations. No torque and no lashing sound of the engine propeller. Accompanied by a whistling sound, my jet shot through the air. Later when asked what it felt like, I said, "It was as though angels were pushing."'

The aircraft's performance was phenomenal. Its speed and rate of climb were hair-raising and only equalled by the weaponry it could carry in a nose unencumbered by an engine and propeller. The threat it could pose to the massive Viermots in particular was a potential game changer. However, the programme was bedevilled by poor decision making and delays at every step. In the summer of 1944, Speer's deputy, Karl-Otto Saur, said to his colleagues:

> We assumed that we would produce at least thirty to forty Me 262s during March ... and soon thereafter seventy-five to eighty per month. It is now June and we do not have a single machine. We have only ourselves to blame, we have been incapable of concentrating our efforts, and incapable of approaching the problem with the energy and determination warranted by its vital importance.

Saur could not have been more right. By the end of the year, the industrial might of Nazi Germany had made just 564 Me 262s. In the last months of the war it would make about the same number again.[251]

Nevertheless, Goebbels and his propaganda machine ceaselessly broadcast that the new jets would help turn the tide of the war, building up a forlorn hope that somehow the Luftwaffe would save Nazi Germany, and many of the men in the line believed him: 'The new jet-propelled fighter planes, which were far superior to the best

British and American planes, were already in action and had caused heavy casualties among their bombers. We knew that even better things were coming. It was only a matter of time, a question of months.'[252]

'New planes flying faster than the speed of sound, turbo-jets which rendered Allied bomber flights into scrap metal. It was said that only a few weeks were needed until their usage was possible'.[253]

Hitler, a military meddler and micro-manager par excellence, took an immediate interest in the plane when it stopped being Messerschmitt's little secret, only he made matters worse by insisting that the aircraft be designed as a fighter-bomber. He was becoming increasingly obsessed that the Luftwaffe was transforming into a purely defensive weapon and that to maintain its offensive capability it needed to keep a bombing facility. This was both technological and strategic madness. In reality, if the Luftwaffe could defend the Reich and the front it would be doing an incredible job. Nevertheless, lip service was paid to the 262 being a fighter-bomber until a Führer conference in April where Milch was deputising for his boss and was directly asked by Hitler how many of the completed Me 262 jets could carry bombs. Milch sheepishly replied, 'None my Führer, the Me-262 is being built exclusively as a fighter.' Galland, who was present, said Hitler actually 'foamed at the mouth' at this news and then flew off the handle at the hapless Milch, lambasting him, Goering, the OKL and the entire Luftwaffe as traitors, incompetents and insubordinates. No one leapt to Milch's defence. His constant intriguing, jockeying for position and naked ambition had made him many enemies and very few friends among senior Nazis and after the conference disaster he was jettisoned by an ungrateful Goering.

As the Luftwaffe's senior leadership became increasingly irrelevant, the structure of the Axis went through meltdown and left the eastern Luftwaffe bereft of the allies it now needed so much. Fascist Italy had long gone of course, its tiny number of aircraft still fighting for Mussolini's puppet Salo Republic in the north barely ever showing themselves in the Allied-dominated sky. The Finns had made a separate peace with Moscow and next to fall were the Romanians. Bagration had stripped Romania and its precious oilfields of Jagdwaffe air cover and left the Romanians with no choice but to pull back their highest-scoring ace, Captain Serbanescu (at least forty-five confirmed kills), and his Grupul 9 Vanatoare from the Eastern Front to try and protect their homeland against the increasing number of USAAF raids. Then, on 7 August, the Romanian Air Ministry issued a secret instruction to its air force to stop attacking Anglo-American planes and conserve their strength for the expected Soviet offensive. That offensive began on 20 August when the 2nd and 3rd Ukrainian Fronts attacked the German-Romanian Army Group South Ukraine. Flush with aircraft, the VVS had massed 1,700 planes against a tiny number of Romanian and German opponents. The FARR somehow managed 800 sorties before their forward airfields were overrun, but it was a snowball in summer. Just five days after the offensive kicked off, young King Michael had arrested the pro-German Romanian *Conducator*, Marshal Ion Antonescu, left the Axis and declared war on Nazi Germany. From the launch of Barbarossa until they switched sides, the FARR claimed that it had shot down 1,500 Soviet aircraft for the loss of about 3,000 pilots, crew and ground staff killed, wounded and missing – many of them in the Stalingrad disaster. Among the pilots there was real despondency. They had flown and fought with their German allies for years – many of them had been trained by them too – and they were now enemies. The German Experte and fighter co-ordinator in the country, Edouard 'Edu' Neumann, said of his Romanian pilot friends, 'We phoned each other for about three days afterwards until our Stukas destroyed the telephone lines. Before that happened we wished each other the best of luck for the future and *au revoir*.' The Romanian pilot Dan Vizanty said, 'A leaden mood, a fog of anxiety that one could almost feel, filled the officers' mess, as if we all had a foreboding of the terrible times ahead. Nobody spoke.'[254]

The last Axis partner with any sort of air force was Horthy's Hungary. The Admiral had tried to pull the country out of the war, only to be strong-armed by the Nazis, who had already kidnapped one of his remaining sons to put pressure on him to 'stay loyal'. The Red Army invaded the country and by Christmas had invested the capital Budapest, both sides carrying out horrific atrocities.

> I clearly remember kneeling among the massacred corpses of our soldiers, hacked to pieces in a frenzy of bloodlust and typical Russian custom, always their genitals cut off and stuffed in their mouth ... less than a couple of hours later we came upon a huge courtyard used by the Hungarian gendarmes as an impromptu POW camp ... .we marched the Russians in small, terrified groups to the nearest site of Soviet butchery where we shot each one through the head in blind reprisal.[255]

In the air, the remaining Magyar air forces were no match for the VVS. During the first eleven days of the siege the Hungarians flew a miserly 291 sorties and shot down just sixteen Soviets, against a VVS tally of 8,490 sorties over the same period as they pounded the city and its defenders.

Despite the Luftwaffe's clearly failing strength, it still had the power to punish the Red Army. However, this was in small, local engagements rather than the grand offensives of the previous years, as witnessed by the Latvian SS volunteer Mintauts Blosfelds: 'The undulating country was full of Red Army tanks and trucks … they were immobilised from the air by a score of Stukas, diving and firing their anti-tank cannons, dropping bombs and machine-gunning the tank crews and Russian infantry.'[256]

It was air attacks like this that made old habits died hard among the solders of the Red Army who continued to look to the skies with trepidation if they heard aircraft engines. Dmitriy Fedorovich Loza, a battalion commander in the 233rd Tank Brigade, 5th Mechanized Corps (later designated a Guards formation), had already been made a Hero of the Soviet Union when he spoke about the Romanian offensive.

The Germans fell upon us with air strikes and we had nothing with which to ward them off [their Lend-Lease supplied Sherman tanks hadn't been fitted with the usual large calibre anti-aircraft guns]. It was the morning of 23 August and already the third air raid. Two tanks had been damaged and one wheeled vehicle set on fire in Ivan Yakushin's company. Ivan Ignat'evich was upset and assembled his commanders. It was noted that some crews halted their vehicles during enemy air attacks. 'This is a big mistake. It is more difficult for the enemy to hit a moving target.' Ivan then proposed what seemed an improbable course of action. Later we heard a loud warning 'Air!' as the German bombers circled above. The decisive moment had arrived. The tank commander spotted a bomb separating from the Ju 87 Stuka diving on his vehicle, and the bomb grew larger with every second of its flight. The officer, calculating the trajectory of its flight, adjusted the Sherman's movement, a spurt forward and the bomb fell behind the tank. The *Emcha** then escaped the danger zone.[257] [*Emcha was the Soviets affectionate nickname for the Sherman, derived from the first letter and numeral of its alphanumeric designation – 'M4' in Russian being 'M-Chetyrye'.]

It wasn't just Lend-Lease tanks that were helping the Soviet advance, as noticed by the ethnic German SS man Sigmund Heinz Landau: 'The Russians were now a well-fed healthy lot, while we were a sorry-looking lot of flea-bitten skeletal scarecrows.' The Soviets were eating American high-protein rations, wearing well-made American leather boots and riding in sturdy American four-wheel-drive trucks. 'Russian morale was at its highest, and ours was at its lowest.'[258]

1944 was the 'black year' for the eastern Luftwaffe. The need to defend the homeland against the growing Anglo-American air offensive and the launching of Overlord had drained the Jagdwaffe of its strength, finally tipping the balance in the east against the Experten and their comrades. The aircraft production lines had finally got into gear, churning out aircraft at a prodigious rate; however the incredibly successful assault on the German synthetic oil industry, and the breakdown in pilot training, had robbed the Luftwaffe in the east of any chance at resurrection.

There was still a sting in the Luftwaffe tail; JG 51 had reached a total of 8,000 kills in May and JG 54 achieved the same milestone in mid-August, while the most successful fighter group in history – JG 52 – actually hit the astronomical 10,000 mark at the beginning of September. Fifty-two eastern Luftwaffe pilots won the Knight's Cross in the year, although increasingly it was a posthumous award. Thirteen winners were killed in action, four died in flying accidents, two were shot down and captured and five were so badly wounded they never flew again, including Norbert Hannig's close friend Hans-Joachim Kroschinski, who was shot down after claiming no fewer than five Pe-2 bombers in a single engagement. Kroschinski survived the crash but lost his right leg and his eyesight.

CHAPTER 26

The VVS Triumphant!

As 1945 dawned, the war in Europe still had over four bloody months to run. The eastern Luftwaffe was a shadow of its former self, with less than 2,000 aircraft to face a VVS that could muster more than six times that number. Men's minds turned inevitably to survival and for the first time Luftwaffe pilots began to use excuses to avoid combat, such as 'engine trouble' and 'undercarriage not retracting'; one pilot was arrested after being seen taking off, flying around aimlessly, firing his guns into nothing and then returning to base. It wasn't just novices either; the 101-score Experte and Kommodore of JG 26 Josef 'Pips' Priller, immortalised as the ranting Luftwaffe fighter pilot in the British-made D-Day film *The Longest Day*, flew his 307th sortie on New Year's Day 1945 and then, despite being uninjured, never flew again for the rest of the war. One veteran said that, 'More senior officers used to fly but that is all over now. They don't do a thing. They don't fancy a hero's death any longer, those days are past.'[259]

Who could blame them?

The Landsers, shorn of the air support they had taken for granted for years, were now reduced to gallows humour about the state of their air force: 'If they're silver they're American, if they're camouflaged they're British, if they're green they're Russian, and if they're not there at all, they're ours!'

Goering decided, at this point, to make one of his by now rare interventions in his service and, as per usual, it was ill-timed, ill-thought out and a disaster – Operation Bodenplatte. The plan was for more or less the entire Jagdwaffe in the West (Luftflotte 3 and Luftflotte Reich's thirty-nine Gruppen of Bf 109s and Fw 190s – about 1,900 aircraft) to strike the packed Anglo-American airfields across Belgium and the

Netherlands at dawn on New Year's Day. To help fill the raiders' tanks, Luftflotte Reich's 732 night fighters (mainly Ju 88s and Me 110s) had their gasoline rations channelled to the day fighters, leaving them immobile on their air bases, and only the barest of reconnaissance was allowed to maintain operational secrecy. Goering believed the Allies would be unprepared for such a stratagem and would suffer a shocking defeat with hundreds, if not thousands, of their aircraft destroyed on the ground. Galland protested vehemently that it was a waste of resources, but was overruled as usual. To add insult to the Jagdwaffe's injury, the operation was put into the exceedingly clumsy hands of none other than Beppo Schmid – the Luftwaffe's ex-head of Intelligence. Goering had sent Schmid to Tunisia back in late 1942 to command the Luftwaffe ground troops encircled there, before he was flown out on Goering's personal orders as the Axis position collapsed. He now proved he was just as capable of fouling up a fighter operation as well as anything else. The Anglo-Americans were not caught off guard by the 'sneak attack' and reacted extremely quickly, engaging the Germans in mass dogfights that ripped the heart out of the western Luftwaffe. The Jagdwaffe lost about 300 planes, but worse still, it also lost 237 irreplaceable pilots killed and missing, including twenty of its most experienced flight leaders.

Hitler fumed at the failure of Bodenplatte. For him, it was yet another example of the incompetence of the Luftwaffe. By now he was routinely blaming the air force, and especially the Jagdwaffe, for the military mess Germany was in. Speer was present at one of the dictator's outbursts. 'He told Galland in a rage that the whole fighter force were good for nothing, that from now on we were only going to produce anti-aircraft guns and that all fighter production would be stopped.'[260]

To his shame, Goering not only didn't step in to defend his men, he even joined in with Hitler's blame game, sacking Galland as General der Jagdflieger and replacing him with the humourless and ambitious Gordon Gollob. Incensed by what they saw as Goering's total lack of leadership, a group of senior fighter leaders confronted the Reichsmarshall in what became known as the 'fighter pilots' mutiny'. One of their number, Johannes 'Macky' Steinhoff, said, 'For most of us the step to insubordination was quite literally appalling, but we had to take it; subordination had become more than we could bear.' The list of those involved read like a roll of honour of the Jagdwaffe's best and bravest: Günther Lützow, Hermann Graf, Edu Neumann, Hannes Trautloft, Heinz Bär, Gustav Rödel, Josef Priller, Gerhard Michalski, Helmut Bennemann and Steinhoff himself. Galland, having been sacked, was under Gestapo surveillance and could play no part in the attempted coup, but there was no doubt he agreed with the group's aims of forcing Goering to relinquish his authority, to reinstate Galland and concentrate the entire Luftwaffe on one final effort to halt the bombing of the homeland. Before they confronted Goering himself, Steinhoff and Lützow went on 13 January to see probably the only senior commander in the Luftwaffe they still trusted, the commander of Luftflotte 6, Robert Ritter von Greim, at his headquarters at Lodz in occupied Poland. They appealed directly to 'Papa' Greim, begging him to go and see Hitler and ask him to relieve Goering immediately. As they sat in front of the fireplace Greim listened to them and then turned them down: 'I have served the Reichsmarshall faithfully all these many years. I believe in the Führer – and damn it I still believe in him, at least I try to ... No, gentlemen, you're asking too much of me. I can't become a traitor, I just can't. Least of all against Hermann Goering. Do you understand that? I can't!'

He slumped back in his chair, his head in his hands and burst into tears. Composing himself, Greim went on to warn the two young officers that Goering knew of their plans and was intent on crushing the mutiny. When he heard of the meeting with Greim, Goering, for once, acted quickly and succeeded in turning the tables on his fighter leaders to such a degree that most of them rightly feared for their lives. Steinhoff in particular was targeted by Goering for revenge and only a take-off accident that left him with extremely severe burns saved him from a court-martial and possible execution. As for the rest, Goering cast them to the four winds, with most of them like Trautloft and Lützow 'exiled' to non-jobs far from their Staffeln.

Luftwaffe morale did not crack, though, as secret recordings of captured pilots attested.

'What was the morale of the officers and men like?'
'On the whole our morale is still quite good. It's obvious the present situation is lousy, but there still exists the great hope that things won't turn out as bad as they look.'[261]

Away from the malaise affecting the Luftwaffe's senior ranks, the front-line pilots in the east just got on with it. Norbert Hannig, now flying with Luftflotte 1 in the cut-off Courland Pocket, was a typical example, concentrating on the task at hand.

As usual, the enemy's infantry and armour were supported by hordes of low-flying ground-attack Il-2s and their escorting fighters. We did what we could to protect our own troops from this ever-present scourge, but our supply of aviation fuel was now running low.

Missions could only be flown upon receipt of a specific order ... If possible, I always attacked from an advantage of height. In diving on the enemy this height was traded for speed. One quick pass at my opponent – either in close or from a distance using the correct amount of lead – and away again before he knew what had hit him. It was a tactic that allowed me to down several Il-2s and escorting fighters.[262]

Elsewhere in the east, the five Bf 109 Gruppen of Luftflotte 6 were trying to help fend off the Soviet thrust into East Prussia. The local Nazi Party leaders across the eastern *Länder* (Germany's regions, then as now, are administratively distinct) failed in their duty to their citizens and waited far too long to order the evacuation away from the advancing Soviets. The result was roads choked with hundreds of thousands of people fleeing to the west through the snow and ice, with their worldly goods packed into wagons, suitcases and simple bundles.

Thirteen-year-old Hannelore Thiele and her family were among the refugees. 'What a way to leave! The stalls were full of livestock, the cows were untied, the pig pens opened, the chicken and geese scattered. It was bitterly cold. The roads were clogged with refugees and again and again low flying Russian aircraft passed over, shooting at us.'[263]

The Nazis had deliberately whipped up the population with tales of what awaited anyone who fell into the hands of the 'Asiatic hordes of sub-humans' as they termed them, but for once their propaganda wasn't too far off the mark. One eyewitness of the Soviet treatment of German civilians wrote, 'An old man was nailed upside down on the door of a shed. Along the wall of a house was a row of bodies, all old men and young boys, shot in the back.'

The murder of German civilians by the Red Army was horrific and fairly widespread, but it was also sporadic and unplanned, whereas Soviet records have now confirmed that the systematic rape of German women and girls was more or less official Soviet policy. 'Shut your eyes, clench your teeth, and don't utter a sound. Only when your underwear is ripped apart with a tearing sound, the teeth grind involuntarily. I feel the fingers at my mouth, smell the reek of horses and tobacco. Then the man above me slowly lets his spittle dribble into my mouth.'[264]

Hundreds of thousands of German women were assaulted, many of them raped repeatedly by gangs of soldiers who then moved on and were replaced by other abusers. So bad was it that some victims committed suicide to escape the horror.

These were despicable acts – war crimes by any standards – but it should also be stated that the Wehrmacht was just as guilty of such crimes itself during its time in the Soviet Union. Two captured Luftwaffe NCOs were secretly recorded discussing their own behaviour in the occupied territories.

Müller: 'When I was at Kharkov the whole place had been destroyed, except the centre of town. It was a delightful town, a delightful memory! Everyone spoke a little German – they'd learnt it at school. Taganrog was the same. We did a lot of flying near the junction of the Don and Donets. Its beautiful country ... everywhere we saw women doing compulsory labour service.'
Faust: 'How frightful!'
Müller: 'They were employed on road making – extraordinarily lovely girls; we drove past, simply pulled them into the armoured car, raped them and threw them out again, and did they curse!'[265]

The Soviet advance was now even touching Goering himself. He ordered 'Emmyhall' burnt to the ground to stop it falling into Soviet hands and then on 31 January ordered his wife to leave Carinhall with the female servants and four trucks full of art treasures – most of them looted earlier in the war, of course. He stayed on, wandering the deserted halls and corridors and spending time with the rare and exotic animals in his private zoo.

By now, the Red Army was on the Oder River at Küstrin, where the Germans put up a furious defence. Hans von Luck, late of the 7th Panzer Division and now a colonel with the 21st Panzers, was there.

We had been promised that we would receive support from the famous fighter-bombers of our most highly decorated soldier, Colonel Rudel. His speciality was to use his Ju-87 dive-bombers, equipped with anti-tank guns, to swoop down on Russian armoured units and destroy their tanks with direct hits. At first the battle on 9 February raged back and forth, then Rudel's fighter-bombers appeared and dived on the Russian tanks, anti-tank guns and artillery positions. After so long it was a great feeling for us old hands to no longer be exposed without cover to the enemy air force. Much more important however was the effect on the morale of our youngsters who were seeing action for the first time.[266]

Rudel had been awarded the diamonds to his Knight's Cross the previous year after getting shot down behind enemy lines, swimming the near-frozen Dniester River and then trekking fifty kilometres back to safety through enemy lines. The Nazis would eventually run out of medals for him and had to create one – the Golden Knight's Cross – of which he was the only ever recipient. Back in November he had been wounded in the thigh and flew subsequent missions with his leg in a plaster cast. Now, as he led his men to support von Luck, a 40 mm anti-aircraft shell hit his aircraft. His right foot took the force of the blast, his Stuka pouring smoke. In a lot of pain, he managed to crash land the plane behind German lines. His life was saved by his rear gunner, Ernst Gadermann, who happened to be a medical doctor as well as a machine-gunner. Gadermann stopped the bleeding from Rudel's shattered foot, but couldn't save the limb. Taken to a hospital, Rudel's right leg was amputated below the knee. Unbelievably, he somehow returned to active flying before the war ended.

As von Luck and his now ragtag force defended Küstrin, Wilhelmstrasse reorganised the remnants of the Luftwaffe to try and co-ordinate some sort of last-ditch resistance in the East. Luftflotte 4 and its three Bf 109 Gruppen down in Hungary and on the Yugoslavian border, was disbanded and merged with von Greim's Luftflotte 6. Von Greim now had formal responsibility for air operations over eastern Germany, Poland, Slovakia, Bohemia, Moravia and Croatia; in effect he was in overall charge of the battle against the VVS and its now 15,000-aircraft strong Air Armies. But all titles were as empty now as the fuel tanks of most of the Jagdwaffe's 2,200 stranded aircraft. What little gasoline that was left was hoarded and sent to Greim's units in a desperate bid to try and hold the Soviets. Luftflotte 2 in northern Italy was effectively grounded for lack of fuel, but it only had night fighters and reconnaissance planes in any case, and Luftflotte 5, which had been in Finland, was now sitting idle on Norwegian airstrips awaiting the inevitable. Stumpff's men in the west were so outnumbered and outclassed that all knew it more or less suicide to take to the skies. New pilots still arrived at the Staffeln, albeit only at a trickle. Eighteen or nineteen-year-old boys, they were counted lucky if they had received forty hours of flying training time. Many went up for their first operational sortie and were never seen again. The last few surviving Experten still had fangs, but it was hopeless and several were killed almost within sight of the war's end, among them Norbert Hannig's comrade in JG 54 Otto 'Bruno' Kittel. Kittel, a softly spoken Sudeten German, was the fourth-highest-scoring ace in the Jagdwaffe, with 267 kills. He was engaging a number of Shturmoviks over Courland in his Fw 190 when he was hit by the rear gunner of the Il-2 he was attacking. His plane crashed into the ground and exploded.

On the ground the barrel was busily being scraped as well. One Waffen-SS veteran remembers the state of the reinforcements they received from the depots: 'We could not believe our own eyes. Some of these poor devils had a pronounced limp, one was deaf, another could not see very well, and one was a hunchback.' As his comrade joked, 'We'll have to put two of them on sentry together, one who can see and one who can hear.'[267]

Come April, the Red Army launched its final offensive aimed at capturing Berlin. Simultaneously, the STAVKA ordered that East Prussia be finished off and the fortress city of Königsberg taken. The Jagdwaffe only had enough strength for one battle, so Königsberg was abandoned to its fate, the VVS being given a free hand by their exhausted opponents. 'We raided Heiligenbal Airfield, south of Königsberg. I led a group of 12 fighters ... We dropped our bombs from a horizontal flight path. There were plenty of German planes on the ground so it was impossible to miss. No one attacked us.'[268]

Novikov was overseeing the VVS assault on the Baltic coast city personally and had concentrated over 2,400 aircraft to support the assault force of 137,000 soldiers and 530 tanks. Opposing them were 35,000 German defenders with fifty panzers. Novikov masterminded a devastating aerial offensive, using waves of heavy bombers attacking at low-level to maximise the impact of their payloads as they dropped 514 tons of high-explosive on their enemy. Clouds of Shturmoviks bombed and strafed everything in sight, knocking out strongpoints, panzers and gun positions. The VVS pilots didn't even have to fear German flak as the batteries had run out of ammunition before the attack began. As a *coup de grace*, on the morning of the 7th a total of 256 bombers in three waves went in and hammered the battered city. As the smoke cleared, there was only ruins: 90 per cent of Königsberg had been flattened. For his part in the operation, Novikov was made a Hero of the Soviet Union.

The Silesian regional capital, Breslau, was also besieged and under attack: 'It rained death out of the sky from Soviet bombers that systematically bombed what was left of the residential areas, square metre by square metre.'[269]

However, the Luftwaffe was still able to offer the hard-pressed defenders some support. One of the soldiers trapped inside Breslau was the Dutch Waffen-SS volunteer Hendrik Verton: 'Our only remaining line of communication was the Gandau aerodrome ... Deliveries were made by our reliable and proven '*Tante*' [Auntie] Ju 52 transports. They took the wounded out on the return journeys ... Frequently we saw our planes in flames, falling from the skies with their helpless passengers on board.'

Casualties among the remaining few air transport Staffeln were high, as noted by the Fortress Commander, General Hermann Niehoff, in his diary in late March: 'The supply line for Breslau has become extremely difficult to protect because of increasingly heavy anti-aircraft guns and searchlights. On 15 March, from a total of 55 machines that tried to land, only half of them managed to do so. Despite this, 150 of our wounded were flown out, most of the machines being able to take 20 wounded per flight.'

To the south-west, on the Oder, the Wehrmacht made one last gasp effort to stop the Soviets. Hans von Luck and his remaining men were rushed north to help hold the line.

During the night of 12 and 13 April 45 our division rolled north in express troop trains, but owing to the great air superiority of the Russians we could only travel by night. The relative strength of the Russian and German forces was as follows; infantry 6:1, artillery 10:1, panzers 20:1, aircraft 30:1. On 16 April the great Russian offensive began, when from 5 am the Russians opened a massive bombardment with over 40,000 guns, supported by fighter-bombers and bombers. The Russian tank armies moved forward and in the first onslaught broke through our positions.

From the sky a Soviet fighter plane suddenly came diving like a falcon ... Like an arrow the plane dived down at the gun emplacement ... Just a hair's breadth over the gun the plane dropped a bomb, turned its nose a few metres over the ground and up into the sky.

The Swedish Waffen-SS grenadier who had seen this low-level attack couldn't help admire the skill of the VVS pilot: 'What an amazingly gifted pilot, what a dive!'[270]

The VVS now had around 17,000 aircraft in theatre and dedicated almost half of those to the assault on Berlin, the Guards regiments in particular taking a heavy toll of Luftwaffe pilots.

The difference between Russian and German pilots? Of course the Germans had more experience and better training. We could sense this, especially in the early part of the war. When they'd beaten us up we concentrated more and began hitting back. Then they became very careful, only attacking when they saw a clear advantage. By the end of the war many German aces were dead and we came across 'losers' as we called them. They didn't have the skills of the aces and we beat them up good.[271]

The Luftwaffe put up one final showing. Von Greim ordered 1,000 sorties against the Soviets on 16 April, including from a patched-up Hans-Ulrich Rudel, minus his amputated right leg. The Stuka ace claimed another twenty-six Soviet tanks destroyed, but it was a drop in the ocean and he, along with all his remaining comrades, could make no discernible difference to the outcome now. By the 25th the capital was surrounded and the Luftwaffe scattered.

Goering was still at Carinhall when the Soviet offensive was launched. He took one last look at his pleasure palace, leafing through the guestbook, pausing as he saw once again the signatures of ex-US President Herbert Hoover, Charles Lindbergh the aviator, the Duke and Duchess of Windsor and most of Europe's other royalty including the kings of Bulgaria, Romania and Yugoslavia. He then walked out to his zoo and shot his four favourite pet North American bison before shaking hands with his foresters, getting into his car and being driven away. He didn't look back. Carinhall was then blown up. Only the monumental entrance gates were left untouched. Today a few foundations and some decorative stones remain from the building and that's about it. A bronze statue by Franz von Stuck, *Kämpfende Amazone* (1897), once at Carinhall, is now on display at Eberswalde.

Goering then cabled his Führer informing him that as his designated successor he would take over leadership of the Reich if he didn't hear anything by return. Adolf Hitler, sitting in his underground bunker, listening to the explosions in the streets above him, cried 'Traitor!' and disowned Goering, ordering him relieved of all posts and arrested. It was the final fall from grace for the creator of the Luftwaffe.

With Goering gone, the eastern Luftwaffe now had one more role to play as the Reich collapsed and Ritter von Greim would take centre stage in that.

Von Greim was ordered into Berlin by Hitler himself, flying in with the famous and celebrated female pilot Hanna Reitsch. Injured by ground fire on his way in, von Greim was dumbfounded on arrival in the bunker to be promoted on the spot to the rank of field marshal and given command of the Luftwaffe as Goering's replacement. In the surreal atmosphere of the bunker, Greim then spoke by phone to the last Chief of the Luftwaffe General Staff, Karl Koller, at his headquarters in the woods near Fuerstenberg: 'Just don't lose hope! Everything will turn out alright. My contact with the Führer and his strength has strengthened me like a dip in the fountain of youth … He retracted all his of his accusations against the Luftwaffe and is aware of what our service branch has accomplished … He had the highest praise for our forces, this made me exceedingly happy.'

The next morning von Greim and Reitsch flew out of Berlin and on to Ploem – the headquarters of Grand Admiral Karl Dönitz. He was in Ploem when he heard that Hitler had committed suicide after naming Dönitz his successor. The Admiral tried to get Greim to stay on as commander-in-chief of the Luftwaffe but he declined. Dönitz said, 'He did not wish, he said, to go on living, and we parted, deeply moved.'

With Hitler's death the Luftwaffe ceased all operations against the Anglo-Americans and the 29,000 aircraft they had in the ETO (European Theatre of Operations), but they continued to fight the Soviets – just as the Army and Navy did – the Kriegsmarine to evacuate as many soldiers and civilians as it could from East Prussia and the Heer as it attempted to hold off the Red Army and get over the Elbe River to surrender to the Anglo-Americans. Greim went south to the Luftwaffe in Bohemia and northern Austria, where it concentrated to make its last stand. It still had 1,500 aircraft, but there was very little fuel, spares or ammunition. Ground services and transportation had broken down and the men were close to being finished. Somehow the eastern Luftwaffe managed to send up around fifty sorties a day for the last days running up to the formal surrender on 8 May. Nine more eastern Jagdwaffe pilots won Knight's Crosses in 1945: three were posthumous and a fourth was killed by anti-aircraft fire soon after. Eight existing Jagdwaffe Knight's Cross holders were also killed, half of them attacking ground targets.

Above the ruins of Berlin, VVS pilots flew low, gazing down at the capital they had fought so long and hard to reach.

The VVS technician Viktor Sinaisky, who had faithfully serviced his pilots' aircraft since the very start of Barbarossa, was recovering in hospital from the shell-shock he had suffered during a stint with Soviet airborne troops during the capture of Vienna. 'I lost both my hearing and my speech. It was on 9 May 1945 when my hearing returned. They gave me a radio set. I was listening to Radio Moscow in bed and weeping with joy.'[272]

CHAPTER 27

As the Sky Cleared

For the eastern Luftwaffe – or what remained of it – the war petered out. They still had some aircraft to fly – even the vaunted Me 262 jet fighters, but there was hardly a drop of fuel and in any case, what was the point, the war was over. Thoughts turned to family and friends and especially for those from Germany's eastern Länder, there was worry at what the future held with the Red Army occupying their homes.

For Norbert Hannig, his journey home took him east to Silesia and the unwelcome attentions of the local Red Army garrison. Picked up for questioning, he was paraded in front of a gaggle of Soviet officers and asked;

'We would like to know your opinion of the Soviet Air Force?'
'Not a lot. It was only your vast superiority in numbers, often 10:1 or more, which defeated us.'

To Hannig's total surprise the Soviets burst out laughing, stood up and saluted him, with the senior officer, a general, saying, 'We Soviet officers know how to respect the courageous German soldiers. You may go.' He was released – it would seem these Red Army men didn't think overly much of their VVS comrades.

This view found an echo through the decades and down into the Cold War, when Soviet soldiers used to tell a joke that went something like this. Two Red Army tank generals met on a railway platform in Paris after the successful Soviet invasion of the West. The two tankers get chatting, and one mentioned the campaigns air war, whereupon the other enquired politely, 'Who won it?'

Perhaps the air war in the Soviet Union was always going to be invisible to a degree to the respective soldiers on the ground. The country was just too big. The Wehrmacht occupied Estonia, Latvia, Lithuania, Belorussia, the Ukraine and huge chunks of the Caucasus and Russia itself, yet it never touched over 80 per cent of a land that was forty-six times the size of Nazi Germany. Günther Rall and Gordon Gollob interviewed a shot down VVS pilot at their air base in late August 1942. His name was Major Yakov Antonov and he was a Hero of the Soviet Union. Antonov had suffered minor head injuries but was otherwise unscathed. A medic patched him up and he sat with Rall and Gollob drinking tea, smoking cigarettes and chatting while they waited for his escort to arrive to take him away to a POW camp. The Wehrmacht was streaming east towards the Volga and the Caucasus at the time but Antonov was unconcerned, pointing to the map on the wall of the German command post and saying, 'Look at the map, and you will see large areas of the USSR that you haven't captured. You will never be able to defeat the Soviet Union.'[273]

The sheer size of the battlefield meant that even thousands of aircraft were simply swallowed up in the vastness of space. The front line at the opening of Barbarossa was 1,600 km long and would expand to over 3,000 km during the height of Case Blue in the autumn of 1942. Army staffs at the time estimated a full-strength division of 10,000 to 12,000 men could effectively control a ten-square-kilometre block of land, so even the mass of the over 400 divisions facing each other were dwarfed by the landscape around them. Churchill had written of the First World War's Eastern Front, 'In the West the armies were too big for the country; in the East the country was too big for the armies.' The same was true for the air of course and so the relatively compressed nature of the front in the west after D-Day lent itself to, if not the primacy of air forces, their huge importance at the very least. This had its downsides though, mainly from what have always been euphemistically called 'friendly fire incidents', although what is 'friendly' about them is open to debate.

So bad did the situation become in the confused close-quarter fighting in Normandy's *bocage* country after Overlord that among the American GIs the rule was 'if it flies it dies', so sick were they of being attacked by their own air force. By December that year matters hadn't improved overly much, with a report from George 'Blood and Guts' Patton's Third Army fighting in the Ardennes stating that, 'Bombers from the Eighth Air Force unfortunately bombed the headquarters of 4th Armoured Division, the town of Wecker, and that part of the 4th Infantry Division at Echternach.' The incident led to a high level bust up between the US army and air commanders, but was hushed up so as not to shake the faith of the troops.[274]

Not that the Americans weren't the only ones to make mistakes – far from it. Mussolini's heir apparent, the bearded, energetic Marshal Italo Balbo – ex-head of Italy's Air Ministry and in 1940 the new commander of the Italian Army of North Africa – was killed when his Regia Aeronautica SM 79 was mistaken for a British bomber and shot down over Tobruk by Italian anti-aircraft gunners as it came into land.

In the east, a lieutenant from the Red Army's 859th Rifle Regiment complained, 'Our own air force is ridiculous in comparison to the German aviation. They arrive five minutes at a time, drop half their bombs on our own troops, the remainder over deserted places, and scram at full speed back home in order to evade the Messerschmitts!'

The Germans were by no means faultless themselves though; von Richthofen himself had seen the results of Luftwaffe friendly fire in the Crimea in 1942 on the combined Romanian/German Grodeck Brigade as it 'advanced so fast that when it reached the eastern Tatar Ditch it ran straight into our bombs. There were several losses.'

For those men of the VVS and the eastern Luftwaffe who survived, the end of the war brought an uncertain future, albeit one of almost unalloyed joy for the vast majority of the VVS and less so for their former Luftwaffe foes. Rudel, back from injury and still Nazi Germany's foremost Stuka ace, was determined not to fall into Soviet hands once hostilities ceased. He ordered his men into three Ju 87s and four Fw 190s and took off from Bohemia to head west. After a nervy flight, all seven aircraft touched down at Kitzingen airfield in Bavaria, newly occupied by the US 405th Fighter Group. As the bemused Americans looked on, Rudel had his men lock their brakes and collapse their landing gear to render the aircraft useless to their captors. This last act of defiance also blocked the runway. Rudel then climbed out of his cockpit, hobbled over to the nearest American and surrendered. He would spend the next eleven months in various prisoner of war camps before being released. Like so many former Nazis who hankered after the 'good old days', he emigrated to Argentina and finally passed away there in 1982 as his adopted country went to war with Great Britain over the Falkland Islands – he might have told General Galtieri's *junta* it was probably not a good idea to take on the British.

Not all the eastern Luftwaffe tried to escape westwards.

Erich Hartmann, the VVS's dreaded 'Black Devil', had never left his beloved JG 52, despite Galland's attempts to entice him to join his jet programme and Wilhelmstrasse's determination to 'retire' him to a safe posting out of harm's way back in the Reich. Now, with the war ending, Hans Seidemann (of Kursk fame) ordered both Hartmann and his fellow Experte Hermann Graf to fly west to avoid capture by the Soviets. Hartmann's reply was blunt. 'I must say that during the war I never disobeyed an order, but when General Seidemann ordered Graf and me to fly to the British sector and surrender to avoid the Soviets, with the rest of the wing to surrender to the Soviets, I could not leave my men. That would have been bad leadership.'

Instead he fought on, shooting down one last Yak-9 before heading home, touching down and being told that the Soviets would be at the airfield in hours. Hartmann instructed his men to destroy their aircraft, including his own cherished Bf 109 – *Karaya One* – and burn everything that could be of value to the enemy. 'We destroyed the aircraft and all munitions, everything. I sat in my fighter and fired the guns into the woods where all the fuel had been dropped, and then jumped out. We destroyed twenty-five perfectly good fighters. They would be nice to have in museums now.'

Hartmann surrendered his unit en masse to the Americans, but like so many others they were all handed over to the Soviets.

The first thing the Russians did was to separate the German women and girls from the men. What followed was a brutal orgy of rape and debauchery by Red Army soldiers. When the greatly outnumbered Americans tried to intervene, the Russians charged towards them firing into the air and threatening to kill them if they interfered. The raping continued throughout the night. The next day a Russian General arrived at the encampment and immediately ordered a cessation ... Later when a few Russians violated the order again and assaulted a German girl, she was asked to identify them from a line-up. There were no formalities, no court martial. The guilty parties were immediately hanged in front of all their comrades. The point was made.

The Soviets wished to extract the maximum benefit from their high-profile prisoners and, along with many others, put huge pressure on Hartmann to collaborate with them. They used a carrot and stick approach, alternating between mistreating Hartmann and offering him a senior position in the soon-to-be created East German air force. Hartmann lived through the former and flatly rejected the latter. 'If, after I am home in the west, you make me a normal contract offer, a business deal such as people sign every day all over the world, and I like your offer, then I will come back and work with you in accordance with the contract. But if you try to put me to work under coercion of any kind, then I will resist to my dying gasp.'

Eventually the Soviets ran out of patience with the stubborn Württemburger and he was charged with various trumped-up crimes, including the 'deliberate shooting of 780 Soviet civilians' and destroying '345 expensive Soviet aircraft'. Convicted and sentenced to twenty-five years' hard labour, Hartmann continued to resist the Soviet authorities and was passed around from camp to camp, ending up in 1955 at Diaterka in the Ural Mountains. He was finally released that year, along with 16,000 other former German military personnel (the so-called *Heimkehrer*) as part of a trade deal between West Germany and the Soviet Union.

Hartmann's fellow JG 52 Experte Hermann Graf followed an altogether different path. His 212 victories made him one of the top scoring fighter pilots of all time and another prime target for the Soviets to turn if they could. They went to work on him and had much more success than with Hartmann. 'We have to begin a new thinking, I am on the Russian side, and therefore I would like to live with the Russians ... I am happy now to be a Russian prisoner. I know that all I have done is wrong and I have now only one wish. That is to fly with the Russian Air Force.' Graf was released on Christmas Day 1949, but his 'conversion' to the Soviet cause was publicised in a 1950s book by fellow fighter ace and Soviet POW Hans 'Assi' Hahn, entitled *I Speak the Truth*. As a result Graf was ostracised by most of his former comrades. One man who didn't turn his back on Graf was his old wingman, Alfred Grislawski, who said of him: 'He was a really great guy, respected by everyone. It is a pity that some people today hold his personal convictions against him.'

Pilots like Hartmann, Graf and a number of others from the Jagdwaffe had chalked up scores that were far in excess of anything achieved by any other air force in the war – why? Unquestionably they were extremely able and sometimes brilliant flyers, but that doesn't account for the astronomical nature of their kill rates in comparison to their VVS opposite numbers. Men like Ivan Kozhedub, a Hero of the Soviet Union three times over and his own country's highest scoring ace with sixty-two kills in his La-5 from 520 sorties, was a superb and courageous pilot yet his score wouldn't even put him in the Jagdwaffe's top 100. Those men benefited from a unique set of circumstances that would propel their tallies ever higher, the first being the machines they flew, which began Barbarossa with a 'best in class' label that was only ever matched by the Soviets and never exceeded. Most of them had precious operational experience garnered from Spain, Poland and the invasion of the West and they came up against often poorly trained and equipped VVS pilots who were up in the skies in droves. This gave them the opportunity to score highly – what a later generation of movie-goers might refer to as a 'target rich environment', as Walter Nowotny testified.

> It was a clear blue sky and it as filled with Soviet fighters trying to attack our bombers. I picked an I-18 and made a sharp turn to place my 109 in a good firing position. A few bursts sent the Russian fighter to the ground burning. The remaining fighters tried to escape but my 109 was faster. Flying above the docks on the Neva mouth, I put the rear plane in a four-finger formation in my gunsight. Two bursts of fire and the Rata blew up. The burning fuselage and wings tumbled down ... I spotted four I-18s attacking our bombers from behind. By pulling up the nose of my plane I made one of the Soviet fighters pass through my tracer bullets. The success stunned me. He immediately went into an almost vertical descent, started spinning, and left a thick, black oily trail of smoke. This was my sixth victor today. Number seven didn't last long. I was just about to return home, when suddenly a Rata pulled up beneath me. I pushed my stick forward, and seconds later the enemy went down in a spiral.

The Austrian-born Nowotny would eventually achieve 258 kills (255 of them against the VVS) before his own death in November 1944.[275]

A Soviet pilot, Aleksey Ryazanov, said of men like Nowotny, 'The German aces decorated their wings and fuselage with badges such as dragons, snakes, scary monsters, and coffins in order to affect the minds of our pilots. Whether it's a 'von', or a baron, or a dragon – it's the same bastard ... We have to beat them.'[276]

The Experten also had two more huge advantages, one of which was their tactics, a system of operation designed to maximise the kill chances of the very best, as evidenced by this description by the Bf 109 pilot Norbert Hannig of a German bombing raid on an enemy-held bridge over the Volkhov River:

> The unit's Experten, those highly decorated members of the Geschwader who already had large numbers of enemy aircraft to their credit, were given a *freie Jagd* [literally 'free hunting'] role and not tied to the bombers. Allowed to range far and wide they had the best chance of scoring. Next came those flying indirect escort, who could engage any enemy fighter getting closer than 500 metres to the bombers or dive-bombers they were protecting. Finally there were the pilots like myself who were assigned to direct

escort duties. We were to stick close to the bombers – no more than 100 metres away at any time – and provide the last line of fighter defence before the bombers' own gunners opened up.

That *'freie Jagd'* role was lifted directly out of the Red Baron's playbook, giving Jagdwaffe pilots the freedom to pile up their scores. 'During one air battle on the Kalinin Front I turned round and saw my friend, Valentin Soloviev, being attacked by a Messer from behind. His plane was immediately devoured by flames. It all happened in a matter of seconds – I didn't even have time to shout.'[277]

Secondly, the Luftwaffe did not operate a rotation scheme as most other air forces did. Pilots did not carry out a certain number of sorties and then move back to rest, recuperate and fill other duties such as instructor posts. A man could reasonably expect to spend the vast majority of his time at the front with his Staffel, flying operational sorties pretty much constantly. Anton 'Toni' Hackl was one such pilot, remaining in front-line service throughout the war with JG 77, surviving more than 1,000 sorties and scoring 192 confirmed kills; the Black Sea naval aviator Mikhail Avdeyev wrote of one engagement against him:

Then, from somewhere high above, beyond the dogfight, a lone Messer, which no one had detected, came rushing downward like a vulture. It set one of the Shturmoviks on fire and disappeared at tree-top level. Together with Danilko I tried to pursue him as he levelled out from the dive but we were intercepted by four Messers. We caught a quick glimpse of a black 'Z' on the hunter's fuselage.

Avdeyev, an ace himself and the man who had shot down the Experte Wolf-Dietrich Huy, back in early 1942, dedicated a whole chapter of his memoirs to Hackl and his attempts to catch and kill him.

It was clear that 'Z' was an outstanding pilot, definitely someone from von Richthofen's inner circle ... That damned 'Z' deprived us of our sleep and never left us in peace. A hundred times I examined in my mind different ways to attack him – from above, from below, from the clouds, or from the sun. But these fine theories were always shattered by the realities. 'Z' wasn't someone whom you could lure into a trap ... he was a worthy opponent, and he definitely gave us a lot of headaches.

Avdeyev would eventually achieve a partial success against his arch-adversary. 'Finally, and not without sensing a fiendish pleasure,

I saw my "carrot" cross the threads of my gunsight. I fired one burst, a second, a third. The plane passed by. I turned my head and looked back. Trailing smoke, 'Z' raced toward German territory. I turned to follow him, but too late, a pack of Messers intercepted me ...'[278]

Very few Anglo-American pilots flew more than 300 sorties throughout the war, yet large numbers of the Jagdwaffe flew over 500 and a sizeable number, like Hackl, over 1,000. This wasn't just a fighter pilot phenomenon either. The famous German bomber pilot Hansgeorg Bätcher flew 658 sorties – only a few Soviet night bomber pilots flew more – and he was awarded the Knight's Cross for his achievements.

As for their old boss, Ritter von Greim, he was ill, on crutches with his wounded foot and close to a nervous breakdown. Captured by an American patrol in Austria, his first words to them were, 'I am the head of the Luftwaffe, but I have no Luftwaffe.' Sent to a hospital in Salzburg, he was scheduled to be handed over to the Soviets in a prisoner exchange. Fearing the worst, he committed suicide by swallowing cyanide, probably using the capsule Hitler had given him in the bunker.

Greim's boss – Hermann Goering himself – also ended up in Austria, at his castle at Mauterndorf, to the south of Salzburg. Like Greim and Rudel, the Reichsmarshall surrendered to the Americans and was imprisoned for trial at Nuremburg. As he languished in gaol, he was weaned off his addiction to Paracodeine and lost seven stone in weight as his body adjusted to a prison diet and a life without drugs. He was the most senior Nazi put on trial at Nuremburg and, unlike most of his co-defendants, put up a spirited defence, defying his prosecutors. It was, rightly, never going to be enough and he was convicted and sentenced to death on 1 October 1946. During the trials he heard von Manstein testifying as to Hitler's mismanagement of the war effort as illustrated by the fate of the seventeen field marshals he had created; only one managed to survive the war in post, with a full half given the boot by the Nazi leader.

Von Manstein was not alone in laying the blame for military failure at Hitler's door.

Some in the Luftwaffe's senior ranks were keen to obtain a modicum of revenge for Hitler's denigration of their service during the later war years, epitomised by his constant contemptuous references to them as 'the gentlemen of the Luftwaffe'. The air force's last chief of staff, General Karl Koller (Günther Korten had died in the 20 July 1944 Stauffenberg bomb plot), said of him, 'He had no understanding of the needs of the Luftwaffe, remaining an infantryman in outlook throughout his life.'[279]

True or not, none of this mattered to Hermann Wilhelm Goering, who, at about 10.40 p.m. on 15 October, roughly two hours before he was due to hang, took cyanide and died in his cell. The next morning his body – along with that of the other major executed war criminals: Wilhelm Keitel, Ernst Kaltenbrunner, Alfred Rosenberg, Hans Frank, Wilhelm Frick, Julius Streicher, Arthur Seyss-Inquart, Fritz Sauckel and Alfred Jodl – was taken to a Munich crematorium and burned. The ashes were put in a box, taken by car into the countryside and scattered in a roadside ditch outside the city.

In the topsy-turvy world of Stalin's Soviet Union, the same fate almost befell Alexander Novikov, Hero of the Soviet Union and the conqueror of the eastern Luftwaffe. Attending the Potsdam Conference with his political master, he was arrested on Stalin's order when the dictator discovered the Americans had developed high-flying spy planes that were far better than anything the VVS possessed – Stalin blamed Novikov for the deficiency. Thrown into prison, he was tortured and then blackmailed by the sadistic NKVD chief Lavrenti Beria into making a false confession which implicated Beria's rival – Marshal Gheorgy Zhukov – in a non-existent conspiracy. Novikov was sentenced to fifteen years' hard labour and served over half his sentence before he was released on Stalin's death in 1953. Rehabilitated, he returned to the VVS as the Chief Marshal of Aviation. Now answering to Nikita Khrushchev as premier, Novikov drafted plans for equipping a fleet of jet aircraft with nuclear weapons, only for Khrushchev to reject the idea as he preferred ballistic missiles. Novikov retired from military service in 1958, was awarded the Order of the Red Banner and worked as head of the Higher Civil Aviation School in Leningrad before his death in 1976.

Most of Novikov's men fared better than he did in the immediate aftermath of the war against the eastern Luftwaffe. A few were warned off for service in the Far East against the Japanese, but that far-off conflict ended before many of them could reach it. The majority served occupation duties in Germany, kicking their heels until sent home for well-earned leave and the search for surviving family that so many had to undertake in the wreckage of their country. This was not the fate of all, though. The Soviet system had perversely decreed that any member of the armed forces, or civilian for that matter, who fell into German hands during the war had committed a crime and on liberation the millions trapped in this idiocy were treated as such.

Several thousand VVS members were included in this benighted group. One such was the fighter pilot Alexander Khaila. Shot down in April 1945 over the Baltic coast, he managed to bail out of his aircraft but was badly burnt. In horrendous pain and requiring his dressings to be constantly changed, Khaila spent ten days in German captivity before escaping back to his own lines. When his squadron comrades saw him in the hospital they gagged; half his face had been burnt away, including his nose and cheeks. Despite this, and his excellent service record, in the autumn he was ordered to a detention camp near Ufa to be screened, along with thousands of other ex-POWs and ex-partisans. Held there and intermittently interrogated, he wasn't released until the following January. Returning to duty in the 72nd Guards Fighter Regiment, the 'Former POW' label stuck and made life very difficult indeed. As late as 1949, he was interrogated again by an NKVD inspector. 'He interrogated me and then asked "Why didn't you shoot yourself?" I had to stop myself shooting him on the spot. What an asshole!'

Another VVS pilot shown the darker side of Soviet 'hospitality' was Mikhail Petrovich Devyataev, a fighter pilot from Soviet Moldova. He was shot down over Lvov by an Fw 190 in July 1944, bailed out and broke his leg on landing. Captured, he was sent from camp to camp, surviving them all, including the notorious Sachsenhausen concentration camp. In one camp he even swapped his own identity discs and papers with a dead comrade to convince the Nazis he wasn't an officer and survive another arbitrary sweep. Sent to Peenemünde rocket testing centre on the Baltic coast as slave labour, starvation and maltreatment reduced his weight to a miniscule forty-one kilograms. Along with some other prisoners, he finally escaped by stealing an He 111 bomber in February 1945 and flying east to crash land behind Soviet lines. The former POWs were very quickly disabused of any notions they may have had of being treated as long-lost comrades. All of them were sent to penal battalions to be used as cannon fodder; given the most dangerous jobs, the least support and terrible rations to boot. When the fighting finally ended, Devyataev was transferred to prison, held in solitary confinement and subjected to months of interrogation and poor treatment. Released in 1947, his papers were, like Khaila's, stamped as 'Former POW' – a situation that dogged him for years, stopping him finding work, from getting a flat, indeed from anything but existing on the margins of the society he had given so much to defend. Then again that was the system; there was little reason to it a lot of the time. One of Devyataev's fellow pilots, Captain Nikolai Gastello, was lauded during the war for killing himself by supposedly diving into a column of panzers and destroying several in a taran in early July 1941 – children's books, films and even postage stamps were named after him and a famous song, 'Captain Gastello', was penned about him. However, it was all nothing but official fantasy and in 1996 the Russian President, Boris Yeltsin, acknowledged the falsehood of the story and instead credited another VVS flyer as the real hero who had died unheralded at the time. He was even awarded a posthumous medal.[280]

For the ex-VVS men who had thrown in their lot with the Nazis, the end was predictable and final. Semyon Bytchkov, along with other ROA members hoping to escape their countrymen's retribution, surrendered to Patton's Third Army. Interned in the French port city of Cherbourg on the Atlantic coast, they may even have allowed themselves a glimmer of hope for survival, but they were unaware of the terms of the Allied Yalta Agreement that condemned them, and hundreds of thousands like them, to be handed over to the Soviets to meet their fate. Bytchkov was sent east in September, along with his commander, Viktor Maltsev, who had attempted suicide but failed. Maltsev was tried in the first tranche of senior ex-Soviet collaborators along with the likes of Andrei Vlasov. All were convicted, condemned to death and hanged in Moscow on 2 August 1946. Bytchkov was up next and duly convicted, but submitted an appeal for clemency. Needless to say, the appeal was rejected and he was hanged on 4 November. The following year he was posthumously stripped of all honours awarded to him by the Soviet Union before his defection.

The Luftwaffe's quest for victory in the east came up against the same barriers that Germany had encountered before in her drive for continental dominance; an enemy that was part of a grand alliance, the need to fight on multiple fronts and being made to engage in a war of attrition for which it was totally unsuited.

It could have been said that on the eve of Barbarossa, the war in the air would be unequal in the extreme. The Luftwaffe was hugely experienced, with major technical and tactical advantages, and possessed of the finest core of flyers in any air force in the world. Their opponents were nowhere near as well trained, were flying obsolete aircraft using obsolete tactics and the Purges had crippled their leadership. This analysis would only be skin-deep at best. The VVS's main job in 1941 and 1942 was to survive until it could buy enough time to re-equip and bring its practically limitless resources to bear. Lieutenant General Klaus Uebe, a Luftwaffe officer who wrote several treatises on the German experience against the VVS after the war for the American military, said: 'Russian reaction to German Air Force operations, however primitive and makeshift in character, and however crude they might have first appeared to be to their more enlightened Western opponents, proved throughout the course of the war to be highly efficient, effective, and ultimately an important factor in the defeat of Germany.'[281]

In the meantime the Soviet Union and the VVS would suffer a bloodletting never equalled since – 1 in 7 of the Soviet population died during the war (it was 1 in 6 in the Ukraine) and the VVS lost 45,000 aircraft.

As for the young men and women behind the controls, for many it would be their end: 'Most of the experienced pilots are gone, and our aviation is replenished with youngsters, sergeants who have no experience – either in combat or in their outlook. They are poorly trained, don't know how to fly in a formation, disperse when attacked, and get shot down alone – one by one.'[282]

This was true for so many, but the reality was that as long as the VVS resisted, every day was a success.

As for the Nazis, the myth of German 'über-efficiency' was proven to be exactly that – a myth. Behind a façade of technological and industrial superiority lay what can only be described as a bit of a mess. The existing fleet was mostly nearing the end of its useful life, there was no strategic bomber arm and by half-committing to failing models such as the He 177 and the Me 210, the Germans were wasting vast amounts of scarce resources. A senior Luftwaffe officer estimated that approximately 10,000 standard Daimler-Benz DB-601 engines were wasted in these endeavours. 'The military situation would have been entirely different if we had had 10,000 more fighter aircraft – this would have been twice as many as we actually had – at the front at that time ... this is the real reason for the defeat of the German Luftwaffe.'[283]

Was this true? Not necessarily. More aircraft sometimes seemed a hindrance to the Germans rather than a boon. The anonymous author Hauptmann Hermann cited the British capture of hundreds of only slightly damaged Luftwaffe planes in the desert in 1942 as Rommel retreated (perhaps as many as 228 according to some sources) as proof of the lack of investment in repair facilities and spares. However, those planes were just as likely to be grounded by a lack of fuel as anything else. It was probably a mix of the two and could better be described as a failure of logistics. The issue of repairs and the effort invested in it has always been a thorny one for air forces and the Soviets had their own problems with it: 'Aircobra engines were quite sensitive and required good grease and good care. They contained silver-coated bearings; when these were new everything worked OK, but after servicing in a Russian repair shop the engines frequently failed. God knows what kind of bearings they installed there!'[284]

The issue of fuel, and the lack of it, would forever haunt the Luftwaffe.

Any restriction on gasoline is a nightmare for an air force, leading to fewer sorties and higher casualties and when the Nazis suffered the twin disasters of the loss of Ploesti and its oil and the Anglo-American air offensive against its synthetic fuel industry, its number was up. George Ball, the Director of the US Strategic Bombing Survey, understated his case when he remarked, 'Beginning in 1944 when we began to strike the hydrogenation plants which produced the synthetic gasoline, the whole situation began to change.'[285]

That production had climbed to 5.7 million tons in 1943 and collapsed to well under 4 million the following year. In September, as the Luftwaffe was being bundled back west in the wake of the Soviet Bagration offensive, total German stocks of gasoline had dropped from over 1 million tons in April to less than a third of that. In contrast, the VVS could literally bathe in the stuff if it wished. Even during the early years of the war, when the Wehrmacht was seizing vast amounts of territory and industry, Soviet oil production did not dip below 30 million tons a year. Every German commander in service, regardless of their arm, would probably have sold their soul to have such resources at their disposal.

Beyond resources, there was a lack of focus on the main aim, with almost one-third of the Luftwaffe spread over secondary fronts even as the bombers were hitting the VVS's western airfields. The leadership that presided over this jumble was itself amateurish and gravely ill-suited to the strategy it wished to follow. Albert Kesselring, one of the Luftwaffe's more effective commanders, said of the thirty-nine-year-old Hans Jeschonnek:

> During the war years, the most impressive personality among the Chiefs of the General Staff was Jeschonnek – an unusually intelligent and energetic person. Even Jeschonnek, however, was not strong enough to oppose Goering successfully, occasionally he did succeed in opposing Hitler, in matters of decisive importance. A very definite lack of harmony brought effective coordination to a standstill.

As Hermann Plocher wrote, 'Everyone in the Army wanted to take over the Luftwaffe, but the Army was completely unaware of the potentialities of air power.'[286]

The political leadership was worse. In September 1940 the new Spanish dictator, General Francisco Franco, sent his future Foreign Minister (and brother-in-law), Ramón Serrano Suñer, to Berlin. Suñer, an advocate of Spain joining the Axis, met Hitler in the Chancellery and received the complete 'Führer treatment', including his usual rhetoric on history and the power of great men. Suñer went away suitably impressed, but on meeting Hitler for a second time to present him with a personal gift from Franco, he was astonished at the dictator's reaction and childlike pleasure. The eminent historian and biographer of Hitler Alan Bullock said of these events: 'This contrast between the grandiose pretensions of the regime and the underlying vulgarity and childishness of its rulers was the most permanent impression that Suñer carried away from his visit to Berlin.' Needless to say, despite Suñer's urging, Franco steered clear of any firm commitment to Hitler and his Axis.

The whys and wherefores of grand strategy can seem a long way away from the men and women who fight on the front line and for whom victory or defeat are only too real. Yet it would be foolish to dismiss their views and thoughts on the big questions, none more so than the ex-Soviet naval fighter pilot Nikolai G. Golodnikov, who captured the argument in a sentence: 'In the end the Germans failed to produce enough aircraft or train enough pilots to win – but we did. That's the deal.'[287]

CHAPTER 28

Forgiveness

For the veterans of the eastern Luftwaffe and the VVS, the immediate needs of living tended to push their recent experiences to the back of their minds as they focused instead on wives, sweethearts, family and home. Men had to find work, feed themselves and their loved ones and generally get on with life. Across a devastated world that was easier said than done, the sheer scale of the conflict proving a tremendous challenge. Both the Soviets and the United States had 12 million people in uniform as the war ended. For the Soviets the task was one of rebuilding the ruins: an estimated 1,710 towns and 70,000 villages had been destroyed in the fighting – many of them deliberately by one side or the other. The country's infrastructure was ravaged too, with 32,000 factories lost and more than 65,000 km of rail track torn up by the retreating Wehrmacht in a land that only had 80,000 km at the beginning of the war. In the United States it was about demilitarising the economy. The new Truman administration in Washington mothballed 6,000 naval ships, and cancelled $15 billion of defence contracts in a single week, resulting in hundreds of thousands of men being laid off work – Boeing, the manufacturer of the Flying Fortresses that had pulverised Nazi Germany, made 29,000 men redundant in one day.[288]

The war was never forgotten by the airmen though. The savagery of what they endured and, in some cases, inflicted was never far from the surface. Fighter pilots especially tended to view their opponents as 'prey' and the language and terminology of the hunt was often used – the German fighter arm, the Jagdwaffe (literally 'armed hunt'), being a case in point. The pilots talked about their own skills and achievements and this made it difficult to view their enemy as human.

I put the rear gunner out of action first, he had three machine-guns, you could see him firing quite plainly, from the tracers of his machine-guns. I was in a 190 with two machine-guns. I pressed the button for a very short burst, he crumpled up – that's all, not another shot, the barrels were sticking up. Then I put a short burst into the starboard engine, which caught fire, I then turned my cannons onto the port engine. The pilot very probably got hit at that moment. I kept my thumb on the button the whole time – it went down in flames.[289]

For the VVS pilots the feelings were similar:

Did we consider that we were killing fellow human beings? Not at all. We saw the Nazis bombing our country, shooting and killing. Each of us knew they simply had to be shot down. You fired at an enemy plane as if it were a flying target, especially if you'd developed a desire to score. If you didn't shoot him down he'd shoot you down – or one of your friends. You had to shoot him first.[290]

Fear was ever present, despite the urgings of men like Major Vasiliy Zaytsev who tried to imbue new pilots with his maxim, 'Never fear the enemy, he who fears the enemy will be shot down.' Both sides had seen what happened to those who weren't good enough, or who were just unlucky. 'We knew that there was no fighter cover available and that Messers were patrolling ... and the place was thick with anti-aircraft guns ... As I listened to Kholobayev, I thought, "Now we're doomed," and I felt cold in the pit of my stomach.'[291]

I joined our unit, Hauptmann Machfeld was there then, he was later burnt to death ... He landed in an Fw 190 and ran off the runway into all those damned bomb craters, the aircraft turned over and caught fire, he screamed like an animal – it was horrible ... the mechanics couldn't bear to hear it, and they let the aircraft engines run at full speed so that the screams couldn't be heard. I was always terrified of being burnt to death, especially in the 109 – I've seen a great many of those aircraft turn over myself.[292]

A fighter pilot not only bears the burden of stress in battle, he also bears responsibility for his wingmen, for his comrades. He also has to deal with losing close friends. He must be prepared for all situations, all pressures. For example, I never felt fear before a sortie or during briefing, but sometimes we were navigated by a ground station and I couldn't see the enemy – then I was nervous. I felt blind – the enemy is out there somewhere, probably preparing to attack, but I cannot see him. You go nuts. As soon as you see the enemy your nerves are back to normal. Then it all depends on who is stronger.[293]

Pilots also witnessed horrors perpetrated by the other side, brutalising them further. The anonymous Hauptmann Hermann was clear on his views of the Luftwaffe and their attitudes:

The Nazi flyer is very different from the German soldier, the German sailor, or the German man of the merchant marine. Most of these latter were either grown up or at least in their late teens when Hitler came to power. The flyers, on the other hand, are entirely a product of Nazi education. They believe much more strongly in Nazi ideas and in the Führer, and it is difficult, if not impossible, to influence them in any other direction.[294]

Ivan Gaidenko would have agreed with those sentiments whole-heartedly. 'Some say German pilots were 'knights', but when you crash-landed you had to hide behind your plane as they would shoot you.' There are accounts by Luftwaffe pilots themselves of having shot down a VVS aircraft and seeing it crash land, the rules on claiming it as a kill were clear – it had to be seen to burn or explode – so they strafed it on the ground. Hans Strelow, the JG 51 Mölders Experte who would later choose to shoot himself rather than surrender to the Soviets when he was shot down, wrote as such in a combat report during which he and his Katschmarek, Sergeant Wilhelm Mink;

Our mission was free hunting ... I turned sharply to the right and while still turning gave him three brief bursts with my cannon ... While still climbing I saw the Russian fighter make a roll and then it went down in spirals and hit the ground, exploding on impact. Mink's I-18 belly-landed on a field. We came down after it and destroyed it with our guns. Back at home we found I had used no more than ten cannon rounds and forty-five bullets from each machine-gun. This was my nicest victory ever, a fighter in a turning fight with only seven rounds![295]

Alexander Shvarev, who would go on to become a highly decorated major general in the VVS, was another victim of the same tactic after being shot down during the air battles at Stalingrad.

> I landed on my belly, but it was easy as the terrain was even and covered in a layer of snow. I saw Germans diving at me in order to finish me off. Where could I hide? I darted under the engine. One Fritz dived and fired. Then he left and the second one dived and fired. Next thing an armour-piercing shell penetrated the engine, hit my leg and stuck there. The pain was unimaginable. By now my assailants had run out of ammo and left.

Not that the Germans were the only culprits.

> My machine was hit and caught fire as I flew through the bomber formation. I bailed out but didn't open my 'chute until I had fallen well clear of everything that was going on. I finally landed in a potato field. I quickly got out of my 'chute and cleared off as fast as I could. Then I saw four [American] Mustangs coming down in a line ... The Mustangs strafed my parachute one after the other and shot it to shreds. Fortunately they didn't spot me.[296]

Up in the air there was perhaps less ambiguity in a pilot's actions.

> Were pilots executed in the air after bailing out? Yes, Sergei Belusov was killed that way. I was a bit lame after Stalingrad so they didn't send me on many missions, but Sergei took off and as other pilots told me afterwards they ran into He-111s. Sergei hit one of them and it caught fire, but he was shot down by the bomber's gunners. He bailed out and opened his parachute, but German pilots shot him in the air. I never saw our pilots perform such executions.[297]

The same pilot also said: 'As for the war, I still see it in my dreams. Can you understand? All those briefings and battles. And all my friends – those who were killed back then and those who are departing this life now.'

The Soviet gunner and radio operator, Sergeant Vasiliy Vasilyevich Kurayev, had to bail out of his stricken bomber near Königsberg a few weeks before the end of the war. 'After many decades of bitterness towards our enemy, I found tranquillity. But I remember that combat over Königsberg, when the German fighter cut the parachute of my commander with his wing, and I still ask myself – why?'[298]

Perhaps the only solace Vasiliy Vasilyevich can take are the words from Olga Berggolts's poem written about the Siege of Leningrad, which can be found inscribed on every memorial to the Great Patriotic War across Russia and the successor countries to the Soviet Union:

Nikto ne zabyt. Nichto ne zabyto.
No one is forgotten. Nothing is forgotten.

APPENDIX

Rank Equivalences

VVS	Luftwaffe	RAF	USAAF
Marshal Sovetskogo Soyuza	Generalfeldmarschall	Marshal of the RAF	General (5 star)
General Armii	Generaloberst	Air Chief Marshal	General (4 star)
General-Polkovnik	General der Flieger	Air Marshal	Lieutenant-General
General-Leytenant	Generalleutnant	Air Vice-Marshal	Major-General
General-Mayor	Generalmajor	Air Commodore	Brigadier-General
Polkovnik	Oberst	Group Captain	Colonel
Podpolkovnik	Oberstleutnant	Wing Commander	Lieutenant-Colonel
Mayor	Major	Squadron Leader	Major
Kapitan	Hauptmann	Flight Lieutenant	Captain
Starshiy Leytenant	Oberleutnant	Flying Officer	First Lieutenant
Leytenant	Leutnant	Pilot Officer	Second Lieutenant

VVS	Luftwaffe	RAF	USAAF
Mladshiy Leytenant			Flight Officer
Starshina	Oberfeldwebel	Flight Sergeant	Master Sergeant
Starshiy Serzhant	Feldwebel	Staff Sergeant	Staff Sergeant
Serzhant	Unteroffizier	Sergeant	Sergeant
Yefreytor	Obergefreiter	Corporal	Corporal
Krasnoarmeyets	Flieger	Aircraftsman	Private

Notes

Chapter One

1. Hastings, Max, *Warriors* (HarperCollins).
2. Ibid.
3. Jones, Michael, *The Retreat – Hitler's First Defeat* (John Murray).

Chapter Two

4. Hastings, *Warriors*.
5. Twenty-one-year-old Luftwaffe pilot Helmut-Peter Rix, cited in Holmes, Tony (ed.), *Dogfight – The Greatest Air Duels of World War II* (Osprey).

Chapter Three

6. Blokhin officially holds the *Guinness Book of World Records* title as the Most Prolific Executioner in history for individually murdering 7,000 Polish prisoners at Katyn in 1940.
7. Bergstrom, Christer, and Mikhailov, Andrey, *Black Cross Red Star: The Air War Over the Eastern Front Volume 2* (Pacifica Military History).
8. Bellamy, Chris, *Absolute War – Soviet Russia in the Second World War* (Macmillan).
9. Bullock, Alan, *Hitler – A Study in Tyranny* (Pelican).

Chapter Four

10. Interview with Alexander E. Shvarev in 2005, cited in Drabkin, Artem, *Barbarossa and the Retreat to Moscow – Recollections of Soviet Fighter Pilots on the Eastern Front* (Pen & Sword).
11. Edwards, Robert, *White Death – Russia's War on Finland 1939–40* (Weidenfeld & Nicolson).

12. Drabkin, *Barbarossa and the Retreat to Moscow*.

13. Ibid.

14. Ibid., comment from Commissar Moses S. Tokarev.

15. Von Luck, Hans, *Panzer Commander – The Memoirs of Colonel Hans von Luck* (Cassell).

Chapter Five

16. Bullock, *Hitler – A Study in Tyranny*.

17. Mitcham Jr, Samuel W., *Eagles of the Third Reich – Leaders of the Luftwaffe in the Second World War* (Crécy Publishing).

18. Ibid.

19. Ibid.

20. Davies, Norman, *Europe At War 1939–1945, No Simple Victory* (Macmillan).

21. Drabkin, *Barbarossa and the Retreat to Moscow*.

22. Hannig, Norbert, *Luftwaffe Fighter Ace – From the Eastern Front to the Defence of the Homeland*, translated and edited by John Weal (Bounty Books).

23. McNab, Chris, *The Luftwaffe 1933–45: Hitler's Eagles* (Osprey).

24. Hooton, E. R., *Eagle in Flames – The Fall of the Luftwaffe* (Arms & Armour Press).

25. Ibid.

26. Sources differ on the exact numbers; see Davies, *Europe At War*.

27. Captured Luftwaffe pilots Maschel and Höhn, cited in Neitzel, Sönke and Welzer, Harald, *Soldaten on Fighting, Killing and Dying – The Secret Second World War Tapes of German POWs* (Simon & Schuster).

28. Ibid., citing captured Luftwaffe observer Lieutenant Pohl.

29. Ibid.

30. *Diary of Franz Halder*.

31. Bullock, *Hitler – A Study in Tyranny*.

32. Murray, Williamson, *Strategy for Defeat – The Luftwaffe 1933–1945* (Chartwell).

33. Major General I. I. Kopets committed suicide on 23 June.

34. Interview with Viktor M. Sinaisky cited in Drabkin, *Barbarossa and the Retreat to Moscow*.

35. When the Gestapo finally caught up with Schulze-Boysen at the end of August 1942, they arrested him and his wife Libertas, tortured them and then executed them both at Berlin's Plötenzee Prison just before Christmas that same year. Their bodies were then given to a university anatomist for medical research.

36. Interview with Viktor M. Sinaisky cited in Drabkin, *Barbarossa and the Retreat to Moscow*.

37. Captain Hans 'Assi' von Hahn. Already an ace from the battles in the West, Hahn would go on to achieve a total of 108 kills before being shot down and taken prisoner by the Soviets in February 1943. He would stay a POW until 1950, denied release on several occasions due to his stubborn resistance to his Soviet captors.

38. Murray, *Strategy for Defeat*.
39. Jones, *The Retreat*.
40. Ibid., citing VVS pilot Stepan Mikoyan. Stepan was the son of the one-time Soviet Trade Minister Anastas Mikoyan. Anastas had five sons, of whom three became pilots. The Armenian Mikoyans were, of course, the original designers of the famous MiG aircraft series.
41. Carell, Paul, *Hitler's War on Russia Volume 1: Hitler Moves East* (George G. Harrap & Co.).
42. Interview with Vitaly I. Klimenko, cited in Drabkin, *Barbarossa and the Retreat to Moscow*.
43. McNab, *The Luftwaffe 1933–45*.
44. Ibid.
45. Sources differ; see Bellamy, Harwood or Hooton.
46. Sources differ; see Bellamy, McNab or Spick.
47. Captain Hans von Luck, the divisional Adjutant for General Hans Freiherr von Funk's 7th Panzer Division.
48. Interview with Alexander E. Shvarev, cited in Drabkin, *Barbarossa and the Retreat to Moscow*.
49. Bellamy, *Absolute War*.
50. POW Höschler, cited in Neitzel and Welzer, *Soldaten on Fighting, Killing and Dying*.

Chapter Six

51. Bellamy, *Absolute War*.
52. Neitzel and Welzer, *Soldaten on Fighting, Killing and Dying*.
53. Ibid., citing POW Faller talking to POW Schmidt.
54. Ibid., citing SS-Untersturmführer Schreiber.
55. Spick, Mike, *Aces of the Reich – The Making of a Luftwaffe Fighter Pilot* (Greenhill).
56. Neulen, Hans Werner, *In the Skies of Europe – Air Forces Allied to the Luftwaffe 1939–1945* (Crowood Press).
57. Jones, *The Retreat*.
58. Vasiliy Kurayev, radio operator in a Soviet DB3-F bomber, cited in Bergstrom and Mikhailov, *Black Cross Red Star* vol. 2.
59. Jones, *The Retreat*.
60. Carell, *Hitler's War on Russia*.
61. Jones, *The Retreat*.
62. Captain Alexsandr Pokryshkin, cited in Bergstrom and Mikhailov, *Black Cross Red Star* vol. 2.
63. Beevor, Antony, *The Second World War* (Weidenfeld & Nicolson).

Chapter Seven

64. Mitter, Rana, *China's War with Japan 1937–1945* (Penguin).
65. Bellamy, *Absolute War*.

66. Drabkin, *Barbarossa and the Retreat to Moscow*.
67. Ibid.
68. Young, Brigadier Peter and Everett, Susan, *The Two World Wars* (W H Smith & Son).
69. Cloutier, Patrick, *Three Kings: Axis Royal Armies on the Russian Front 1941* (Patrick Cloutier).
70. Interview with Ivan D. Gaidenko, cited in Drabkin, *Barbarossa and the Retreat to Moscow*.
71. Interview with Anthony Eden, cited in Holmes, Richard, *The World At War* (Ebury Press).
72. Holmes, *The World At War*.
73. Bellamy, *Absolute War*.

Chapter Eight

74. Gerhard Lilienthal was the pilot and Hans Stopf the radio operator – no mention was made in the paper about the Bf 110's commander, Captain Elmar Hornung. None of the three crewmen ever returned to Germany. Hans Stopf was reported to have died in Soviet captivity on 14 September 1942 but Lilienthal and Hornung simply disappeared off the face of the earth.
75. Jones, *The Retreat*.
76. McNab, *The Luftwaffe 1933–45*.
77. Bellamy, *Absolute War*.
78. Jones, Michael, *Leningrad – State of Siege* (John Murray).
79. Ibid.
80. Hermann, Hauptmann, *The Rise and Fall of the Luftwaffe* (Fonthill Media, 2012; originally published in 1943). The identity of the author – Hauptmann Hermann – is, as far as this author is aware, still unknown. He wrote his book in exile (probably in the United States) at the time of the Nazi regime and no doubt was fearful of Nazi reprisals on his family and friends back home if his identity was revealed as the book was very critical indeed of the Nazis.
81. *Diary of Franz Halder*.
82. Interview with Viktor M. Sinaisky, cited in Drabkin, *Barbarossa and the Retreat to Moscow*.
83. Ibid.
84. Carell, *Hitler's War on Russia* vol. 1.
85. Luftwaffe Bf 109 pilot Norbert Hannig would serve on the Eastern Front throughout his war service and survive. Hannig, *Luftwaffe Fighter Ace*.
86. Bergstrom, Christer, Dikov, Andrey and Antipov, Vlad, *Black Cross Red Star: The Air War Over the Eastern Front Volume 3* (Eagle Editions).
87. Lieutenant Wolfgang Koch of Walther Nehring's Saxon 18th Panzer Division. The 18th was equipped with submersible tanks and was earmarked to use them for the invasion of Great Britain, Operation Sea Lion, but instead used them to cross the River Bug, their first ever recorded use in war.
88. The diary of NKVD Major Ivan Shabalin. Major Shabalin would be killed on 20 October trying to lead a breakout from a pocket. Jones, *The Retreat*.

89. Heinz Otto Fausten of Walter Krüger's elite 1st Panzer Division, part of Panzer Group 3. Jones, *The Retreat*.

90. Jones, *The Retreat*.

91. The Soviet war reporter and propagandist Vasiliy Grossman.

92. Interview with Anthony Eden cited in Holmes, *The World at War*.

93. Interview with Major Hinrichs, an officer of engineers in the German Army, cited in Holmes, *The World at War*.

94. This was from the Soviet general Konstantin Rokossovsky as he visited General Ivan Panfilov's 316th Division. Panfilov himself died defending his command post on 19 November, the same day his division was awarded the Order of the Red Banner and the honorary title of a 'Guards' division in recognition of their outstanding bravery. Jones, *The Retreat*.

95. Gustav Fehn would go on to command the Afrika Corps in its dying days before being captured by Tito's Communist Partisans in Yugoslavia in June 1945. The partisans shot him summarily.

Chapter Nine

96. Faber, Harold (ed.), *Luftwaffe – An Analysis by Former Luftwaffe Generals* (Sidgwick & Jackson).

97. Interview with General of Panzers Hasso von Manteuffel, cited in Holmes, *The World at War*.

98. From General Heinz Guderian's book *Panzer Leader*.

99. Jones, *The Retreat*.

100. Davies, *Europe At War 1939–1945*.

101. Interview with Alexander E. Shvarev, cited in Drabkin, *Barbarossa and the Retreat to Moscow*.

102. Bergstrom, Dikov and Antipov, *Black Cross Red Star* vol. 3.

103. Interview with Vitaly I. Klimenko, cited in Drabkin, *Barbarossa and the Retreat to Moscow*.

104. Leo Tolstoy's famous estate, Krasnaya Polyana, was home to a memorial to the great Russian writer. Heinz Guderian had taken it as his headquarters and saved it from destruction at the hands of German troops.

105. Osadchinsky would be promoted to platoon leader in time, but would see his beloved brigade cut to pieces in the German counter-offensive at Rzhev in January 1942.

Chapter Ten

106. Jones, *The Retreat*.

107. The noted historian of JG 52, Heinz Kiehl.

108. Bergstrom and Mikhailov, *Black Cross Red Star* vol. 2.

109. Jones, *The Retreat*.

110. German army private Reinhold Pabel, cited in Jones, *The Retreat*.

111. See Jones and Bergstrom.

Chapter Eleven

112. Lieutenant Klein, cited in Neitzel and Welzer, *Soldaten on Fighting, Killing and Dying*.
113. Ibid.
114. Lieutenant Heinrich Freitag survived the war and eventually returned to Germany on 4 December 1949.

Chapter Twelve

115. Kulakov ended up volunteering for a German-controlled, anti-Soviet air force unit. He was later captured by Soviet partisans, who executed him for treason. Bergstrom and Mikhailov, *Black Cross Red Star* vol. 2.
116. Ibid.
117. Ibid.
118. Leopold Höglinger, cited in Jones, *The Retreat*.
119. Johannes 'Macky' Steinhoff, cited in Bergstrom and Mikhailov, *Black Cross Red Star* vol. 2.
120. Drabkin, *Barbarossa and the Retreat to Moscow*.
121. Bergstrom and Mikhailov, *Black Cross Red Star* vol. 2.
122. Ibid.
123. Ibid., citing Lieutenant Alexsandr Pavlichenko.
124. Ibid.
125. Ibid.
126. Ibid.

Chapter Thirteen

127. Harwood, Jeremy, *Hitler's War* (Quantum).
128. Faber, *Luftwaffe*.
129. Mitcham, *Eagles of the Third Reich*.
130. Faber, *Luftwaffe*.
131. Hooton, *Eagle in Flames*.
132. Murray, *Strategy for Defeat*.
133. Davies, *Europe At War 1939–1945*.
134. Holmes, *The World At War*.
135. MacLean, French, *The Cruel Hunters – SS-Sonderkommando Dirlewanger* (Schiffer).
136. Neulen, *In the Skies of Europe*.
137. Interview with Ivan D. Gaidenko, cited in Drabkin, *Barbarossa and the Retreat to Moscow*.
138. Bergstrom and Mikhailov, *Black Cross Red Star* vol. 2.
139. Ibid.
140. Bergstrom, Dikov and Antipov, *Black Cross Red Star* vol. 3.

Chapter Fourteen

141. Neitzel and Welzer, *Soldaten on Fighting, Killing and Dying*.
142. Landau, Sigmund Heinz, *Goodbye Transylvania* (Stackpole).

143. Ibid.

144. Historian Edgar Röhricht, cited in Bergstrom and Mikhailov, *Black Cross Red Star* vol. 2.

145. Ibid. Kurt Schade miraculously survived and was finally repatriated back to West Germany on Christmas Day 1949.

146. Neitzel and Welzer, *Soldaten on Fighting, Killing and Dying*.

147. Interview with Alexander E. Shvarev, cited in Drabkin, *Barbarossa and the Retreat to Moscow*.

148. Bergstrom and Mikhailov, *Black Cross Red Star* vol. 2.

149. Ibid.

150. Ibid.

151. Ibid.

152. Beevor, Antony, *Ardennes 1944 – Hitler's Last Gamble* (Viking).

153. Beevor, Antony, *Stalingrad* (Viking).

154. Hermann, *The Rise and Fall of the Luftwaffe*.

Chapter Fifteen

155. Interview with Ivan D. Gaidenko, cited in Drabkin, *Barbarossa and the Retreat to Moscow*.

156. Bergstrom and Mikhailov, *Black Cross Red Star* vol. 2.

157. Bergstrom, Dikov and Antipov, *Black Cross Red Star* vol. 3.

158. Ibid. Captain Hajo Hermann in his He-111.

159. Ibid. Lieutenant Georg Kannmayer; his He-111 ditched in the sea and he and his crew were rescued from freezing to death by the British destroyer HMS *Ledbury*.

160. Diary of Jagdwaffe pilot Heinrich Setz, cited in Bergstrom and Mikhailov, *Black Cross Red Star* vol. 2.

161. Ibid. The shaven-headed commander of the Coastal Army, Major General Ivan Yefemovich Petrov. Petrov was a much decorated hero of the Russian Civil War.

162. Ibid. Avokian was an Armenian, captured by the crew of the USS *Eberle* on Monday 21 August 1944 at the Île de Porquerolles in France and interrogated by Lieutenant Carl A. Keyser, USNR. After Sevastopol, Avokian and some of his fellow Armenian prisoners were pressed into service by the Germans; Avokian stated that the Germans told them to 'fight for us or starve'. The Armenians were eventually turned over to Soviet authorities and were almost certainly transported to the Gulag.

163. Ibid.

164. Ibid.

Chapter Sixteen

165. Captain Friedrich Lang, cited in Bergstrom, Dikov, and Antipov, *Black Cross Red Star* vol. 3.

166. Neulen, *In the Skies of Europe*.

167. Ibid.

168. Drabkin, *Barbarossa and the Retreat to Moscow*.
169. Ibid., citing an interview with Vitaly I. Klimenko.
170. Bellamy, *Absolute War*.
171. Turner, Jason, *Stalingrad – Day by Day* (Brown Bear).
172. Lieutenant Arkady Kovachevich, cited in Bergstrom, Dikov and Antipov, *Black Cross Red Star* vol. 3.
173. Interview with Ivan D. Gaidenko, cited in Drabkin, *Barbarossa and the Retreat to Moscow*.
174. Lieutenant Fyodor Arkhipenko, cited in Bergstrom, Dikov and Antipov, *Black Cross Red Star* vol. 3.
175. Ibid., citing Unteroffizier Walter Tödt.
176. Ibid., citing Captain Wolf-Dietrich Wilke.
177. Ibid., citing Lieutenant Otto Decker during an interrogation with his Soviet captors. Decker died during his captivity.
178. Bergstrom and Mikhailov, *Black Cross Red Star* vol. 2.
179. Lieutenant Timofey Lyadskiy, cited in Bergstrom, Dikov and Antipov, *Black Cross Red Star* vol. 3.

Chapter Seventeen

180. Nikolai Krylov was a highly decorated and extremely courageous officer. He had been seriously wounded in Sevastopol back in January, but had fought his way back to fitness to serve as Chuikov's chief of staff. He would later go after the war to serve as the commander of the USSR's Strategic Rocket Forces and Deputy Minister of Defence in 1963.
181. Joachim Stempel, a company commander in the 103rd Panzer Grenadier Regiment, cited in Turner, *Stalingrad*.
182. A soldier from Major General Erich Magnus's German 389th Infantry Division. This division, nicknamed the Rheingold Division – 'Rhine Gold' – was only formed in January 1942 in Milowitz near Prague, however its ranks were primarily experienced men drawn from other front-line units. Cited in Bergstrom, Dikov and Antipov, *Black Cross Red Star* vol. 3.
183. Ibid.
184. Holmes, *The World At War*.
185. Bergstrom, Dikov and Antipov, *Black Cross Red Star* vol. 3.
186. Hayward, Joel S. A., *Stopped at Stalingrad – The Luftwaffe and Hitler's Defeat in the East 1942–1943* (University Press of Kansas).
187. Interview with Alexander E. Shvarev, cited in Drabkin, *Barbarossa and the Retreat to Moscow*.
188. Bellamy, *Absolute War*.
189. Bergstrom and Mikhailov, *Black Cross Red Star* vol. 2.
190. Interview with Vitaly I. Klimenko, cited in Drabkin, *Barbarossa and the Retreat to Moscow*.

Chapter Eighteen

191. See Neulen, Faber and Mitcham.
192. Interview with Alexander F. Khaila, cited in Drabkin, *Barbarossa and the Retreat to Moscow*.

193. Holmes, *The World At War*.
194. Carell, Paul, *Hitler's War on Russia Volume 2: Scorched Earth* (Corgi).

Chapter Nineteen

195. Interview with Viktor M. Sinaisky, cited in Drabkin, *Barbarossa and the Retreat to Moscow*.
196. Neitzel and Welzer, *Soldaten on Fighting, Killing and Dying*.
197. Despite the criticism from his fellow generals, Chistyakov would end the war still in command of the Sixth Guards Army, leading it in the capture of the Baltic city of Memel in January 1945.
198. Rudel would eventually fly 2,530 combat sorties, survive thirty-two forced landings, have a 100,000 rouble bounty put on his head by the Kremlin, destroy 519 tanks, 700 trucks, 150 artillery batteries, nine aircraft, seventy landing craft, the Soviet cruiser *Murat*, the battleship *October Revolution*, and countless bunkers and bridges. He would become the only person to be awarded the Knight's Cross of the Iron Cross with Golden Oak Leaves, Swords and Diamonds – an award created especially for him.
199. Landau, *Goodbye Transylvania*.
200. See Carrell and Welzer.
201. See Welzer and Mitcham. Alfred Druschel was a winner of the Knight's Cross with Oak Leaves and Swords, credited with seven kills and over 800 combat sorties, mainly in the ground-support role. As a lieutenant colonel he participated in the ill-fated Luftwaffe Bodenplatte offensive in the West on 1 January 1945. Druschel led an attack against the Anglo-American air base at St Trond in Belgium, where he was separated from his formation by heavy anti-aircraft fire. He failed to return to his own base and was reported as Missing in Action.
202. Hannig only discovered the truth during a rare spell of home leave, where he was shown a letter from one of his brother's comrades detailing the circumstances of his brother's death. On reading the letter Hannig joined the dots and realised he had watched his own brother's body being carried off the battlefield.
203. Bergstrom, Dikov, and Antipov, *Black Cross Red Star* vol. 3.
204. Interview with Viktor M. Sinaisky, cited in Drabkin, *Barbarossa and the Retreat to Moscow*.
205. Ibid.
206. Interview with Alexander E. Shvarev, cited in Drabkin, *Barbarossa and the Retreat to Moscow*.
207. The highly decorated Hünersdorff refused to be evacuated and carried on commanding his division, only to be hit in the head by a Red Army sniper two days later. Hünersdorff had led the spearhead of Hermann Hoth's army to within thirty miles of Stalingrad the previous winter and in an effort to save him he was operated on by a renowned brain surgeon, Dr Tönjes, specifically flown in from Germany for the task. After the operation he was nursed by his wife, who was serving in the area with the Red Cross. However, he didn't recover and died three days later.

Chapter Twenty

208. Von Luck, *Panzer Commander*.
209. Interview with Frau Chantrain, cited in Holmes, *The World at War*.
210. Interview with Albert Speer, cited in Holmes, *The World at War*.
211. Hooton, *Eagle in Flames*.
212. Landau, *Goodbye Transylvania*.
213. Hooton, *Eagle in Flames*.
214. See Harwood and McNab.
215. Neitzel and Welzer, *Soldaten on Fighting, Killing and Dying*.
216. Hannig, *Luftwaffe Fighter Ace*.
217. Interview with Vitaly I. Klimenko, cited in Drabkin, *Barbarossa and the Retreat to Moscow*.
218. Hannig, *Luftwaffe Fighter Ace*.
219. As related to Norbert Hannig by a comrade.
220. The thirty-eight-year-old Viennese pilot Wilfried von Müller-Rienzburg. He was shot down in December 1943, was captured and survived the war.

Chapter Twenty-One

221. Interview in 2000 with ex-Soviet naval fighter pilot Nikolai G. Golodnikov, cited in Drabkin, *Barbarossa and the Retreat to Moscow*.
222. Bergstrom and Mikhailov, *Black Cross Red Star* vol. 2.
223. Davies, *Europe At War 1939–1945*.
224. Interview with Viktor M. Sinaisky, cited in Drabkin, *Barbarossa and the Retreat to Moscow*.
225. Neitzel and Welzer, *Soldaten on Fighting, Killing and Dying*.
226. Bergstrom, Dikov and Antipov, *Black Cross Red Star* vol. 3.
227. Interview with Vitaly I. Klimenko, cited in Drabkin, *Barbarossa and the Retreat to Moscow*.
228. Neulen, *In the Skies of Europe*.
229. Bellamy, *Absolute War*.
230. Neulen, *In the Skies of Europe*.
231. Interview with Alexander E. Shvarev, cited in Drabkin, *Barbarossa and the Retreat to Moscow*.
232. The diary of Major Udo von Alvensleben, the divisional Intelligence officer for the 16th Panzer Division.

Chapter Twenty-Two

233. Bullock, *Hitler – A Study in Tyranny*.
234. McNab, *The Luftwaffe 1933–45*.
235. Harwood, *Hitler's War*.
236. Neitzel and Welzer, *Soldaten on Fighting, Killing and Dying*.

Chapter Twenty-Three

237. The diary of Hermann Graf, cited in Bergstrom and Mikhailov, *Black Cross Red Star* vol. 2.
238. Spick, *Aces of the Reich*.
239. Neulen, *In the Skies of Europe*.

Chapter Twenty-Four

240. Murray, *Strategy for Defeat*.
241. Mitcham, *Eagles of the Third Reich*.
242. Drabkin, *Barbarossa and the Retreat to Moscow*.
243. Murray, *Strategy for Defeat*.
244. Excerpt from Friedrich Mellenthin's memoirs, *Panzer Battles*.
245. Mitcham, *Eagles of the Third Reich*.
246. Neitzel and Welzer, *Soldaten on Fighting, Killing and Dying*.

Chapter Twenty-Five

247. Hannig, *Luftwaffe Fighter Ace*.
248. McNab, *The Luftwaffe 1933–45*.
249. Two Bf 109 pilots in conversation, cited in Beevor, *Ardennes 1944*.
250. Spick, *Aces of the Reich*.
251. Faber, *Luftwaffe*.
252. Hillblad, Thorolf (ed.), *Twilight of the Gods* (Helion & Company).
253. Verton, Hendrik C., *In the Fire of the Eastern Front* (Helion & Company).
254. Neulen, *In the Skies of Europe*.
255. Landau, *Goodbye Transylvania*.
256. Blosfelds, Mintauts, *Stormtrooper on the Eastern Front* (Pen & Sword).
257. Rogers, Duncan and Williams, Sarah (eds), *On the Bloody Road to Berlin – Frontline Accounts From North-West Europe and the Eastern Front 1944–45* (Helion).
258. Landau, *Goodbye Transylvania*.

Chapter Twenty-Six

259. Beevor, *Ardennes 1944*.
260. Interview with Albert Speer, cited in Holmes, *The World at War*.
261. Lieutenants Hans Hartigs and Hans Wöffen, cited in Neitzel and Welzer, *Soldaten on Fighting, Killing and Dying*.
262. Hannig, *Luftwaffe Fighter Ace*.
263. Denny, Isabel, *The Fall of Hitler's Fortress City – The Battle for Königsberg 1945* (Greenhill Books).
264. Ibid.
265. Neitzel and Welzer, *Soldaten on Fighting, Killing and Dying*.
266. Von Luck, *Panzer Commander*.

267. The ethnic German Transylvanian Saxon Waffen-SS volunteer Sigmund Heinz Landau. Landau, *Goodbye Transylvania*.
268. Interview with Alexander F. Khaila, cited in Drabkin, *Barbarossa and the Retreat to Moscow*.
269. The Dutch Waffen-SS volunteer Hendrik Verton. Verton, *In the Fire of the Eastern Front*.
270. The Swedish Waffen-SS volunteer Erik Wallin. Hillblad, *Twilight of the Gods*.
271. Interview with Alexander E. Shvarev, cited in Drabkin, *Barbarossa and the Retreat to Moscow*.
272. Interview with Viktor M. Sinaisky, cited in Drabkin, *Barbarossa and the Retreat to Moscow*.

Chapter Twenty-Seven

273. Bergstrom, Dikov and Antipov, *Black Cross Red Star* vol. 3.
274. Beevor, *Ardennes 1944*.
275. Bergstrom, Dikov and Antipov, *Black Cross Red Star* vol. 3.
276. Ibid.
277. Interview with Vitaly I. Klimenko, cited in Drabkin, *Barbarossa and the Retreat to Moscow*.
278. Bergstrom and Mikhailov, *Black Cross Red Star* vol. 2.
279. Beevor, *Ardennes 1944*.
280. Davies, *Europe At War 1939–1945*.
281. Faber, *Luftwaffe*.
282. Bergstrom, Dikov and Antipov, *Black Cross Red Star* vol. 3.
283. General Ernst Marquardt, Luftwaffe engineers.
284. Interview with Ivan D. Gaidenko, cited in Drabkin, *Barbarossa and the Retreat to Moscow*.
285. Interview with George Ball, cited in Holmes, *The World at War*.
286. Hermann Plocher would end up writing three excellent studies for the US Air Force in the 1960s on the Luftwaffe.
287. Drabkin, *Barbarossa and the Retreat to Moscow*.

Chapter Twenty-Eight

288. Burleigh, Michael, *Small Wars, Far Away Places, The Genesis of the Modern World: 1945–65* (Macmillan).
289. PoW Fischer, cited in Neitzel and Welzer, *Soldaten on Fighting, Killing and Dying*.
290. Interview with Alexander E. Shvarev, cited in Drabkin, *Barbarossa and the Retreat to Moscow*.
291. Lieutenant Boris Yemelyanenko. He was shot down but survived; the two other aircraft in his flight were both shot down and their crews killed.
292. Luftwaffe Sergeant Rott, cited in Neitzel and Welzer, *Soldaten on Fighting, Killing and Dying*.

293. Interview with Vitaly I. Klimenko, cited in Drabkin, *Barbarossa and the Retreat to Moscow*.
294. Hermann, *The Rise and Fall of the Luftwaffe*.
295. Bergstrom, Christer, and Mikhailov, Andrey, *Black Cross Red Star* vol. 2.
296. Hannig, *Luftwaffe Fighter Ace*.
297. Alexander E. Shvarev passed away on 2 May 2006 at the age of ninety-two.
298. Bergstrom, Dikov and Antipov, *Black Cross Red Star* vol. 3.

Bibliography

Baxter, Ian, *Operation Bagration – The Destruction of Army Group Centre June–July 1944* (Helion & Company, 2007)

Beevor, Antony, *Stalingrad* (Viking, 1998)

Beevor, Antony, *Ardennes 1944 – Hitler's Last Gamble* (Viking, 2015)

Beevor, Antony, *The Second World War* (Weidenfeld & Nicolson, 2012)

Beevor, Antony, *Berlin – The Downfall 1945* (Viking, 2002)

Beevor, Antony, *Crete – The Battle and the Resistance* (John Murray, 1991)

Bellamy, Chris, *Absolute War – Soviet Russia in the Second World War* (Macmillan, 2007)

Bergstrom, Christer and Mikhailov, Andrey, *Black Cross Red Star: The Air War Over the Eastern Front* Volume 2 (Pacifica Military History, 2001)

Bergstrom, Christer, Dikov, Andrey and Antipov, Vlad, *Black Cross Red Star: The Air War Over the Eastern Front* Volume 3 (Eagle Editions, 2006)

Bernad, Denes, Karlenko, Dmitry and Roba, Jean-Louis, *From Barbarossa to Odessa: The Air Battle for Odessa: August to October 1941* (Ian Allan Publishing, 2008)

Blosfelds, Mintauts, *Stormtrooper on the Eastern Front* (Pen & Sword, 2008)

Bullock, Alan, *Hitler – A Study in Tyranny* (Pelican, 1962)

Burleigh, Michael, *Small Wars, Far Away Places, The Genesis of the Modern World: 1945–65* (Macmillan, 2013)

Carell, Paul, *Hitler's War on Russia Volume 1: Hitler Moves East* (George G. Harrap & Co., 1964)

Carell, Paul, *Hitler's War on Russia Volume 2: Scorched Earth* (Corgi, 1971)

Cawthorne, Nigel, *Turning the Tide* (Capella, 2007)

Cloutier, Patrick, *Three Kings: Axis Royal Armies on the Russian Front 1941* (Patrick Cloutier, 2012)

Cloutier, Patrick, *Regio Esercito: The Italian Royal Army in Mussolini's Wars 1935–1943* (Patrick Cloutier, 2013)

Cornish, Nik, *Armageddon Ost: The German Defeat on the Eastern Front 1944–5* (Ian Allan Publishing, 2006)

Davies, Norman, *Europe At War 1939–1945, No Simple Victory* (Macmillan, 2006)

Denny, Isabel, *The Fall of Hitler's Fortress City – The Battle for Königsberg 1945* (Greenhill Books, 2007)

Drabkin, Artem, *Barbarossa and the Retreat to Moscow – Recollections of Soviet Fighter Pilots on the Eastern Front* (Pen & Sword, 2007)

Edwards, Robert, *White Death – Russia's War on Finland 1939–40* (Weidenfeld & Nicolson, 2006)

Faber, Harold (ed.), *Luftwaffe – An Analysis by Former Luftwaffe Generals* (Sidgwick & Jackson, 1979)

Gerasimova, Svetlana, *The Rhzev Slaughterhouse – The Red Army's Forgotten 15-Month Campaign Against Army Group Centre, 1942–1943* (Helion & Company, 2013)

Glantz, David M., *The Battle for Leningrad 1941–1944* (BCA, 2004)

Hannig, Norbert (trans. and ed. John Weal), *Luftwaffe Fighter Ace – From the Eastern Front to the Defence of the Homeland* (Bounty Books, 2015)

Hargreaves, Richard, *The Germans in Normandy* (Pen & Sword, 2006)

Harwood, Jeremy, *Hitler's War* (Quantum, 2014)

Hastings, Max, *Warriors* (HarperCollins, 2005)

Hayward, Joel S. A., *Stopped at Stalingrad – The Luftwaffe and Hitler's Defeat in the East 1942–1943* (University Press of Kansas, 1998)

Hermann, Hauptmann, *The Rise and Fall of the Luftwaffe* (Fonthill Media, 2012; originally published 1943)

Hillblad, Thorolf (ed.), *Twilight of the Gods* (Helion & Company, 2004)

Holmes, Richard, *The World At War* (Ebury Press, 2007)

Holmes, Richard, *Battlefields of the Second World War* (BBC, 2001)

Holmes, Tony (ed.), *Dogfight – The Greatest Air Duels of World War II* (Osprey, 2011)

Hooton, E. R., *Eagle in Flames – The Fall of the Luftwaffe* (Arms & Armour Press, 1997)

Jones, Michael, *The Retreat – Hitler's First Defeat* (John Murray, 2009)

Jones, Michael, *Leningrad – State of Siege* (John Murray, 2009)

Kurowski, Franz, *Bridgehead Kurland: The Six Epic Battles of Heeresgruppe Kurland* (J. J. Fedorowicz Publishing, 2002)

Landau, Sigmund Heinz, *Goodbye Transylvania* (Stackpole, 2015)

Macksey, Kenneth, *Kesselring – The Making of the Luftwaffe* (Greenhill, 2000)

MacLean, French, *The Cruel Hunters – SS-Sonderkommando Dirlewanger* (Schiffer, 1998)

Matthews, Rupert, *Hitler – Military Commander* (Capella, 2007)

McNab, Chris, *The Luftwaffe 1933–45: Hitler's Eagles* (Osprey, 2012)

Mitcham Jr, Samuel W., *Eagles of the Third Reich – Leaders of the Luftwaffe in the Second World War* (Crécy Publishing, 2010)

Mitter, Rana, *China's War with Japan 1937–1945* (Penguin, 2014)

Murray, Williamson, *Strategy for Defeat – The Luftwaffe 1933–1945* (Chartwell, 1986)

Neitzel, Sönke and Welzer, Harald, *Soldaten on Fighting, Killing and Dying – The Secret Second World War Tapes of German PoWs* (Simon & Schuster, 2012)

Neulen, Hans Werner, *In the Skies of Europe – Air Forces Allied to the Luftwaffe 1939–1945* (Crowood Press, 2000)

Perrett, Bryan, *Knights of the Black Cross* (Robert Hale, 1986)

Ries, Karl, *The Luftwaffe – A Photographic Record 1919–1945* (B. T. Batsford, 1987)

Rogers, Duncan and Williams, Sarah (eds), *On the Bloody Road to Berlin – Frontline Accounts From North-West Europe and the Eastern Front 1944–45* (Helion, 2005)

Spick, Mike, *Aces of the Reich – The Making of a Luftwaffe Fighter Pilot* (Greenhill, 2006)

Taylor, Brian, *Barbarossa to Berlin, Volume Two – The Defeat of Germany* (Spellmount, 2004)

Tolstoy, Nikolai, *Stalin's Secret War* (Pan, 1982)

Turner, Jason, *Stalingrad – Day by Day* (Brown Bear, 2012)

Verton, Hendrik C., *In the Fire of the Eastern Front* (Helion & Company, 2007)

Von Luck, Hans, *Panzer Commander – The Memoirs of Colonel Hans von Luck* (Cassell, 1989)

Young, Brigadier Peter and Everett, Susan, *The Two World Wars* (W H Smith & Son, 1982)

Index

List of Illustrations

All photos are from the author's personal collection except for the following: